Sulpicia

WOMEN IN ANTIQUITY

Series Editors: Ronnie Ancona and Sarah B. Pomeroy

This book series provides compact and accessible introductions to the life and historical times of women from the ancient world. Approaching ancient history and culture broadly, the series selects figures from the earliest of times to late antiquity.

Cleopatra
A Biography
Duane W. Roller

Clodia Metelli
The Tribune's Sister
Marilyn B. Skinner

Galla Placidia
The Last Roman Empress
Hagith Sivan

Arsinoë of Egypt and Macedon
A Royal Life
Elizabeth Donnelly Carney

Berenice II and the Golden Age of Ptolemaic Egypt
Dee L. Clayman

Faustina I and II
Imperial Women of the Golden Age
Barbara M. Levick

Turia
A Roman Woman's Civil War
Josiah Osgood

Monica
An Ordinary Saint
Gillian Clark

Theodora
Actress, Empress, Saint
David Potter

Hypatia
The Life and Legend of an Ancient Philosopher
Edward J. Watts

Boudica
Warrior Woman of Roman Britain
Caitlin C. Gillespie

Sabina Augusta
An Imperial Journey
T. Corey Brennan

Cleopatra's Daughter
And Other Royal Women of the Augustan Era
Duane W. Roller

Sulpicia

Life, Love, and Literature in Ancient Rome

ALISON KEITH

OXFORD
UNIVERSITY PRESS

OXFORD
UNIVERSITY PRESS

Oxford University Press is a department of the University of Oxford.
It furthers the University's objective of excellence in research, scholarship,
and education by publishing worldwide. Oxford is a registered trade mark of
Oxford University Press in the UK and in certain other countries.

Published in the United States of America by Oxford University Press
198 Madison Avenue, New York, NY 10016, United States of America.

CIP data is on file at the Library of Congress.

ISBN 9780197606964 (hbk)
ISBN 9780197606971 (pbk)

DOI: 10.1093/9780197607008.001.0001

Printed by Marquis Book Printing, Canada

The manufacturer's authorized representative in the EU for product safety is
Oxford University Press España S.A. of Parque Empresarial San Fernando de Henares,
Avenida de Castilla, 2 – 28830 Madrid (www.oup.es/en or product.safety@oup.com).
OUP España S.A. also acts as importer into Spain of products made by the manufacturer.

Contents

Contents

Acknowledgments

Servius' daughter Sulpicia and her poetry have long been of interest to me, as to so many of my friends and colleagues amongst contemporary feminist Latinists and Roman historians. I first read the cycle in graduate school and saw almost nothing there except difficult syntax. Since then, I have reread Sulpicia's poems in the very different contexts of teaching women in classical antiquity; comparing Sulpicia's themes of modesty and reputation to those of Vergil's Dido-narrative in the *Aeneid*; investigating the codes and conventions of both Roman dress and Roman onomastics in Sulpicia's verse; exploring androcentric critical assumptions in male-authored scholarship on the cycle; and honing feminist theoretical arguments to rebut them. But it would never have occurred to me to write a biography of Sulpicia, had Ronnie Ancona not invited me to contribute one to this series. Thank you, Ronnie!

At the time I received the invitation, however, I was astonished and more than a little perplexed. How could anyone (let alone a Latin philologist like myself) write the biography of a woman whose very existence was not just in doubt but actually denied in the most recent scholarship on her oeuvre? Yet in the course of researching and writing this book, I have discovered such compelling evidence for both female authorship in classical antiquity and the keen interest in women's writings in ancient Rome that I have convinced myself, at least, of her historical existence and literary talent. I am grateful to the many interlocutors who have allowed me to enthuse about my discoveries, and especially to Stefan Vranka, Ronnie Ancona, and Sarah B. Pomeroy for commissioning this volume and bearing with me as it has expanded beyond the parameters we originally envisaged. The OUP Production team and their partner production company Straive have managed all the moving parts of the production process with consummate professionalism: I am grateful to Stefan Vranka, Rachel Ruisard and Teddy Reiner at OUP and Thomas Deva and Tim Beck at Straive.

I have had the opportunity to present various parts of the discussions in this volume to a wide range of audiences, at first online but latterly in person, and I thank my interlocutors at Emory University, the National and

Kapodistrian University of Athens, Oriel College Oxford, Princeton University, the Scuola Normale Superiore, and the Universities of Alberta, British Columbia, Calgary, Chicago, Cincinnati, Manitoba, Queensland, Sydney, Torino, Toronto, Winnipeg, Victoria, and Virginia; the Historical Fictions Research Network; Massey College in Toronto and Victoria College in the University of Toronto; the Classical Association of Canada, Classical Association of the Middle West and South Southern Section, Ontario Classical Association, and North Toronto Collegiate Institute Classics Club. I am grateful to the audiences on those occasions and especially to friends and colleagues who read part or all of the manuscript: Lorenza Bennardo, Caitlin Hines, †Sharon James, Sarah McCallum, Anita Minerva, Melanie-Racette Campbell, Stephen Rupp, and Jessica Westerhold. Their enthusiasm for the project has sustained me through global plague and domestic affliction. Particular thanks are owed to my superlative research assistants Georgia Ferentinou, Donald McCarthy, and Angus Wilson whose keen eyes and critical skills have saved me from numerous errors and enlivened the journey throughout.

I am very happy to acknowledge my gratitude to Victoria College in the University of Toronto which has provided me not only with abundant conference travel, research funds, and publication assistance in support of this project over the last five years but also with the academic office and intellectual fellowship in which I completed the volume while on leave from the Jackman Humanities Institute in the spring of 2023. I am also grateful to the *Classical World* for permission to reprint a portion of my article "Critical Trends in the Interpretation of Sulpicia" from *CW* 100.1 (2005[2006]) in Ch. 8.

Since the innovative series "Women in Antiquity" is conceived as furnishing women of the ancient world with biographies, it seems only fitting to dedicate this work to my mother and sister. I am fortunate in having a librarian for mother, who introduced me in my youth to the full range of female-authored literature from children's books to murder mysteries, and an English teacher for sister, who shares my feminist passion for both literature and learning. To them both I offer this feminist biography of the earliest extant female author of Latin poetry by way of explanation for how a classical scholar can combine a love of literature with a feminist engagement in the Roman past.

Alison Keith
Toronto 2025

List of Figures

List of Tables

Abbreviations

Abbreviations of classical authors and their works follow, or are fuller than, those of Liddell-Scott-Jones's *Greek Lexicon* and the *Oxford Latin Dictionary*; abbreviations of journal titles follow, or are fuller than, those of *L'année philologique*.

CIL   *Corpus Inscriptionum Latinarum.* Berlin 1863–.

IGR   *Inscriptiones Graecae ad Res Romanae pertinentes.* Paris 1901–.

L-S   C. T. Lewis and C. Short (eds.), *A Latin Dictionary.* Oxford 1879.

OLD   P. G. W. Glare (ed.), *Oxford Latin Dictionary.* Oxford 1968–82.

PIR   *Prosopographia Imperii Romani Saeculi I, II, III* (Berlin 1897–99, 2nd edition 1933–).

P.Oxy. B. P. Grenfell, A. S. Hunt, and N. Gonis (eds.), *The Oxyrhynchus Papyri.* London 1898–.

RE   Pauly-Wissowa (eds.), *Real-Encylopädie der classischen Altertumswissenschaft.* Stuttgart 1893–1978.

TLL   *Thesaurus Linguae Latinae.* Leipzig-Stuttgart 1900–.

Introduction

> I hate and I love. How can I do that, perhaps you ask?
> I don't know, but I feel it happening and it's torture.[1]

For over two millenia, Latin students have encountered Catullus' expression of amatory despair in this epigram with the shock of recognition born of fellow feeling. Many of us read the epigram—Catullus' most famous poem—early on in our exposure to Latin literature and/or Roman culture and are gripped by the speaker's emotional anguish. When the couplet is placed in the context of the poet's all-engrossing love affair with an idealized but apparently faithless mistress Lesbia—a recurrent focus of Catullus' poetry—it also seems to offer disillusioned commentary on the outcome of their erotic adventure. The figure of Lesbia holds such sway over the Catullan ego and his verse that there are few readers who haven't desired to know more about the historical person presumed to be refracted in the poems.[2]

The biographical interpretation of literature is far from fashionable today, but it was the norm in Catullus' own time.[3] He even seems to invite such a reading of his verse, especially of the Lesbia cycle, in another caustic epigram that unites amatory, social, and political invective to devastating effect:[4]

> Lesbius is Pretty. Why not? Lesbia would rather have him
> than you, Catullus, along with your whole family.
> But yet this pretty-boy would sell Catullus out, along with his family,
> if he could find three kisses among his acquaintance.

In the first couplet, Catullus (ca. 84–54 BCE) implies Lesbia's descent from the powerful Claudian family, whose "Pretty" (Pulcher) branch was prominent in the senatorial politics of late republican Rome. He thereby strips the veil of pseudonymity from his beloved to name—and shame—her publicly as a Claudia (or Clodia, a less elevated by-form of her patrician name). He further hints at her incestuous relations with her brother, a charge repeatedly made against Publius Clodius Pulcher and his sister Clodia, Metellus' wife, by the contemporary politician Cicero (106–43 BCE),[5] who reviled Clodius as the author of his exile in 58 BCE. In the second couplet, moreover, Catullus has added a socio-political dimension to his vituperation by insinuating that Pulcher, along with his loving sister, was so arrogant and unscrupulous as to sell free men into slavery, in order to sustain the social ties crucial to his electoral success.[6]

Among Catullus' readers, the figure of Lesbia/Clodia has excited intense interest, as much because of the scathing portrait the poet draws of her "Claudian" arrogance and sexual depravity as because of his flattering picture of her wit and charm.[7] Especially intriguing is his depiction of her as a playful literary critic:[8]

> Volusius' *Annales*, shitty sheets,
> discharge an oath for my girlfriend.
> For to holy Venus and Cupid
> she vowed—if I had been restored to her
> and ceased to brandish fierce iambs—
> to give the choicest writings of the
> very worst poet to the lame god,
> to be toasted on unlucky wood.
> And the wicked girl saw her vow
> to the gods as a charming joke.

Catullus parries Lesbia's witty oath to consign his poetry to the flames with his own clever counterproposal to sacrifice instead Volusius' long-winded *Annales*, excoriated elsewhere as fit only to wrap fish.[9]

Nor is Lesbia the only literature-loving girlfriend to be found in Catullus' poetry. When Catullus writes to his fellow poet Caecilius, asking to see more of his new poem on the Great Mother of the gods, he expresses some concern that his friend's girlfriend is delaying completion of the project:[10]

> If he's smart, Caecilius will eat up the road,
> even if his fair girlfriend should recall him
> a thousand times as he's on the point of leaving,
> and ask him to stay, casting both her hands round his neck.
> She now, if the reports that reach me are true,
> is desperately, madly in love with him.

> For from the time when she read the beginning
> of his poem "Mistress of Dindymon," the poor girl's
> been consumed to her very marrow by the flames of love.
> I forgive you, girl more learned than
> the Sapphic muse; Caecilius has indeed made
> a charming start on his "Great Mother."

Catullus' praise of Caecilius' girlfriend sheds further light on his own mistress' literary discernment, for it implicitly glosses the pseudonym "Lesbia" as homage to Sappho of Lesbos (as do the Sapphic stanzas of poems 11 and 51) and confirms Clodia's interest in, and knowledge of, literature—especially, perhaps, women's writings. Might Clodia even have been a poet herself? If so, nothing survives from her pen.

From the next generation, however, there comes a cycle of Latin love poems exploring an upper-class Roman woman's relationship with her lover Cerinthus and her guardians, her mother Valeria and her kinsman Messalla. The cycle, included in the third book of the elegiac poet Tibullus' works (3.8–18), opens with the name "Sulpicia," the first word of the first poem (3.8.1), while the first-person voice of the sequence (speaking in 3.9, 11, 13–18) names herself toward the end of the collection as "Servius' daughter Sulpicia" (3.16.4). Unlike other ancient Mediterranean women who have received modern biographies, however, the poet/lover Sulpicia is not mentioned anywhere else in classical literature. Our knowledge of her historical existence and literary activity derives solely from the poems in which she speaks and is named. This constitutes a distinct challenge for constructing her biography, and one not shared by other prominent ancient women like Sappho, Cleopatra, and even Catullus' Lesbia (Clodia), who were the targets of copious, often critical, commentary in the male-authored literature of classical antiquity but whose words have been so appropriated and ventriloquized by male authors that they may as well have left no first-person accounts of their lives and loves.[11] If other volumes in this series have asked how it is possible to write biographies of women whose life-histories are known to us only in refraction, filtered through ancient preconceptions of gender and sexuality,[12] this study explores the possibility of direct contact with a historical Roman woman.

Sulpicia: Life, Love, and Literature in Ancient Rome. Alison Keith, Oxford University Press.
© Oxford University Press 2026. DOI: 10.1093/9780197607008.003.0001

I
TEXTS

1

Discovery

The transmission of Sulpicia's poetry from classical antiquity to the present day is itself an exciting tale of near destruction, chance discovery, and repeated misidentification. The survival of her poetry depends on a single manuscript of the so-called Tibullan corpus, now lost, that was unearthed in medieval France and copied in renaissance Italy before vanishing for good. The manuscript occasioned immediate interest in the contents of its first two books of elegies, which were recognized as the work of Albius Tibullus (ca. 55–19 BCE), the leading poet of Latin elegy, a genre focused on the poet's erotic tribulations with a capricious beloved.[1] But the manuscript also included a third book, consisting of a poetic miscellany apparently associated with Tibullus' literary patron Marcus Valerius Messalla Corvinus (64 BCE–8 CE).[2]

The contents and authorship of the poems collected in this third book of the Tibullan corpus sparked scholarly interest upon its print publication in the late fifteenth century CE, and debate continues to this day. Particular disagreement has focused on the poetic sequence 3.8–18 that explores the love of an elegiac "mistress" or "girlfriend" (*puella*)[3] named Sulpicia for her beloved Cerinthus.[4] The elegies about the lovers are voiced both by an unnamed third-person speaker (3.8, 10, 12) and by a first-person female speaker (3.9, 11, 13–18), who identifies herself by her family name and filiation as "Servius' daughter Sulpicia" (3.16.4).[5] Here I review Sulpicia's fortunes from her first appearance in the literary record, in the Carolingian renaissance, to the twentieth-century consensus identifying her as a patrician woman writing Latin love poetry early in the reign of the first Roman emperor, Augustus.

In the estimation of classical antiquity, the foremost poet of Latin elegiac verse was Albius Tibullus, the author of love poems celebrating a youth named Marathus (1.4, 8, 9) and two different mistresses, commemorated under the pseudonyms Delia (1.2, 3, 5, 6) and Nemesis (2.3–6).[6] Tibullus' poetry survived classical antiquity in a medieval manuscript tradition that transmited two books of his elegies along with a third book, conventionally known as the *Appendix Tibulliana*, containing a miscellany of Latin verse by authors apparently connected with his patron Messalla.[7] The relationship between the three books of the Tibullan corpus has long been a vexed question of classical scholarship, and one to which a definitive answer is not forthcoming on the basis of our current knowledge. Yet the medieval manuscript tradition can at least shed some faint light on the problem.

The earliest reference to a manuscript of Tibullus dates from 790 CE, in a register of Charlemagne's court library at Aachen in modern Germany. The court catalogue records two books of Tibullus, but we cannot determine from the registry whether or not the third book miscellany later associated with Tibullus' two books of elegies was also contained in the manuscript since, strictly speaking, the poems in the third-book miscellany are not the work of Tibullus. To complicate matters further, the codex itself does not survive. Two of its descendants, however, have been identified. The earlier, a late tenth- or early eleventh-century anthology of Latin verse (a medieval *florilegium*) for teaching grammar, is known from Freising.[8] This manuscript contains excerpts from every book recorded in the Aachen court catalogue and includes extracts from all three books of the Tibullan corpus (citing, from the Sulpicia sequence, 3.8.3–4 and 3.9.10).[9] The second descendant of the Carolingian manuscript is a twelfth-century catalogue from Lobbes, which records three books of Tibullus in that library.[10] Since textual scholars have found no evidence of an independent witness to the Tibullan corpus beyond the Carolingian codex, it has been conjectured that the Aachen court registry erred in attributing two, rather than three, books to Tibullus.[11] The earliest evidence of the medieval manuscript tradition would thus seem to imply that the poetic miscellany was already closely associated with Tibullus' two books of elegies by the time of the Carolingian classical renaissance.

After Charlemagne's death in 814 CE, perhaps even earlier, his court library was broken up and sent to leading monasteries in France. The codex containing the Tibullan corpus must have been among them, since all but one of the subsequent medieval attestations of Tibullus' verse come from France. The sole attestation from outside of France is an eleventh-century medieval *florilegium* containing extracts from across the Tibullan corpus (including 3.11.7 from the Sulpicia cycle). This manuscript, known as the *Excerpta Veneta*, was compiled at Montecassino, south of Rome, by Lorenzo of Amalfi, tutor to the future pope Gregory VII (1010–85; papacy 1073–85).[12] It is not known where Lorenzo took these extracts from, though they have been thought to derive from the Carolingian codex, which seems to have spent some time at Fleury, a monastery with which the monks of Montecassino maintained a longstanding connection.

Eventually, however, the Carolingian codex reached the vicinity of Orléans, where we know that a text of the Tibullan corpus resided from the late eleventh century through the twelfth.[13] From this codex was compiled the *florilegium Gallicum*, an anthology of Latin verse excerpted for moral instruction in the mid-twelfth century and extant in four French manuscripts dating from the long thirteenth century.[14] Another nine *florilegia*, shorter and later, contain a collection of brief extracts from the Tibullan corpus compiled at Orléans in the early thirteenth century for use in teaching Latin verse composition in the schools there.[15] Also in the thirteenth century, the chancellor of the cathedral at Amiens, Richard de Fournival, possessed a copy of the Orléans Tibullus.[16] At his death in 1260, this copy (no longer extant) was transferred to Paris along with many of his other books to establish the library of the newly founded Collège de la Sorbonne.

The only known copy of the Tibullan corpus to have survived the Middle Ages apparently derives from this French tradition. Its owner was the Italian humanist Coluccio Salutati (1331–1406),[17] chancellor of Florence from 1375 until his death. Learned in classical Latin literature and Roman republican history, he corresponded with the poet Petrarch (1304–74), collected classical manuscripts, and eventually amassed a personal library of some eight hundred volumes, including our earliest extant manuscript of the Tibullan corpus.[18] It has been conjectured that Salutati's manuscript of Tibullus (or at least that from which he had it copied) reached Italy in the previous generation, brought from France in 1333 by Petrarch himself, as his characteristic *nota* sign has been recognized in the margin of the text (f. 9ᵛ).[19] Salutati's codex dates from 1374, but it is not until the 1420s, when five manuscripts appeared in quick succession,[20] that we can see sustained interest in Tibullus' poetry. In the next twenty-five years another hundred or so manuscripts (almost all Italian) appeared, although neither their relationship to Salutati's codex, nor to one another, has been studied.[21]

The first printed editions of the Tibullan corpus were published in Venice in 1472, some hundred years after Salutati obtained his codex.[22] Already in 1475, moreover, just three years later, there was published at Rome a commentary on the full Tibullan corpus by an obscure Italian humanist named Bernardinus Cyllenius,[23] and it was continuously reprinted for over a hundred years.[24] In his commentaries on individual poems, Bernardinus briefly summarizes the contents and explains the action according to masculine norms of literary discourse and social intercourse. In the case of the first-person Sulpicia poems, this practice obscures the distinctively female voice and gynocentric focus of the verse by stabilizing her elegiac rhetoric in terms of the masculine orientation familiar from Catullus, Propertius, and Tibullus.[25] In this regard, Bernardinus' commentary reflects the Christian context in which it was composed.

Bernardinus' commentary was only superseded in 1577 with the publication of Joseph Justus Scaliger's edition of, and commentary on, Tibullus in his *Castigationes* ("Reproofs"). In his edition, Scaliger marks an important advance in Sulpicia scholarship through his use of the so-called *fragmentum Cuiacianum*, a medieval manuscript containing [Tib.] 3.4.65–3.20.4 that has since disappeared.[26] In the accompanying commentary, Scaliger attends closely to both the narrative action and the aesthetic qualities of the poems in the third book of the Tibullan corpus. His narrativization of the Sulpicia poems clarifies their amatory content to show that this poetry features a female lover speaking about the different phases of a heterosexual love-affair,[27] although Scaliger himself is silent about the immorality of such an affair (in the Christian worldview). Yet, while he explicitly recognizes the feminine gender of the first-person speaking voice in these poems—i.e., their female narrator and agent—he does not acknowledge female authorship. Instead, as Skoie has shown, he views Sulpicia as Tibullus' fiction, an elegiac *puella* through whose eyes the elegiac affair is presented by the master-poet.[28] Yet the qualities of softness, delicacy, and charm which he imputes to elegies 3.14 and 3.16—both voiced in the first-person feminine—were associated with the female in classical, medieval, and early modern European thought. In so characterizing these poems, Scaliger implicitly responds to the female voice and feminine perspective that distinguish Sulpicia's epigrams from Tibullus' elegies.

Despite (or perhaps because of) the widespread interest in Tibullus' poetry in the fifteenth and sixteenth centuries, all our renaissance manuscripts and early published editions of the Tibullan corpus ascribe authorship of the third-book miscellany to Tibullus. Indeed, it was only some one hundred and fifty years after the first printed editions, in 1624, that the German scholar Kaspar von Barth suggested that the first-person Sulpicia poems were composed by a female author. He identified the poet as Sulpicia the satirist, mentioned as a contemporary by the poet Martial, who wrote during the reign of the Roman emperor Domitian (r. 81–96 CE).[29] Yet it is difficult to reconcile the Augustan date of Tibullus with a Domitianic poet, and even harder to reconcile the elegiac form of both Tibullus' verse and the Sulpicia cycle, with Sulpicia the satirist's iambic trimeters and seventy-line hexameter fragment.[30] His proposal has therefore never garnered broad support.[31]

It was over one hundred years later, in the mid-eighteenth century, that the German scholar Christian Gottlob Heyne proposed that seven of the eight poems voiced in the first-person feminine could have been composed by an Augustan Sulpicia (3.9, 11, 13–14, 16–18).[32] He argued that, while:

> there cannot be complete clarity in such a matter, it is probable that these are the playful verses of various elegant and noble people, composed at different times and for different reasons, but in an age when the pursuits of literature flourished in association with urbanity, such as was character-istic of the Augustan age. There is nothing to prevent the belief that the great part proceeded from Sulpicia herself.

Heyne seems to have admired above all the "sincerity" of Sulpicia's verse, characterizing 3.17 as "the sweetest poem of the softest girl,"[33] and reading into the sequence the narrative of a real Roman love affair. Indeed, he deemed the whole series the product of amateur poets, who exhibit "a weakness of care and diligence in polishing the poetry."[34]

But it is the nineteenth-century German polymath Otto Friedrich Gruppe (1804–76), however, who is conventionally credited with the "discovery" of Sulpicia as the author of (most of) the first-person feminine-voiced elegies (3.14–18), and the demarcation of the preceding elegies (3.8–13) as the work of a different (male) poet. In his 1838 monograph *Die römische Elegie*, Gruppe cited the evidence of the *fragmentum Cuiacianum* (as reported by Scaliger), which supplies the heading "Sulpicia" before elegy 3.14, in support of his division, and this evidence was immediately accepted as decisive.[35] Gruppe thus inaugurated the modern division of the cycle into the *amicus*-poems, the so-called "Garland of Sulpicia" (3.8–12), and the Sulpicia poems (3.13–18), attributed to a historical Roman woman of that name. Although he included 3.13 in the roster of elegies composed by the *amicus*-poet, most subsequent scholars have followed A. Rossbach, a later German scholar who, in his 1855 edition of the Tibullan corpus, ascribed elegy 3.13 to Sulpicia as well.[36]

As for her date and identity, our poet's name and filiation ("Servius' daughter Sulpicia," 3.16.4), along with the name of her guardian, "Messalla kinsman" (*Messalla...propinque*, 3.14.5–6), and the literary genres in which she wrote (elegy and epigram), taken together confirm that she belonged to a prominent family at the very pinnacle of the Augustan aristocracy and composed her poetry early in the Roman emperor Augustus' reign. In 1871, the German scholar M. Haupt proposed that she was the granddaughter of Cicero's friend the jurist Servius Sulpicius Rufus[37] (d. 43 BCE) and niece of Augustus' general Messalla Corvinus, and this identification has been accepted by most specialists. From Cicero's correspondence, we know that in 50 BCE Sulpicius and his wife Postumia were looking for a wife for their son, also named Servius Sulpicius Rufus (Ch. 2), while from the Church Father Jerome (ca. 347–420 CE) we know that Messalla's sister Valeria married a Servius Sulpicius Rufus (Ch. 3). Although some scholars have thought Valeria married the elder Servius, there is no evidence either that his wife Postumia predeceased him or that he divorced her (Ch. 2).[38] The identification of Sulpicia as the granddaughter of the jurist would make her a younger contemporary of the elegists Propertius and Tibullus (born in the mid-50s BCE), possibly even closely coeval with the poet Ovid (b. 43 BCE). Latin scholars, moreover, have long dated her elegies to the early years of Augustus' reign (25–20 BCE), on the basis of her lexicon, grammar, and syntax (Ch. 6). This reconstruction of the genealogical and stylistic evidence points to Sulpicia's composition of her elegiac verses in the middle years of the genre's heyday (ca. 30–15 BCE) in ancient Rome (Ch. 5).

By the beginning of the twentieth century, therefore, there had developed a robust consensus ascribing elegies 3.13–18 (and only those six elegies) to Messalla's niece Sulpicia and the other five Sulpicia elegies (3.8–12) to a shadowy *amicus*-poet or *auctor de Sulpicia* ("author about Sulpicia"). Much scholarly ink has been spilt on the question of the latter's date and identity, with Tibullus and Ovid the most frequently proposed candidates (Ch. 7).[39] This scholarly orthodoxy spans the twentieth century from the 1905 edition of the Oxford don J. P. Postgate and 1913 commentary of the American scholar Kirby Flower Smith, to the German scholars Hermann Tränkle and Georg Luck, at the end of the century, who enshrined the consensus in their 1990 commentary and 1998 Teubner edition respectively.[40]

In 1994, however, Holt N. Parker reviewed the evidence for the ascription to an unknown male author of elegies 3.9 and 3.11, both voiced in the first-person by a female speaker, and argued that they were composed by Sulpicia herself:[41]

> Nowhere in love elegy do we find any case of a poet completely surrendering the ego-figure, not simply to some other *persona* (and this itself is rare),

but to another person: that is, writing "Subjective" love poetry while pre-
tending to be one of his friends, a poet in her own right, well known both
to the immediate and the wider audience.

Parker's findings have been bolstered by the work of Judith Hallett, Peter
Dronke, and Jacqueline Fabre-Serris, among others,[42] and this is the position I take in this volume. Almost a century ago, moreover, it was proposed
to add a ninth poem to Sulpicia's small corpus, with the inclusion of a
funerary epigram for Sulpicia Petale, a freed slave whose epitaph records
her position as a "reader" (*lectrix*) in the household of a Sulpicius or Sulpicia
(Ch. 4).[43] In an Appendix, I provide Latin text and English translation of
the complete Sulpicia cycle transmitted in manuscript ([Tib.] 3.8–18),
along with the Sulpicia Petale epitaph and Tibullus' elegy 2.2, addressed to
Messalla's friend Cornutus, whom many scholars have identified as Sulpicia's
pseudonymous lover Cerinthus and/or her husband (Ch. 4).

Since this innovative Oxford series is conceived as furnishing women of
the ancient world with biographies, Sulpicia's life-story takes pride of place
in Part II, which focuses on her paternal heritage, maternal lineage, and the
social roles and religious observances for which her aristocratic background
trained her. Sulpicia is nowhere independently attested in the ancient
textual record, however, so Chapters 2 and 3 must inevitably focus on her
male family members and the political background of the period. Family is
always important in life-writing, but for the Romans it was even more so:
names tell us something key about individuals (e.g., "Claudii are arrogant").
For that reason, much of my discussion in these two chapters focuses on the
reconstruction of her family's genealogy, a field of study known to ancient
historians as prosopography. In Chapter 4, I discuss Sulpicia's childhood
and marriage in connection with the social and religious obligations of the
daughters of the Roman elite. The poetry by and about Sulpicia provides
much of the evidence for her life-course including, especially, her courtship
and presumed marriage, which was assuredly the most important aspect of
the life of the ancient Roman woman.

Sulpicia's writings constitute the focus of Part III, which offers an over-
view of her literary formation alongside an interpretation of her poetic
achievement and literary impact. Chapter 5 explores the literary commit-
ments of her father Servius and uncle Messalla, prominent men of letters
in triumviral and Augustan Rome, and considers the vogue for amatory
verse that swept Italy in the wake of the publication of Meleager's *Garland*,

an anthology of Hellenistic Greek epigrams compiled about 100 BCE and very popular with Roman readers as well as Greek audiences. Chapter 6 then discusses the style and themes of Sulpicia's verse in the context of the contemporary popularity of love lyric, erotic elegy, and epigram, while Chapter 7 considers evidence for Sulpicia's own literary impact. A brief Postscript (Ch. 8) surveys the difficulty contemporary (mostly male) scholars have had in believing that an aristocratic Roman woman could write poetry about love and sex, and reviews the rhetorical strategies by which they write her out of both literary and social history.

Sulpicia: Life, Love, and Literature in Ancient Rome. Alison Keith, Oxford University Press.
© Oxford University Press 2026. DOI: 10.1093/9780197607008.003.0002

II
GENEALOGIES

2

Daughter of the Patriciate

Both the name Sulpicia and the filiation our poet asserts, "Servius' daughter" (3.16.4), bespeak her aristocratic lineage from the ancient Roman patrician family of the Sulpicii. Their recorded traditions went back to 500 BCE, ten years after the establishment of republican government at Rome, when a Sulpicius Camerinus Cornutus held one of the two annual consulships. Another Sulpicius Camerinus Cornutus was elected to the consulship of 490, and a third, perhaps the son of the first, was consul in 461 and decemvir in 451. In the following century, the Rufus branch of the family first appears in Roman records, with a Servius Sulpicius Rufus elected consular tribune four times in the first quarter of the fourth century (388, 384, 383, 377), and a Servius Sulpicius Camerinus Rufus holding the consulship in 345. In the third and second centuries BCE, however, during the sustained advance of prominent plebeian families to senatorial office, many early Roman patrician families seem either to have died out or to have fallen to equestrian rank. The latter seems to have happened to the Sulpicii Rufi, of whom there is no record of renewed tenure in office until early in the first century, when a Publius Sulpicius Rufus, brother to a Servius Sulpicius,[1] was elected tribune in 88 BCE,[2] though the collateral branches of Sulpicii Paterculi and Sulpicii Galbae (from whom the emperor Galba descended), enjoyed continuing electoral prominence in the mid-republic.[3] This chapter explores the revival of the political fortunes of the Servii Sulpicii Rufi, in the persons of Sulpicia's grandfather and father, in the late republic.

We begin with her grandfather's circumstances at low ebb, in 63 BCE, when he had failed to secure election to the consulship for 62 BCE and undertook a prosecution for bribery against the successful candidate Murena. In his speech "In Defense of Murena," of 63 BCE, the great republican orator and politician Cicero (Fig. 1) briefly sketches the venerable antiquity of the patrician Sulpicii, in order to underline the contrast between the family's prominence in early Roman republican history and its obscurity in his own day. Addressing Servius Sulpicius Rufus, his client's prosecutor, Cicero remarks:[4]

Fig. 1 Bust of M. Tullius Cicero, first century AD (Musei Capitolini, Rome).

> Although your nobility is of the highest, nonetheless it is better known
> to men of letters and antiquarians, and less known to the people and
> electorate....Thus, the memory of your nobility does not come from recent
> conversation but must be dug up from ancient records.

Cicero here magnifies the insignificance of his adversary's family as part
of his strategy to secure an acquittal for his client. But his reference to the
family's ancient records is of some interest in connection with a tradition,
known from early imperial Latin literature, commemorating the virtue of a
mid-republican Sulpicia, whose noble parentage and illustrious marriage
were scrupulously preserved in the notices of her personal probity.

Indeed, the only republican member of Sulpicius' family whose career
is known to us now in any detail is this Sulpicia, recorded as the daughter
of Servius Sulpicius Paterculus and wife of Quintus Fulvius Flaccus.[5] The
moralist Valerius Maximus, writing under the emperor Tiberius (r. 14–37
CE), explains that she was selected by her peers, as the "most blameless of
her sex," to dedicate a statue of Venus Verticordia:[6]

To the commemoration of men, there deserves to be added [the commemoration of a woman named] Sulpicia, daughter of Ser. [Sulpicius]
Paterculus and wife of Q. Fulvius Flaccus. After the Sibylline books had
been inspected by the Board of Ten, the Senate ordained that an image of
Venus Verticordia be consecrated, the more easily to turn the minds of
virgins and married women from lust to chastity; and that from all the
matrons one hundred and from the one hundred ten drawn by lot should
make a judgment, who was the most blameless of the sex. Sulpicia was
placed above them all for her chastity.

In her guise as Verticordia ("changer of hearts"), Venus was venerated for
turning women's thoughts to virtue and reputation, "the natural concerns"
of Roman wives.[7] The cult was established by Sulpicia, either just before or
early in the second Punic war (218–201 BCE), when she consecrated the
goddess' image at the instigation of a special magisterial commission. The
story is repeated by the elder Pliny in his *Natural History*:[8]

The first case of a woman judged by a vote of the matrons to be the most
modest (*pudicissima*) was Sulpicia, daughter of [Sulpicius] Paterculus and
wife of Fulvius Flaccus, who was elected from a previously chosen list of
one hundred to dedicate the image of Venus [Verticordia] in accordance
with the Sibylline books.

This virtuous Sulpicia was among the most distinguished members of her
noble patrician family in the late third century BCE, and won the acclaim of
her peers and regard of posterity for her exemplary morality.

The dates and political pre-eminence of her male kin document the
social prominence of both her natal and marital families in mid-republican
Rome. Her father, the patrician Ser. Sulpicius Paterculus, is conjectured to
have been the brother of the consul of 258 BCE, Gaius Sulpicius Paterculus,[9]
while her husband Quintus Fulvius Flaccus was one of the leading generals
and politicians of the second Punic war. There is no record of her father
holding office, but her husband held four consulships in the second half of
the third century BCE (237, 224, 212, 209) and was elected to numerous other
curule offices in this period, including the censorship (231), praetorship
(215, 214), proconsulship (211, 208, 207), and the dictatorship to oversee
elections (210).[10] In 216 BCE, moreover, he was elected to the pontifical
college. The social, religious, and political standing of her menfolk

undoubtedly enhanced Sulpicia's reputation among the elite Roman wives, and her peers' recognition of her moral probity will have enhanced in turn the military, political, and religious authority of her male kin.

This Sulpicia may also have played a role in Roman politics early in the following century. The Augustan historian Livy records the actions of a certain Sulpicia behind the scenes in the Bacchanalian affair of 186 BCE. In his account of the Roman senatorial supervision of Bacchus' rites in Italy, he reports that information about the cult was laid before one of the consuls of 186 BCE, the patrician Postumius Albinus,[11] by a disenfranchised youth named Aebutius.[12] Three women figure prominently in Livy's narrative: Aebutius' aunt, Aebutia, who urged him to report the affair; Aebutius' mistress, the freed slave Hispala Faecenia, who testified to the obscene rites of the cult; and the consul Postumius' mother-in-law, Sulpicia, who vouched for Aebutia's "probity and ancient moral standards."[13] Livy characterizes Sulpicia as "a venerable woman,"[14] of "the utmost dignity,"[15] and he thereby implies her pre-eminence among the Roman matrons of her day. Her moral authority was clearly enough to confirm both Aebutia's good repute and her own reputability, and this has led scholars to identify her with the Sulpicia who dedicated the statue of Venus Verticordia at the end of the previous century. Livy's subsequent description of her as "such an outstanding woman"[16] is highly appropriate for a leading Roman noblewoman of an age and stature to have consecrated the statue of Venus Verticordia.[17]

Livy reports that the consul drew his mother-in-law into his political investigation by making use of her standing among her peers to have her invite first Aebutius' aunt and then his mistress Hispala Faecenia into her Roman townhouse, where he could question them in person. After satisfying himself that he had secured credible testimony from them both, moreover, Postumius assigned Aebutius and Hispala, for their safety, to appropriately gendered quarters:[18]

> The consul asked his mother-in-law to vacate some part of the house into which Hispala could move. An apartment above the house was granted, with the stairs leading to the street closed up and the approach turned into the house. All Faecenia's property was immediately brought over and her household slaves summoned, and Aebutius was ordered to move to the house of one of the consul's clients.

In Livy's narrative, we see an expectation of the involvement of elite Roman women, on behalf of their male kin, in the political and religious matters of the day.[19] Thus, both Aebutius and Postumius draw not only on networks of male patronage and kin but also on female channels. By harnessing his mother-in-law's female networks and allowing her to remain behind the scenes (at least according to Livy), Postumius acquired crucial information in his investigation of the Bacchanalian affair and protected his witnesses. The participation of a freedwoman/courtesan in these networks is treated as conventional—not only by Postumius and Livy, but also, apparently, by the consul's mother-in-law Sulpicia, who was herself entrusted with the obligation of supporting the entire establishment of a courtesan from the servile class in her own house. Indeed, the relocation of Hispala's household— both furnishings and slaves—apparently required extensive reconfiguration of Sulpicia's townhouse to accommodate the establishment.

Whatever the historical value of Livy's report,[20] his narrative testifies to Augustan cultural expectations concerning elite Roman matronal intervention into affairs of state in mid-republican Rome. It is very likely, moreover, that Sulpicia's family carefully preserved (and burnished) the tales of her exemplary modesty, her social and religious standing, and her political involvement, in order to enhance their own social prestige.[21] The name Sulpicia was thus one to conjure with in the first century BCE. Moreover, it is striking that, in the interval between the political activity of Postumius' mother-in-law Sulpicia and that of the tribune Publius Sulpicius of 88 BCE, there is limited evidence for politically active men in the clan.

The family's fortunes changed dramatically, however, in the final generation of the republic. The tribune of 88 has been conjectured to have been a close relative of Servius Sulpicius Rufus, the eminent jurist whom M. Haupt identified as our poet's grandfather.[22] In his voluminous writings, the late republican orator and politician Cicero offers a good deal of information about his friend Sulpicius' illustrious legal career and less distinguished political attainments.[23] The two men seem to have been close coevals— Cicero born in 106 BCE and Sulpicius probably the following year, to judge by the date of his praetorship forty years later in 65 BCE.[24] Cicero and Sulpicius studied together from boyhood and traveled with one another to Athens and Rhodes in 79 BCE to study philosophy and rhetoric.[25] On Sulpicius' return to Rome, however, perhaps in 77, he transferred his attention from philosophy and rhetoric (Cicero's fields) to legal studies.[26] Elected quaestor for 75 BCE, he was assigned the port of Ostia as his province, an assignment "not so much agreeable and illustrious as laborious and troublesome," according to Cicero.[27]

After his quaestorship, Sulpicius devoted himself to full time study of the Roman civil law and was ultimately to become the foremost jurisconsult, or legal scholar, of his day. Cicero describes him, in his speech in defense of Murena, working on the routine matters of jurisprudence, giving responses, preparing documents, advising on legal procedure, and starting to teach.[28] His legal studies may have impeded his political ambitions. He never stood for the aedileship but was elected praetor for 65 BCE and allotted the presidency of the court for embezzlement of public money or property. In this capacity, it has been conjectured, his innate probity was unlikely to win him any political support. Certainly, when he first stood for election to the consulate, in 63 BCE (the year of Cicero's famous tenure of the office), he was unsuccessful, losing to Murena and Silanus, who—like their fellow candidate, the impoverished aristocrat Catiline—practiced corruption on a grand scale. In defeat, Catiline inaugurated the conspiracy that absorbed most of Cicero's attention in the last quarter of his consular year, but Sulpicius pursued legal redress through the courts, accusing Murena, who had been his colleague in the quaestorship, of electoral corruption (*ambitus*).

In his speech in defense of Murena, Cicero sketches Sulpicius' illustrious genealogy and personal rectitude, lauding him for "the height of dignity" with which he was endowed by "his family lineage, upright character, hard work and all the rest of the distinctions appropriate to a consular candidate."[29] As we have seen, however, while conceding that Sulpicius' lineage derived from the ancient nobility, Cicero emphasizes the obscurity of his friend's immediate ascendants, since neither his father nor his grandfather had reached curule office. Indeed, although his grandfather had at least been a senator, his father was only of equestrian rank according to Cicero— presumably either unsuccessful or uninterested in pursuing a senatorial career. In Cicero's eyes, the electoral setback of 63 BCE, when Sulpicius failed to win the consulship of 62, confirmed the obscurity of his family:[30]

> Therefore, I am always in the habit of including you in our number [i.e., in the ranks of new men] because by your moral excellence and diligent application you have achieved the reputation of being thought worthy of the highest office though you are the son of a Roman equestrian.

The political maneuvering of the decade that followed Sulpicius' defeat in the consular elections for 62 BCE suited neither his juridical sense of probity nor his political preference for compromise. There is some evidence that he contemplated standing for the consulship of 58,[31] but in the event he did not put his name forward.[32] Instead, the compact of the consul of 59, Julius Caesar (Fig. 2), with the consuls of 70, Crassus and Pompey the Great (Fig. 3)—the so-called First Triumvirate, struck in late 60—easily secured the election of Caesar's father-in-law Piso and Pompey's henchman Gabinius as the consuls of 58. After the second consulship of Crassus and Pompey in 55, moreover, scandals and violence repeatedly impeded the regular election process at Rome. Both the consuls of 54 were involved in electoral scandals and civil disturbances that delayed the polls for the following year, with the result that the consuls of 53 were only finally able to enter office in July of that year. Their attempts to hold the elections for 52 were in turn frustrated by the violence of several of the candidates for office. As a result, the year 52 opened without consuls and with continuing violent unrest, culminating in the murder of Cicero's enemy Clodius Pulcher on January 18.[33] The subsequent disorder in Rome united the opposing political factions and resulted in a senatorial deal to elect Pompey as sole Consul for the year.

Fig. 2 Bust of C. Julius Caesar, ca. 44 BCE (Museo di Antichità, Turin).

Fig. 3 Bust of Cn. Pompeius Magnus. Claudian period copy of a post-60 BCE original. (Museo Archeologico Nazionale, Venice).

It is in this context that Servius Sulpicius Rufus reappears in Rome's political annals, his name preserved as that of the magistrate who successfully presided over Pompey's election to the consulship in the last days of February 52.[34]

After this, Sulpicius presented himself as a candidate for the consulship of 51 BCE and was finally elected to that office. His candidacy was immeasurably aided by the hostility, to both Caesar and Pompey, of another candidate for the consulship, Cato, and the generals' opposition to Cato's candidature proved decisive for the outcome of the election. The imperial Roman historian Dio Cassius reports that Sulpicius was elected for his knowledge of the law, but it is clear that he reached office primarily as a result of Cato's alienation of Caesar and Pompey, who backed his rivals.

Sulpicius' political career reached its apex with his election to the consulate, but his tenure of the office fell at a turbulent time. The years 52 to 50 saw tense and protracted political maneuvering at Rome—between Caesar and Pompey, formerly allied but estranged as a result of the successive deaths of Caesar's daughter Julia, Pompey's fourth wife, in 54 and Crassus, their erstwhile colleague in the compact, at the battle of Carrhae in 53; between the senate and Pompey, who was driven to treat with the optimate senatorial faction because of Caesar's growing military reputation and enrichment in Gaul; and between the senate and Caesar, who was threatened with prosecution upon laying down his Gallic command in 49. The imperial biographer Suetonius, in his *Life of Caesar*, records Sulpicius' steadfast support of an embattled Caesar in the face of his colleague's efforts to cut short his Gallic command a year early: "Caesar stoutly resisted Marcellus, partly through vetoes of the tribunes and partly through the other consul, Servius Sulpicius."[35]

Dio (40.59.1) attributes Sulpicius' actions in his consular year to his innate respect for the law—in contrast, he implies, to the illegal tactics of Pompey's partisan, the other consul Marcellus. Certainly, Sulpicius is consistently characterized in Cicero's voluminous writings as "conservative by training and temperament" and "devoted to the cause of constitutional government."[36] Cicero's correspondent Caelius complained about Sulpicius' delaying tactics in his year of office,[37] but Cicero himself respected Sulpicius' unswerving defense of peace, both during the difficult year of his consulship and afterwards,[38] and he recognized that his friend's counsel was resolutely offered with a view to political compromise and senatorial concord.[39] In the end, however, on January 7, 49 BCE, the Pompeian party secured passage of a senatorial decree declaring the republic in danger and summoning office-holders to Rome in order to prevent the state from suffering any damage (i.e., from Caesar). Four days later, Caesar responded by crossing the Rubicon, the river that separated the province of Gaul from Roman Italy, and the long threatened civil war broke out.

As the civil war clouds were gathering in the years 51–50 BCE, both Sulpicius and Cicero were trying to arrange marriages for their adult children—Sulpicius' youthful son (our poet's father), the homonymous Servius Sulpicius Rufus,[40] for the first time, and Cicero's daughter Tullia, for the third.[41] The younger Sulpicius' mother was a Postumia, from an ancient patrician family even older than her husband's, with consuls dating back to 505 BCE, when Publius Postumius Tubertus first held the office.[42] But there may have been some scandal attached to Postumia (or a sister?) at the time of her son's marriage.[43] She is named by the biographer Suetonius as one of Caesar's many amatory conquests,[44] though Cicero calls her "a very loyal wife" in his eulogy of Sulpicius some years later.[45] In Cicero's correspondence, Postumia figures as a socially shrewd and politically engaged Roman matron, much like his own wife Terentia, Tullia's mother.[46] Certainly, Postumia and Terentia took leading roles in arranging the marriages of their children.[47] Indeed, Cicero's letters reveal that both families drew on women's networks to make suitable marriages for their offspring. The younger Sulpicius' candidacy for marriage with Tullia was promoted not only by Sulpicius' wife Postumia but also by Servilia,[48] another prominent matron and Caesarian partisan, while Tullia and Terentia pursued a quite different marital alliance. Postumia, her husband, and her son remained on friendly terms with Cicero even after his own wife and daughter settled on a rival candidate for Tullia's third husband.[49] The younger Sulpicius, moreover, made an even more advantageous marriage, to a patrician Valeria, the sister of Messalla Corvinus (Ch. 3).[50]

Like Cicero, the Sulpicii father and son had to balance personal friendships against constitutional principles throughout the ensuing years of civil war (49–46 BCE). The jurist seems to have left Rome during Caesar's march on Rome but returned in March with several others in the senatorial party. In late March, Cicero reveals in correspondence with his friend Atticus that the jurist had sent his son to Caesar's camp in Brindisi, where Pompey's forces were besieged.[51] Shortly afterwards, on the first of April, the elder Sulpicius seems to have entered Caesar's senate, though apparently reluctantly as on that occasion he "gave a courageous speech on peace and the war in Spain which Caesar was about to begin."[52] In his letters from this period, Cicero portrays Sulpicius as a Caesarian partisan, sending his son to besiege Pompey and legitimizing Caesar's senate by his attendance. Later, however, he implies that Sulpicius had sent his son about peace,[53] at more or less the same time that the senate was debating sending legates to approach Pompey for the same reason, though in the end no official embassy was sent. In early May, Cicero reported to Atticus that Sulpicius had consulted him about their duty—even though he had already attended Caesar's senate in April.[54] Against Cicero's advice, Sulpicius declined to leave Italy, and his allegiance and motives in this period remain unclear to us, just as the situation in which they were caught up must have seemed perilously uncertain to many at the time.

In a series of speeches against Mark Antony, Cicero offers some late, ambiguous evidence that purports to place Sulpicius, like himself, in Pompey's camp in Greece, naming him among ten consular senators who would "not despise Pompey's senate"—i.e., his camp at Dyrrhachium.[55] But we lack reliable information about Sulpicius' movements or whereabouts from mid-May 49 until early July 47 BCE. Sulpicius' modern biographer has interpreted a statement in the *Digest* as suggesting that he spent this period outside of Italy, at work on his legal writings,[56] and it is certain that, when Sulpicius recurs in Cicero's writings in early July 47, he was on the island of Samos, discoursing on pontifical law and its relations with Roman civil law to the future tyrannicide Brutus.[57] In late September of that year, Cicero applauded Caesar's appointment of a trio of governors, including that of Sulpicius to the province of Achaea (i.e., Greece) for 46–45: "[Caesar] has commissioned Cassius as his legate, appointed Brutus governor of Gaul and Sulpicius of Greece...."[58] Perhaps Caesar required for Achaea not only a governor of good reputation and unquestioned authority, whose skills encompassed both compromise and diplomacy, but also, above all, a proconsular senator in possession of Pompeian connections, in order to diffuse enduring disaffection among the senatorial class.[59] Cicero implies that his friend struggled over the decision to accept Caesar's appointment[60] and the company in which he locates Sulpicius here must confirm his republican sympathies, since a few years later Brutus and Cassius formulated the plot that ended Caesar's life.

Sulpicius returned to Rome after his governorship, in late summer or autumn of 45 BCE. Caesar's assassination on the Ides of March 44 found him a senior consular in the Roman senate, but the conflict had taken a terrible toll on his health. He died less than a year later, in January 43, while on an embassy to negotiate peace with Mark Antony at Mutina.[61] On February 2, 43, the senate received the ambassadors' report about their meeting with Antony and proceeded to declare a state of public emergency. Two days later, the senate convened to discuss honors for the deceased Sulpicius. Cicero's ninth *Philippic* oration preserves the details of the senatorial debate. The consul spoke first, offering fulsome praise of Sulpicius and proposing the erection of a statue in his honor. A former consul, however, opposed the erection of a statue, on the grounds that Sulpicius had died of illness rather than on the battlefield, and proposed that Sulpicius be honored with a public tomb instead. Finally, Cicero himself spoke in praise of his old friend, paying tribute to his acceptance of a place in the embassy to Antony despite the gravity of his illness.[62] He argued for the propriety and precedent of the erection of a statue to honor Sulpicius, inasmuch as he had died while on active service for the senate. Since he had been a preeminent jurist and man of peace, however, Cicero proposed that he receive a pedestrian statue (i.e., standing on foot), as well as a public tomb and a state funeral.[63] The senate voted to accept Cicero's motion.[64]

With Sulpicius, Roman jurisprudence became a scientific study. In his day, jurisconsults engaged in three activities: responding to queries, drawing up formulas of security for clients, and advising on legal process.[65] The *Digest* preserves the names of some of his students—Alfenus Varus,[66] Aufidius Mamusa, and C. Ateius. His adherents seem to have systematized his responses, of which one hundred and fifty are reported, in eight books.[67] He is also credited with the refinement of two legal processes (regarding an owner's estate and a creditor's pledge)[68] and the authorship of as many as one hundred and eighty books on points of law.[69] His most famous work seems to have consisted of annotations, perhaps for clarification, of his teacher Scaevola's rulings.[70] We hear too of a treatise on dowries in one book, which was very influential in later centuries,[71] and a work on abjuring one's familial rites in at least two books.[72] His less securely attested titles include two books of notes on the praetor's edict, apparently dedicated to Brutus,[73] and perhaps a treatise on the laws of the Twelve Tables.[74]

Cicero, throughout his writings, bears witness to his friend's reputation as the leading jurisconsult of the day—perhaps as early as in his speech on behalf of Caecina in 69 BCE,[75] and certainly in his treatise of 52 BCE *On Laws*;[76] in the *Brutus*, his history of Roman eloquence from 46 BCE;[77] and in his eulogy in the ninth *Philippic*.[78] In the latter, he applauds

Sulpicius' "gravity, steadfastness, loyalty, and outstanding care and wisdom in guarding the republic," and credits his friend with "an amazing, unbelievable and nearly divine expertise in the interpretation of law and the explanation of equity." Cicero deems Sulpicius head and shoulders above all previous jurisconsults as "an expert not only in jurisprudence but equally in justice" and sums up his unique combination of juridical expertise and personal probity in his assessment that "to the interpretation of statutes and the civil law he always brought flexibility and a sense of fair play; he was not fonder of setting up processes of litigation than of clearing away disputes."

In his eulogy, Cicero depicts the younger Ser. Sulpicius Rufus as "too grief-stricken" to attend the meeting of the senate on that occasion.[79] He was perhaps not yet forty years old when his father died, born ca. 80 BCE as has been conjectured from his possible assistance in his father's prosecution of Murena in 63 BCE, when Cicero described him as "a talented and upright youth."[80] In his letters, the orator praises the jurist's son for his culture and wit.[81] He also mentions the youth's cousin, the tyrannicide Decimus Junius Brutus,[82] to whom he was presumably related through their mothers, since Servius' mother was a Postumia and his cousin changed his name upon his adoption by a Postumius Albinus (implying a familial connection with the Postumii).[83]

Cicero's daughter Tullia and the jurist's son, the younger Sulpicius, went their separate marital ways in 50 BCE, and the Church Father Jerome records the marriage of Ser. Sulpicius Rufus to Messalla's sister Valeria (Ch. 3).[84] Like his father, he seems to have avoided service in Caesar's civil war, and he also survived the turmoil unleashed by Caesar's assassination. Cicero records his presence in Rome in the first half of 43 BCE, unable to attend the meeting of the senate that celebrated his deceased father in early February but in June still "most loving" toward his cousin Brutus, who perished during a senatorial campaign against Mark Antony and Caesar's heir Octavian the following year.

This was a dangerous time for wealthy and prominent Roman citizens. Pre-empting senatorial governance, Octavian (the dictator's great nephew and adoptive son, the future emperor Augustus) made common cause with his great uncle's military commanders Mark Antony and Lepidus (Caesar's Master of the Horse) at a face-to-face meeting in October of 43 at Bononia (modern Bologna), where they concluded a formal pact to cooperate. Their control of Rome's legions induced the senate to appoint them as a "board of three for the ordering of the state," the so-called Second Triumvirate.[85] The triumvirs took advantage of their control of the state to draw up a list of proscribed citizens—men outside the protection of the law (effectively condemned to death), whose wealth they needed to pay their soldiers as civil war loomed between them and the republicans (led by the tyrannicides Brutus and Cassius).

In this troubled period, another exemplary Sulpicia emerges in our sources, daughter of an otherwise unknown Julia and wife of a certain Lentulus Cruscellio. Valerius Maximus preserves the notice of this late republican Sulpicia's exemplary conjugal loyalty:[86]

> Sulpicia was watched most carefully by her mother Julia to prevent her from following Lentulus Cruscellio, her husband proscribed by the Triumvirs, to Sicily. Nonetheless she reached him in a secret flight dressed in servile clothing along with two female slaves and the same number of male slaves. Nor did she refuse to proscribe herself in order to remain faithful to her proscribed husband.

As with his report of the exemplary chastity of the mid-republican Sulpicia (wife of Fulvius Flaccus) at the start of the second Punic war (quoted above, p. 19), Valerius here commemorates a paragon of wifely virtue whom he introduces under the rubric "of the fidelity of wives toward their husbands."[87] This tale too seems to have circulated widely, for Appian repeats it a century later in his history of Rome's civil wars.[88] While we cannot now discern the relationship of the jurist and his son to this exemplar of marital chastity, we can be sure that her ordeal was also commemorated in the family annals.[89]

Cicero's own death in December of 43, a victim of the proscriptions, leaves us without a contemporary witness to the subsequent career of the jurist's son. Later sources record the fame he achieved as an orator, primarily for his speech *Pro Aufidia*, on behalf of a female family client whom he defended against the prosecution of his brother-in-law Messalla.[90] The imperial rhetor and educator Quintilian knew three of his speeches and on their evidence deemed Sulpicius to possess "shrewd judgment,"[91] declaring him fully deserving of his "outstanding fame."[92] Since Quintilian records the name of Ser. Sulpicius Rufus in the ranks of orators prominent in the generation after Cicero—among them his brother-in-law Messalla (64 BCE–8 CE), Catullus' friend L. Licinius Calvus (82–47 BCE), the tyrannicide M. Junius Brutus (85–42 BCE), and the great Augustan orator Cassius

Severus (d. 32 CE)[93]—it has been thought that he embarked on his oratorical career in the 30s BCE, after the convulsions of Caesar's civil wars (49–46)
and the republicans' last stand at Philippi (42), during the relative stability
of the decade of triumviral rule after the proscriptions (42–32 BCE).[94] If so,
Sulpicius may have died toward the end of that decade, as our sources for
the reign of Augustus (31 BCE–14 CE) are silent about him.[95]

By his marriage, the younger Servius Sulpicius Rufus fathered a son, Servius
Sulpicius Postumius, and at least one daughter, our poet, and possibly two
(Table 1). The name of the younger Sulpicius' son, our poet's brother Sulpicius
Postumius, combines the family names of both his paternal grandparents,
the elder Sulpicius and his wife Postumia, in a manner calculated to recall
the antiquity of their patrician genealogies.[96] Sulpicius Postumius apparently followed family tradition and enjoyed a senatorial career under the
emperor Augustus. The imperial senator, engineer, and bureaucrat Frontinus
(ca. 40–103 CE) attests to Postumius' tenure of the praetorship in his history
of Rome's aqueducts. He records the information that in 11 BCE, a year after
the death of Augustus' friend Agrippa, who served as the first commissioner
of Rome's aqueducts, Messalla succeeded to the office on the emperor's
appointment "and was given as his assistants Postumius Sulpicius, an ex-
praetor [praetorius], and L. Cominius, a junior senator."[97]

Sulpicia and her brother must have been born between 50 at the earliest
(given the date of their father's marriage) and 33 at the latest (given his disappearance from the historical record in Augustus' reign), perhaps most
likely in the year Caesar crossed the Rubicon or after his assassination
(when Cicero locates their father in Rome).[98] Some have thought that the
younger Sulpicius was killed during the proscriptions, but Syme has argued
that he more likely escaped this fate, like his brother-in-law Messalla; and,
indeed, we shall see that the poet Horace places him in Rome in 35 BCE
(Ch. 5).[99] If the minimum age requirement of 39 for tenure of the office of
praetor was still in force in this period (though there is some evidence that
it could be waived for elite youth in Augustus' day), Sulpicius Postumius is
likely to have been the eldest child, born in 50 or 49 BCE. That would place
Sulpicia's birth some years later, given the civil wars of the following years,
either during Caesar's dictatorship or its immediate aftermath, in the mid-
to late 40s BCE, when we can place her father in Rome.

In addition to his son (our poet's father), the jurist sired at least one and
possibly two or even three daughters,[100] our poet's aunts, who will also have
been named Sulpicia in accordance with Roman onomastic convention.

Table 1 Sulpicia's Paternal Lineage

(Adapted from Syme 1986, Table XXIV and Münzer, *RE* IV A. 879–80)

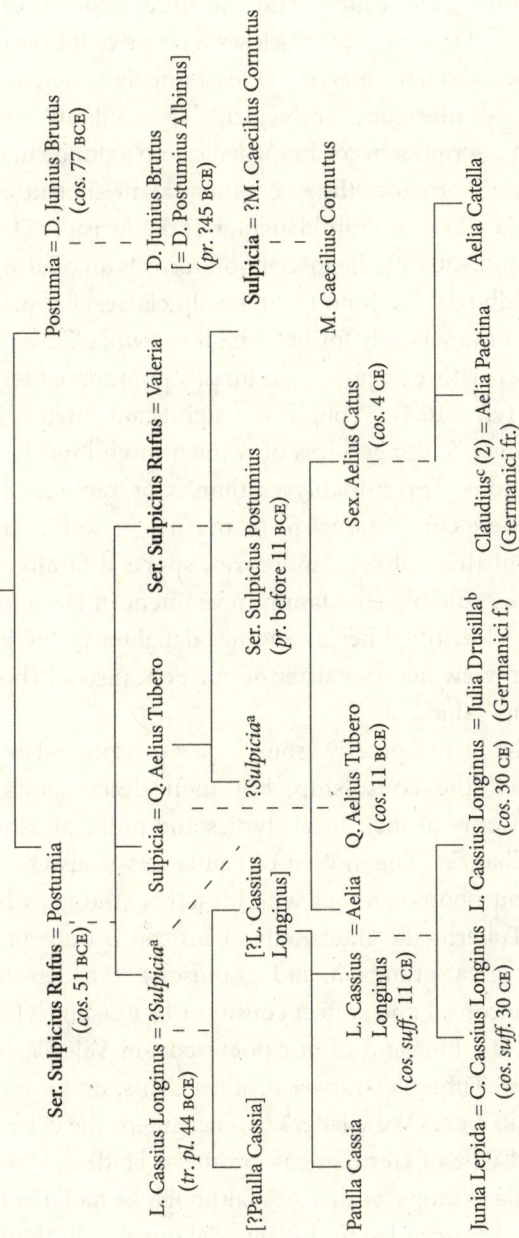

a The dedicant of *ILS* 3103 (= *CIL* I² 979 = *CIL* VI 361), identified by Münzer as a daughter of the jurist; alternately, by Syme, as the jurist's granddaughter, sister of our poet.

b The daughter of Germanicus Caesar and sister of the emperor Caligula (r. 37–41 CE).

c The brother of Germanicus Caesar, the emperor Claudius (r. 41–54 CE).

The *Digest* records the marriage of the distinguished lawyer and historian Tubero[101] to a daughter of the jurist in a reference to Tubero's son-in-law Cassius Longinus, also a jurist and the suffect consul of 30 CE, late in Tiberius' reign.[102] The comment discloses a nexus of juridical intermarriage, as Sulpicius seems to have married at least one daughter, and possibly two, to a younger legal colleague. For the jurists' descendants, see Table 1.

An Augustan inscription recording a dedication to Juno Lucina by "Sulpicia, Servius' daughter" provides the only other extant ancient evidence for the marriage of a daughter or granddaughter of the jurist.[103] Dated to the early principate (30 BCE–30 CE), the inscription records an offering to the Roman goddess of childbirth: "To Juno Lucina, Sulpicia Servius' daughter gave this gift willingly and deservedly for her daughter Paulla Cassia." Strikingly, the dedicant shares with our poet (the jurist's granddaughter) not only her nomenclature (cf. 3.16.4),[104] but also a significant interest in Juno Lucina ("the light-bringer"), the goddess of women in childbirth (cf. 3.8.1–2), to whom dedications, "presumably as thanks or requests for a return to good health," were conventional from an early period in ancient Rome.[105] The husband of this Sulpicia, moreover, sports a family name, Cassius, that belongs to a suitably elite family, prominent in law and politics of the period. Münzer identified her as another daughter of the jurist, but Syme may be right to view her as a sister of our poet instead (both possibilities are canvassed in Table 1).[106]

Neither of the jurist's putative sons-in-law (or son-in-law and grandson-in-law) attained the consulship, but their descendants distinguished themselves not only in their legal studies and political careers but also in their marital alliances. The mother of Paulla Cassia also bore a son named Cassius Longinus, homonymous with his father (though whether it was he who married Tubero's daughter Aelia or his son is uncertain). The jurists' grandsons (or great-grandson and grandson), the cousins Tubero and Longinus, were consul and suffect consul in 11 BCE and 11 CE respectively, the latter with the husband of our poet's cousin Valeria, Statilius Taurus (Table 2, Ch. 3). Tubero's younger brother Catus, moreover, also achieved the consulship in 4 CE. Of the latter's two daughters, the elder (Aelia Paetina) was the second wife of Germanicus' brother Claudius, who succeeded his nephew Caligula as emperor in 41 CE (although he had divorced her almost a decade before he ascended to the imperial purple). Both of Aelia Paetina's cousins (her aunt Aelia's sons), attained the consulship in 30 CE—Lucius Cassius Longinus as *consul ordinarius* and Gaius Cassius Longinus as suffect consul—and both also married into the imperial house. Lucius married the emperor Caligula's sister Julia Livilla, a daughter of Germanicus (the emperor Tiberius' nephew and adoptive son) and Augustus' granddaughter Agrippina (the elder), while Gaius married Junia Lepida, the granddaughter of Augustus' granddaughter Julia (daughter of his daughter Julia).

We have no information about the childhood household of the poet Sulpicia and her brother. Nonetheless, we can conjecture much about the siblings' upbringing on the basis of that of their contemporaries (Ch. 4). On the younger Sulpicius' death, his children seem to have passed into the guardianship of their mother Valeria's natal family, the subject of the next chapter.

Sulpicia: Life, Love, and Literature in Ancient Rome. Alison Keith, Oxford University Press.
© Oxford University Press 2026. DOI: 10.1093/9780197607008.003.0003

3

Niece of the Augustan Aristocracy

The Church Father Jerome, in his treatise *Against Jovinian* in defense of celibacy, records the marriage of Valeria to Servius Sulpicius Rufus. Jerome excerpted the information from the younger Seneca's treatise on marriage, no longer extant, for inclusion in his notice about "famous Roman wives" who chose a celibate life:[1]

> Let me pass to Roman women; and let me put Lucretia first…Valeria, Messalla's sister, after she lost her husband Servius, was not willing to marry anyone. Asked why she would do this, she said that, for her, her husband Servius would always live.

Writing in an early Christian context, Jerome reframes the Roman ideal of female sexual fidelity to a single husband as the precursor to a newly emergent theological model of celibate widowhood spent in pious devotion. Seneca's report of Valeria's decision not to remarry, however, must be interpreted in the early imperial context of Augustus' marriage and adultery legislation of 18–16 BCE, which required elite Roman women between the ages of 18 and 50 (i.e., in their childbearing years) to remarry within ten months of divorce or their husband's death.[2] The legislation was so unpopular that it had to be repeated a generation later, in 9 CE, though it remained valid (and could be enforced) throughout the principate. Nonetheless, women like Augustus' granddaughter the elder Agrippina, who declined to remarry after the death of her husband Germanicus (Augustus' step-grandson), continued to be celebrated in the ancient Roman exemplary tradition for chaste devotion to their deceased spouses. Valerius Maximus' near contemporary notice about the mid-Republican Sulpicia who dedicated the statue of Venus Verticordia (Ch. 2) bears witness to this longstanding Roman ideal of female sexual virtue and marital chastity. As a widow, moreover, Valeria will have gained both a financial autonomy and a personal authority unlikely to have been available to Christian women in the same circumstances.[3] In this regard, it will have helped that her own lineage was still more distinguished than that of her husband. For the Valerii were an even older patrician family than the Sulpicii and one that enjoyed both longer-lasting, and far greater, electoral success at Rome.

The Valerian family, of ancient Sabine stock, went back to the very foundation of the Roman republic when Valerius Publicola ("friend of the people") helped Brutus "the Liberator" overthrow the Etruscan kings and joined him as suffect consul (replacing Lucretia's husband Tarquin Collatinus) in the first year of the newly constituted republican state (509 BCE).[4] In the same year, he celebrated a triumph for his victory over the Etruscans at the battle in which Brutus was killed.[5] Publicola went on to hold three more consulships in close succession (508, 507, 504)[6] and to celebrate a second triumph for victories over the Sabines and Veientines (504).[7] His cognomen Publicola passed into the family—we shall see that it was held by Valeria's half-brother Gellius.

The early republican Publicola's fame was so great that his sister and daughter (both named Valeria) earn a reflected prestige in Roman legend. Along with the Roman antiquarian Dionysius of Halicarnassus and historian Appian, Publicola's biographer Plutarch names his sister Valeria as the leader of a delegation of Roman women sent to intercede with the wife and mother of another legendary Roman general, Coriolanus, when he raised an army against Rome. Plutarch implies that she was selected for this role (presumably by her peers) because of the prestige she enjoyed as a result of her brother's outstanding military and political career.[8] Publicola's daughter, moreover, is occasionally credited with the feat, more commonly attributed to an otherwise unknown Cloelia,[9] of leading the group of Roman female hostages who escaped from the Etruscan king Lars Porsenna by swimming across the Tiber. According to the elder Pliny, this Valeria was recognized for her bravery by the receipt of an equestrian statue.[10]

Another illustrious male ancestor of Sulpicia's mother was Valerius Maximus Corvus ("Raven"),[11] from whom Valeria's brother Messalla derived his cognomen Corvinus ("of or belonging to a raven").[12] Corvus (371–271 BCE) won his cognomen at the age of twenty-two when, as a military tribune in 349 BCE, he defeated a Gaul in single combat with the help of a divinely sent raven.[13] He went on to hold six consulships, serve three times as dictator[14] and four times as praetor,[15] as well as to take part in a special commission of three to found a Latin colony at Saticula;[16] and he also celebrated five triumphs, military victory parades voted by the senate in recognition of success in battle.[17] Reported to have been nearly one hundred years of age at his death, he lived to see his son hold the consulship three times and the censorship once.[18] His military and political renown remained so great in Augustus' day that the emperor erected a statue of him in the gallery of Rome's "greatest men" in his forum.[19]

Valeria's brother gained his other cognomen, Messalla, from a third famous Valerian ancestor, the grandson of Corvus, Valerius Maximus Messalla.[20] As consul in 263 BCE, at the beginning of the first Punic war (264–241 BCE), he captured many Sicilian towns, including Messana and Syracuse, and he celebrated a triumph over the Carthaginians and Hiero, king of Syracuse.[21] The Capitoline *Fasti* (Roman calendar records) report that he earned the cognomen Messalla during his consulship, and later sources explain the form as a corruption of the city-name Messana.[22] As censor in 252,[23] he went on to expel sixteen men from the senate and demote four hundred knights to the lowest census class because of their disobedience in Sicily.[24]

The *gens Valeria* even boasted a famous man of letters, Valerius Antias, a Roman historian,[25] whose lost history of Rome began with the city's origins and covered events down to ca. 91 BCE in at least seventy-five books. He is generally held to have been of Sullan date (i.e., writing in the 80s BCE), and seems to have been a major source for the Augustan historian Livy.[26] His lack of a first name and his Greek cognomen imply servile origin in the household of a wealthy Valerius of the first half of the first century BCE. It has therefore been conjectured that he celebrated Valerian family history in his work and that the Augustan currency of the exploits of the many republican Valerii was due to him.[27]

Our poet's mother Valeria was the daughter of Valerius Messalla Niger. He was appointed to the pontifical college (perhaps by Sulla) and elected to the quaestorship before 70 BCE, when the censors are reported to have expelled him from the senate.[28] If so, he returned soon enough, elected to the praetorship of 64 BCE, the year his son—Valeria's brother—Messalla Corvinus was probably born. Niger was consul in 61 BCE, the first of his line to hold curule office in a hundred years.[29] He went on to serve on Caesar's agrarian commission in 59 and to hold the censorship in 55/4: an extant inscription records his regulation of the Tiber in that capacity after a flood in 54 (*ILLRP* 476). In the violence and disorder of the late 50s, Niger also served three times as *interrex*, the magistrate presiding over irregular consular elections, and apparently died shortly thereafter. Cicero records his prominence as an orator and pleader in the courts:[30]

M. Messalla [Niger], younger than I, was not without resource, but his diction possessed no great distinction; as a pleader he showed judgement, shrewdness and caution, diligence in mastering and arranging his case, great industry and devotion, and was engaged in many cases.

We have no information about Niger's marriages or the dates of his children's births, but some details can be deduced from the dates of the consulships of his son and stepson, as well as from the date of his daughter's marriage. The first name and gentilician (family name) of Messalla's stepbrother[31] Lucius Gellius Publicola proclaim him the son by blood of the homonymous consul of 72 BCE, while the date of his consulship (36 BCE) implies a birthyear in the mid-70s BCE. His mother's name is not recorded, but she will have been divorced from Gellius senior by the end of the 70s and remarried to Niger soon after. The date of their daughter Valeria's birth must be conjectured on the basis of the date of her own marriage to Servius Sulpicius Rufus in 50 BCE, and is plausibly placed in the early 60s, as that would make her a little over a decade younger than her husband, in accordance with elite Roman marital conventions.[32]

Jerome dates her brother Messalla's birth to 59 BCE and his death to 11 CE, but he also reports that Messalla died at the age of 72, which would place his death two years later, in 13 CE.[33] These dates, however, cohere neither with the evidence of Messalla's command on Brutus' right wing at Philippi in 42 BCE (i.e., at the implausibly young age of 17), nor with the poet Ovid's eyewitness account of his funeral in Rome (i.e., before December, 8 CE, when the elegist was relegated to Tomis on the Black Sea).[34] H. Schulz therefore argued that Jerome confused the consuls of 59 (Gaius Julius Caesar and Bibulus) with those of 64 (Lucius Julius Caesar and Figulus), and placed Messalla's birth in 64 BCE and his death (at age 72) in 8 CE.[35] These dates align well with the full evidence for Messalla's life and career, and they have been widely accepted for over a century.[36]

Born in 64 BCE then, Messalla was a close contemporary of both Cicero's son Marcus (b. 65 BCE)[37] and Octavian, the future emperor Augustus (b. 63 BCE).[38] Messalla Niger was a noted pleader, and it is likely that he saw to it that his son received a traditional Roman education in oratory: first in grammar (via poetry, both Greek and Latin) and then in rhetoric (via declamation, again both Greek and Latin) and later in philosophy (in Greece).[39] Moreover, just as Servius Sulpicius' father attached himself to the leading jurisconsults in his youth, in order to pursue his studies in jurisprudence

(Ch. 2), so Messalla, after his father's death, seems to have attached himself to Cicero, the leading speaker of the day, to further his oratorical studies. Cicero records Messalla's intention to study in Greece in late March 45 BCE, when his own son Marcus was preparing to go to Athens.[40] Two decades later, the Augustan poet Horace recalls Messalla's commitment while there to the study of philosophy at Plato's Academy: "he drenched himself in Socratic discourses."[41] In a letter of reference to Brutus the tyrannicide, moreover, Cicero lauds the young Messalla's talent and experience: "thus with serious judgment and much artistry he has applied himself in the most severe style of speaking."[42]

After the murder of Caesar, on the Ides of March in 44 BCE, Brutus and Cassius along with many of the other republican "liberators" fled Rome for her eastern provinces in Asia Minor, where they proceeded to exact funds to finance their troops in anticipation of further civil warfare. Messalla returned to Rome that spring, calling on Cicero in June of 44 to give him a good report of his son Marcus, who remained in Athens.[43] In the midst of the turmoil, Messalla seems to have begun his political career in earnest and, while continuing to polish his oratorical skills, was perhaps still attached in some capacity to Cicero.[44] In a letter to Brutus, written at the beginning of July 43, Cicero mentions entrusting to Messalla a letter for him of some political import,[45] and in a later letter to Brutus, from the middle of the same month, Cicero introduces his protégé with a glowing reference, praising his "virtue, loyalty, diligence, and love of the republic."[46] Messalla was thus likely in town when his niece Sulpicia was born, if indeed she was born that year.

That fall, Cicero began to deliver the series of senatorial speeches, known as the *Philippics*, which rendered him odious to the Caesarian party of Mark Antony, Octavian, and Lepidus. After their appointment by the senate as a Board of Three for the Ordering of the State, they therefore included Cicero's name at the top of their list of proscribed citizens. Messalla's longstanding association with Cicero may explain why the triumvirs entered his name, along with Cicero's, onto the list of the proscribed. It has been conjectured that the younger Servius Sulpicius was also proscribed (Ch. 2), but in the event both he and his brother-in-law Messalla escaped—as Cicero did not.

After Cicero's death in December of 43 BCE, we have no further first-hand testimony about the movements of Messalla or his brother-in-law Sulpicius during the civil wars. The historian Appian reports that Messalla was proscribed by the triumvirs, "because they feared his courageous spirit,"[47] and that he fled to Brutus,[48] although he himself claimed allegiance to Cassius.[49] Messalla's modern biographer, Jakob Hammer, suggests that Messalla reached Cassius late in 43 at Smyrna, where he and Brutus had joined forces to prepare for battle against the Caesarians.[50] Dio records Cassius' military actions against Cappadocia and Rhodes in this period, and Hammer suggests that this is where Messalla may first have distinguished himself in battle.[51]

The historian Velleius (writing under the emperor Tiberius) reports that Messalla's authority in the republican camp was second only to that of Brutus and Cassius,[52] a formulation that may well derive from Messalla's *Memoirs* (no longer extant), which we know Plutarch drew on in his account of the two engagements between the Caesarian and republican forces collectively known as the battle of Philippi (October, 42 BCE).[53] Plutarch records Cassius' placement of Messalla on Brutus' right wing in the first engagement, in which Brutus routed Octavian's forces (capturing three eagles) but Cassius was defeated by Antony's army and committed suicide, mistakenly believing that Brutus had also been defeated. In a second engagement, two weeks later, the republican forces were decisively defeated and Brutus himself committed suicide. The republican forces retreated to the island of Thasos, where Messalla was offered, but declined, command of the army.[54] Instead, he and Bibulus reached an agreement with Antony, and committed their supplies, funds, troops, and ships to him when he reached Thasos.[55] Hammer conjectures that Messalla traveled with Antony in the aftermath, including on the trip to Tarsus in 41 BCE, where Antony summoned Cleopatra to explain her conduct in the civil war but ended up succumbing to her charms (no doubt financial, political, and military as much as sexual).[56] On Antony's tour of the east in 41–40, we also hear of Messalla continuing to practice oratory: at Antioch, where a Jewish embassy complained that the brothers Herodes and Phaselus ruled by force, Messalla defended them so successfully that Antony appointed them tetrarchs of Judea.[57]

The ancient sources explain Messalla's transfer of allegiance from Antony to Octavian as resulting from his disgust at the debauchery of court life under Antony and Cleopatra in Egypt,[58] but we do not know when or why the final break occurred. Antony spent the winter of 41–40 with Cleopatra, fathering her twins (b. 40 BCE) before marrying Octavian's sister Octavia in the autumn of 40. Horace places Messalla in Rome in 35, pleading in the courts,[59] a year after the historians record his presence with Octavian's forces in the naval war against Sextus Pompey off Sicily. Syme hazards that he had brought a squadron from Mark Antony.[60] Appian reports that in the initial stages of the naval action Messalla "commanded in Agrippa's absence,"[61] brokering the surrender of one of Sextus' captains[62] and facilitating Octavian's recovery of his forces after being trapped by Sextus.[63] Early in September of 36, however, when Agrippa decisively defeated Sextus at Naulochos, Messalla is nowhere mentioned as having participated in the sea battle. Yet in the aftermath, Octavian rewarded him among his other lieutenants, appointing him (supernumerary) to the college of augurs, a position with a lifetime tenure.[64] Perhaps it was then that Messalla transferred his allegiance from Antony to Octavian, for he joined Octavian's campaigns in Illyricum in 35–34, participating in the expedition against the Pannonians (in modern Croatia) in the summer of 35 and the following year leading Roman troops against the Salassi (in northwestern Italy).[65] Messalla's presence in Italy and environs in the mid-30s may have stabilized the fortunes of his sister Valeria's family in the aftermath of her husband's death and her children's entry into his guardianship.

The Tiberian historian Velleius claimed that Augustus "was never happier about anything in his victories than for having saved Corvinus, while there was no greater example of a grateful and dutiful man than Corvinus in regard to him."[66] He gives us no clue about the date of his transfer of allegiance, however, and it has been suggested that Messalla could have maintained a studied independence of allegiance until late in 33 BCE, possibly even into the early weeks of 32, when the consuls—both Antonians— left Italy for Egypt "and the crisis broke."[67] It is in this latter period that we may place Messalla's three pamphlets against Antony, mentioned by a late grammarian but no longer extant:[68] "On Antony's statues," about the sycophantic (to the Roman mind) erection of statues to the dynast in the Greek east; "On Asia's tax system," presumably about such vagaries as Antony's assignment to a flute player of responsibility for collecting taxes in four cities;[69] and "Against Antony's letters," which may have contained "either a personal defence or something to refute scandalous allegations against Italy's leader."[70] The break between the dynasts occurred early in 32 BCE, when Octavian revealed the contents of Antony's will (naming his children by Cleopatra—illegitimate in Roman eyes—as his heirs)[71] and stripped him of the following year's consulship. With another civil war inevitable, Messalla's choice was clear for all to see in his receipt of the consulship of 31—in place of Antony and alongside Octavian.[72]

Appian reports that at the battle of Actium (September, 31 BCE) Messalla held a naval command under Agrippa.[73] Plutarch supplements this statement with the report that Octavian lauded Messalla's zeal in the battle.[74] On the other side, Messalla's half-brother Gellius Publicola commanded Antony's right wing.[75] There is no record of Gellius' fate after the battle, which left Octavian master of the Mediterranean, but it has been suggested that the sibling connection may have saved him again in 31.[76] Antony and Cleopatra, besieged the following year in Alexandria by Octavian's forces, committed suicide in August of 30.

Octavian himself took nearly a year to reach Egypt after Actium, having had to settle a mutiny in Italy before traveling through Greece, Asia, and Syria, where Messalla is reported to have destroyed a band of Cyzicene gladiators marching to support Antony in Egypt.[77] In his elegy 1.3, Messalla's protégé Tibullus represents himself as ill at Corcyra, while his patron martials Roman forces for an eastern mission.[78] The poet also mentions this campaign in his elegy 1.7 by reference to cities and landmarks in Cilicia and Syria, two of Rome's eastern provinces unsettled during the conflict between Antony and Octavian.[79] The literary evidence has been interpreted as suggesting that Messalla governed Syria in 30/29 BCE, preceding Cicero's son in the post.[80] Perhaps he returned to Rome in time to witness Octavian's triple triumph the following year, August 13–15, 29 BCE.

The Roman historian Tacitus wryly observed how profitable the civil wars had been for Messalla and Pollio, "stuffed full of spoils in the wars between Antony and Octavian."[81] Messalla had the opportunity to acquire further wealth in 28/27 BCE, when he was sent out to Gaul with proconsular authority to quell an uprising of the Aquitani.[82] The *Acta Triumphalia* record his appointment as governor of the province in that year,[83] and the poet Tibullus also bears witness to his patron's campaign in Aquitania in his encomiastic review of the region's geography in elegy 1.7 (vv. 9–12). Octavian received the title "Augustus" by a vote of the senate in January of 27, when Messalla was still on active military service in Gaul. For his victories there, the *Acta Triumphalia* record his receipt of a triumph celebrated on his birthday, September 25, 27 BCE.[84] Upon his return, Messalla undertook the repair of a stretch of the Via Latina between Tusculum and the Alban hills.[85] Suetonius' report that Augustus "personally undertook to rebuild the Via Flaminia all the way to Rimini, and assigned the rest of the peninsula's roads to men who had been honored with triumphs, asking them to use the money acquired from their spoils to pave them" has led scholars to assume that the wealth that accrued to Messalla from his Gallic campaign paid for his reconstruction of this section of the Via Latina.[86] In this connection, we may also note the elder Pliny's casual mention of Messalla's restoration of two statues of the Sibyl, an ancient prophetess.[87] Their renewal may have been undertaken in conjunction with Augustus' concomitant efforts to beautify the city,[88] as we know that the emperor moved the Sibylline books, a collection of oracles, to the newly built temple of Apollo which adjoined his own residence on the Palatine.[89] In this context, it is surely relevant that in his elegy 2.5 Tibullus celebrated the appointment of his patron's son Messallinus to the Board of Fifteen Men charged with oversight of the Sibylline books.[90]

In his absence from Italy during the final showdown with Antony, Octavian left the peninsula in the informal (and illegitimate) care of his friend Maecenas, patron of the poets Vergil and Horace among others. Upon his departure on campaign in the provinces of Gaul and Spain in the summer of 27 BCE, however, Augustus resurrected the urban prefecture—a monarchal post his adoptive father Julius Caesar had employed during his tenure of the dictatorship in the mid-40s BCE—and he appointed Messalla to the office at the beginning of January the next year.[91] On entering office, Messalla seems to have reacted to his formal appointment as city prefect with a resurgent republican spirit: having initially accepted the post, he resigned it less than a week later, apparently considering the office unconstitutional.[92] Yet his resignation does not seem to have strained relations with the emperor. Dio reports that when, the following year, the house on the Palatine formerly owned by Mark Antony, which Augustus had given to Agrippa and Messalla for their joint occupation (a signal honor), burned down, the emperor compensated Messalla with money for his loss.[93]

After his abortive tenure of the post of urban prefecture, Messalla seems to have retired from active political and military service. During the 20s and 10s BCE, however, he kept on playing a leading role in the cultural life of Rome (see below). No doubt he continued to foster the education of his wards, Sulpicia and her brother, and groom them for their adult roles of marriage for Sulpicia (Ch. 4), and a political career for her brother Sulpicius Postumius. Indeed, when Messalla next appears in the historical record, in 11 BCE upon taking up the newly created position of "keeper of the waters" in charge of Rome's aqueducts after Agrippa's death,[94] Messalla sponsored his nephew as one of his assistants in the post (Ch. 2). Frontinus reports that Messalla remained in office until his death.

His last recorded political act occurred in the year 2 BCE, when Augustus assumed the consulship for the thirteenth time, in order to introduce his second adopted son into public life.[95] In that year, Suetonius reports a spontaneous deputation of citizens to the emperor's estate at Antium, outside Rome, to offer him the title "Father of the Fatherland."[96] Augustus modestly declined the offer, but a second public demonstration occurred on his arrival at the theater in Rome, and he was finally confirmed in the title, according to Suetonius, "not by a decree or by acclamation, but through Valerius Messalla."[97] The senate apparently retained the text of Messalla's exact words: "May good fortune and divine favor attend you and your house, Caesar Augustus. For so we deem we are praying for everlasting felicity for the republic and prosperity for this city: the senate, in agreement with the Roman people, together salutes you as Father of the fatherland." Perhaps Messalla published the speech he pronounced on that historic occasion;[98] it was certainly one of the highlights of his public career.

Cicero's praise of Messalla's oratorical talent already in 43 BCE foreshadowed his pre-eminence in the field in the following generation.[99] The author of the *Panegyric of Messalla* (composed on the occasion of Messalla's consulship in 31 BCE and preserved in the *Appendix Tibulliana*),[100] praises the power of his oratory to calm the rampant mob,[101] and Augustus' stepson, the future emperor Tiberius, is reported to have taken him as a model of eloquence in his youth.[102] Ovid in his exile poetry, asking Messalla's sons to intercede for him with the emperor, recalls their father's "polished eloquence" and "eloquent tongue," and he even claims that Messalla embodied "the eloquence of the Latin language."[103] The poet certainly knew Messalla's eloquence first-hand, for he records the support Messalla gave him as his earliest patron.[104] Messalla's interest in Latin literature thus extended well beyond the years of his active military/political career.

The elder Seneca (ca. 54 BCE–ca. 39 CE), who witnessed the zenith of Augustan oratory, preserves abundant evidence of Messalla's participation in the contemporary vogue for declamation (the performance of practice speeches on historical and legal themes),[105] along with the title of one of his orations (*Pro Pythodoro*).[106] He pronounced Messalla's judgment "of the most exacting, in every branch of study," and deemed his use of the Latin language to show "the most careful precision."[107] A century later, Quintilian and Tacitus attest to his lasting fame as a speaker.[108] Quintilian mentions

Messalla's use of translation exercises in his oratorical training,[109] and he also records the information that Messalla "devoted whole books not only to words but to letters,"[110] including a treatise on the letter "s."[111] Elsewhere he offers fulsome praise of his oratory (10.5.2), remarking its "excellence,"[112] and characterizing his style as "elegant and clear," "somehow exhibiting his distinction in his speaking," even though he was "not outstanding in strength."[113] Indeed, both Quintilian and Tacitus comment on Messalla's characteristically "self-effacing" openings,[114] in which he apparently deprecated his strength, preparation, and/or ability to rise to the occasion. It has been suggested that he perfected a restrained, "low-key" style appropriate not only to an aesthetic standard of linguistic elegance but also to his physical constitution,[115] as there is some evidence that his health may not have been robust. In a lost treatise "On Messalla's health," the polymath Varro (d. 27 BCE) mocks Valerius Messalla for being excessively concerned about his health, while the elder Pliny cites Messalla Corvinus as an example of the fragility of memory.[116] The latter notice, however, may refer to the final two years of Messalla's life when, according to Jerome, he lost both his memory and the ability to speak. It is in this context that Jerome reports that Messalla finally starved himself to death, at the age of 72.

Although Messalla's marriage(s) are not on record, his two sons—Sulpicia's cousins—enjoyed long and illustrious careers under the emperors Augustus and Tiberius, and the dates of their tenures of office can shed some light on their birthyears if not on their maternal lineage. Messalla's elder son, Messalla Messallinus is mentioned as a child in the mid-30s by the poet of *Catalepton* 9,[117] and we know that he was inducted into the Board of Fifteen entrusted with the care of the Sibylline books around 20 BCE, an occasion commemorated in Tibullus' elegy 2.5 (vv. 114–18). Birth in the year 36 has therefore been surmised, since in the principate sons of the nobility could enter into priesthoods as early as their assumption of the adult toga.[118] Messalinus was thus some years younger than his cousin Sulpicia (Table 2).

In 6 CE, nine years after his consulship, he went out to Dalmatia and Pannonia as legate but left to campaign in support of Augustus' heir Tiberius, who held a command against the Marcomani in Bohemia.[119] In his absence, the Illyrian provinces revolted and Tiberius sent him back to deal with the rebellion; at first unsuccessful, he finally defeated the insurgents in an ambush,[120] and was awarded triumphal ornaments for his victory.[121] Ovid addresses three poetic epistles from exile to him, lauding

Table 2 Sulpicia's Maternal Family

(Adapted from Syme 1986, Table IX)

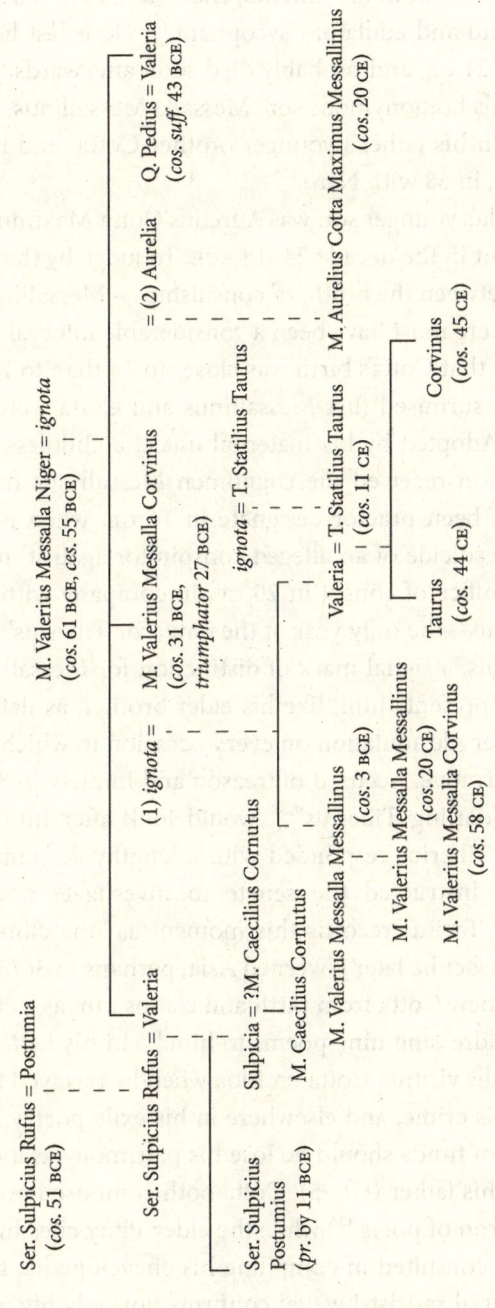

his inherited eloquence and appealing to his close relations with the ruling house.[122] Tacitus, in the *Annales*, characterizes him as the emperor Tiberius' close friend and adulatory sycophant.[123] He is last heard of in a senatorial debate of 21 CE, and probably died soon afterwards,[124] though not without an heir: his homonymous son, Messalla Messallinus, held the consulship in 20 CE with his father's younger brother Cotta, and his son's son, Messalla Corvinus, in 58 with Nero.[125]

Messalla's younger son was Aurelius Cotta Maximus Messallinus, born at some point in the decade 24–14 BCE. To judge by the over twenty-year separation between the brothers' consulships—Messallinus' in 3 BCE, Cotta's in 20 CE—there must have been a considerable interval between their ages, so it is likely that Cotta's birth was closer to 14 than to 24. From the gap it has also been surmised that Messallinus and Cotta were the sons of different wives.[126] Adopted by his maternal uncle, a childless Aurelius Cotta,[127] the younger son received the cognomen Messallinus from his brother.[128] He may have been praetor-designate in 16 CE, when he spoke in the senate about the suicide of an alleged conspirator against imperial rule,[129] and he held the office of consul in 20 CE, in company with his nephew Messalla Messallinus—the only year of the emperor Tiberius' reign that saw no suffect consuls, a signal mark of distinction for Messalla's illustrious progeny. Tacitus represents him, like his elder brother, as flattering Tiberius to the point of servile adulation on every occasion in which he appears in his historical narrative. Accused of treason and impiety in 32 CE, Cotta predicted that his "darling Tiberius"[130] would look after him and appealed to the emperor. Tiberius responded with a lengthy account of their long friendship and instructed the senate to investigate one of Cotta's accusers instead.[131] Tacitus records this moment as "the climax of Cotta's honors," though in fact he later governed Asia, perhaps in 36/37.[132]

Ovid knew Cotta from birth and claims him as a close friend in the exile poetry, addressing nine poems to him.[133] In his *Letters from the Black Sea*, Ovid recalls visiting Cotta on Elba when he received the sentence of relegation for his crime, and elsewhere in his exile poetry he cites Cotta's generous offer of funds should he lose his patrimony as a result.[134] Ovid reports that, like his father (Ch. 5), Cotta both composed poetry[135] and was a generous patron of poets,[136] while the elder Pliny cites him among the authors whom he consulted in compiling his encyclopedia, the *Natural History*.[137] The imperial satirist Juvenal confirms not only his patronage of poets but also his largesse,[138] and the two qualities are jointly commemorated in the funerary epitaph of one of his freedmen, Marcus Aurelius Zosimus, who records his gratitude for Cotta's provision of financial support so munificent as to enable him to attain equestrian status and dower his daughters, as well as providing the five elegiac distichs that graced his tomb.[139]

No descendants of Sulpicia or her brother are discernible in the inscriptional archive, unless Marcus Caecilius Cornutus (*PIR*[2] C35) is her son (Ch. 4; see Table 2). The male line of her maternal uncle Messalla ended with his namesake and great-grandson, Marcus Valerius Messalla Corvinus, consul with Nero in 58 CE. Of Messalla's two presumed wives, only the name (Aurelia)—and not the filiation—of his second is known and that by conjecture from her son's adoption by his maternal uncle and resulting name change. Likewise, neither the name/s of Cotta's wife or wives nor those of his brother Messallinus are recoverable from the historical record.[140] We do, however, have evidence, both direct and indirect, for the existence of several of Sulpicia's female relatives on the maternal side—as, for example, her mother Valeria, Messalla's sister. Valeria and Messalla had another sister, also named Valeria in accordance with the conventions of Roman nomenclature, who married Quintus Pedius, another great-nephew of Julius Caesar and the quaestor of 41 BCE, whose father shared the suffect consulship with Octavian in 43 BCE.[141] It has also been conjectured that Messalla himself had a daughter by his second wife Aurelia—another Valeria, cousin to our poet, who will have married the homonymous son of Augustus' general Statilius Taurus, since one of their two sons bore the cognomen Corvinus, and Suetonius confirms him as Messalla's grandson.[142] Given the reappearance of the cognomen Corvinus in this generation, their father's marriage to a daughter of Messalla Corvinus is inescapable. Either this Corvinus or his brother Taurus, moreover, will have been the father of Statilia Messalina,[143] the third wife of the emperor Nero (in turn her fifth husband). Thus, on her mother's side too, Sulpicia anticipates a distant relationship to the imperial house, as the Julio-Claudian dynasty neared extinction.

Sulpicia: Life, Love, and Literature in Ancient Rome. Alison Keith, Oxford University Press.
© Oxford University Press 2026. DOI: 10.1093/9780197607008.003.0004

4

An Elite Upbringing

Sulpicia's descent from at least three ancient patrician houses, along with the political prominence of her kinsmen in the late republic and early principate, allows us to conjecture a great deal about her upbringing. The textual evidence we have for the daily life of elite Roman girls and women in this period derives from Cicero's copious correspondence as well as from biographical anecdotes about the daughters of the Roman senatorial elite, especially Caesar and the Julio-Claudian dynasts, with many of whom Sulpicia's male relatives could boast strong bonds of personal friendship and political alliance. There is also a considerable body of documentary and archeological evidence for Roman girls' lives in the form of inscriptions, frescoes, and sculpture. In order to sketch a picture of Sulpicia's life, therefore, we shall survey the literary and material records for information about the upbringing of Roman aristocratic girls in the late republic and early principate, and the societal expectations regarding their participation in the religious rituals and social ceremonials of their class.[1] The sociohistorical horizons limned in the poetry by and about Sulpicia will also feature in this discussion.

Religious rites and familial ceremonies began soon after the birth of a child in ancient Rome.[2] Immediately after birth, the midwife placed the newborn on the ground to elicit her first cry. She then examined the child to check her physical health, before lifting her again to sever the umbilical cord.[3] Acceptance of the child was signified by the father's instruction to put the infant to the breast, though whether of mother or wetnurse depended on the family's social standing. Shortly after birth, Roman newborns were differentiated by sex and class through social and religious rites including naming conventions and the formal presentation of the new family member on the "lustral day."[4] Occurring eight days after the birth of a girlchild (nine for a boy), the lustral day was devoted to the ritual purification of the newborn (to protect her from forces that might threaten her safety and health) and her naming, both ceremonies observed in the context of a family party. On our poet's lustral day she will have formally received her family name and paternal filiation, "Servius' daughter Sulpicia" (*Serui filia Sulpicia*, [Tib.] 3.16.4). Celebrated as a family festival, the lustral day was the Roman child's earliest rite of passage, marking her entry into family and society.[5]

Elite Roman mothers like Valeria were not usually closely involved in the physical care of child-rearing despite the prescriptions of ancient moralists that they should breastfeed their infants. Instead, children of the upper classes were normally left to the ministrations of wet-nurses and slave attendants in their infancy and early childhood.[6] Once the child had emerged from swaddling clothes, maternal solicitude manifested itself in the verbal and moral spheres, in order to furnish ethical and linguistic standards.[7] Already in early childhood, upper-class boys were introduced to Roman history and their familial traditions through story-telling and the visual arts, both public and private, and there is no reason to suppose that girls were not.[8] Thus, while Sulpicia may not have known her paternal grandfather (d. January, 43 BCE), she would surely have known his pedestrian statue, erected in the city of Rome (Ch. 2). There is also reason to believe that elite girls were inculcated, similarly to their brothers, in the family's exemplary history. Indeed, it is tempting to speculate that Sulpicia's mother and aunts will have shared the exemplary tales of their own female family members,[9] especially since they could boast such famous ancestors as Sulpicia, the daughter of Ser. Sulpicius Paterculus and wife of Q. Fulvius Flaccus (Ch. 2), and the two Valerias, sister and daughter of P. Valerius Publicola (Ch. 3).[10] They may even have known the wife of Lentulus Cruscellio, Sulpicia Lentuli, whose exemplary fidelity during the proscriptions won her lasting renown (Ch. 2).[11]

In elite households, children were attended by *paedogogi*, slaves who supervised young children's behavior and their earliest education (*OLD* s.v. *paedagogus*). In our period, the offspring of the upper classes were generally educated privately at home, where libraries of both Greek and Latin books could often be found,[12] and this seems to have been especially true for girls. Indeed, by the late republic, the instruction of elite Roman daughters in reading, writing, and literature seems to have superseded the old-fashioned training of daughters in wool-working among the Roman elite.[13] The daughter of Cicero's friend Atticus, Caecilia Attica (b. 51 BCE), for example, received her earliest education from a slave *paedagogus*[14] and her training in literature from her father's freedman grammar-teacher, Q. Caecilius Epirota.[15] Like Cicero (and, we may presume, Sulpicia's grandfather, father and uncle), Atticus had an extensive private library, which his daughter (an only child) likely inherited at his death.[16] When, at fourteen, she married Octavian's friend, the great general Agrippa, her education with Epirota continued, until he was dismissed under suspicion of impropriety toward her.[17] Since the grammarian was responsible for children's moral guidance through literary instruction, such charges were taken very seriously,[18] not least because upper-class daughters seem to have been educated, at least in part, so that they could educate the sons that they would bear once they were married.[19]

Like Caecilia Attica, Sulpicia will have enjoyed home tuition in Greek and Latin letters. Ancient sources attest to her male relatives' extensive writings across a variety of prose and verse genres in both Greek and Latin (Chs. 2, 3, 5). Her brother's tenure of the praetorship confirms his pursuit of a political career under Augustus and that career must also have entailed a literary education in his youth. Sulpicia likely received instruction alongside her brother, at first from a *paedogogus* (or perhaps even a *paedogoga*, a "female slave attendant"), and later from a grammarian like Caecilius Epirota. When her schooling came to an end, moreover, whether at puberty or marriage, she may have continued to enjoy Greek and Latin literature in the company of a female slave trained to read aloud (*lectrix*). A funerary epitaph in Latin elegiacs, contemporary with Sulpicia's own verse, commemorates the recent death of a female "reader-aloud" named Sulpicia Petale (Appendix). Her Greek name confirms Petale's servile status, though her ashes' possession of the name Sulpicia appears to confirm her manumission at her death by her owner, a member of the Sulpician family. Inscriptional evidence suggests that only the wealthiest, most literary Roman families had the resources, and commitment, to employ a dedicated female slave reader. For example, a somewhat later inscription from the imperial household identifies a *lectrix* with the Greek name of Cnide as the enslaved wife of the slave-valet of the emperor Tiberius' daughter-in-law, Livia Drusi (*CIL* VI[2] no. 8786).[20] Linguistic features of Sulpicia Petale's epitaph allow us to date it very precisely to the mid-20s BCE, at the same time as Sulpicia's own foray into elegiac composition (Ch. 6). The French scholar Jérome Carcopino therefore proposed that Petale was Sulpicia's very own *lectrix*, and the verse epitaph another instance of her poetry.[21]

Elite Roman girls and boys dressed in the clothing of their class, wearing the *toga praetexta* (a purple-bordered toga worn by freeborn children) over a tunic that was normally long for girls but short for boys.[22] The south frieze

Fig. 4 South frieze of the *Ara Pacis* (Museo dell'Ara Pacis, Rome).

of the Augustan "Altar of Peace" (*Ara Pacis*) shows three children, two boys and a girl, wearing the *toga praetexta* (Fig. 4), which marked them out as belonging to elite Roman citizen stock and protected them from both physical and moral threats to their safety.[23] There can be no doubt, given their patrician birth, that Sulpicia and her sibling(s) wore such apparel in their childhood, at least on formal occasions. Sulpicia's brother will also have worn the *bulla* (the protective amulet worn by elite Roman boys, visible on the frieze at Fig. 4), while she and any sisters may have worn the *lunula*, the moon-shaped locket of the aristocratic girlchild.[24] The locket was dedicated to the family's household gods at another rite of passage, the coming-of-age ceremony traditionally held at puberty or at the time of the girl's betrothal in her early- or mid-teens.[25]

Alongside the moralizing rhetoric concerning children's upbringing found in classical literary texts, ancient artifacts reveal the ubiquity of play—"with toys, pets, and peers"[26]—in their daily lives. The infant's earliest toys were typically noisy: *crepundia*, "strings dangling with small toys or charms and worn across the shoulders or around the neck," and "rattles, which were recommended for soothing crying or restless infants."[27] Wheeled frames and push-carts are attested in the material record as aids for toddlers learning to walk.[28] For older children of both sexes, gaming

Fig. 5 Giocatrici di astragali (Herculaneum) (Museo Archeologico Nazionale di Napoli).

play with knucklebones, dice, and nuts is widely attested in literature and art. A Roman painting (Fig. 5),[29] for example, shows two of Niobe's daughters playing at knucklebones just as many an upper-class Roman girl must have done in antiquity. Girls' toys also included balls and dolls, as we can see illustrated on imperial sarcophagi: a relief from a second-century CE sarcophagus represents boys playing with nuts and girls playing with balls (Fig. 6),[30] while an early second-century CE sarcophagus lid portrays a young girl resting on a couch and petting a small dog, with two dolls lying at her feet (Fig. 7).[31]

Both the literary evidence and the archeological record associate the use of dolls exclusively with girls in ancient Rome.[32] Surviving dolls depict articulated adult female figures who embody a specifically Roman physical

Fig. 6 A child's sarcophagus depicting children playing with nuts and balls (Lanmas/Alamy Images).

ideal of femininity, with small breasts and wide hips. Scholars have therefore suggested that in playing with their dolls ancient girls were engaged from an early age in mimicking the roles and activities of adult women of their class.[33] John Chrysostom, the late fourth-century CE archbishop of Constantinople, supports this view in his remark (*Hom. in Jo.* 81.3) that girls dressed up their dolls as brides.[34] In this regard, it is especially noteworthy that ancient dolls seem to have been equipped with wardrobes of colorfully dyed garments and accessories (jewelry, shoes, etc.), in addition to elaborate hairstyles.[35] It has accordingly been suggested that dolls embodied an ideal of gender and status of particular application to elite girls and young women as they came to adulthood.[36] Before marriage, Roman girls customarily dedicated their dolls to Diana, the goddess who

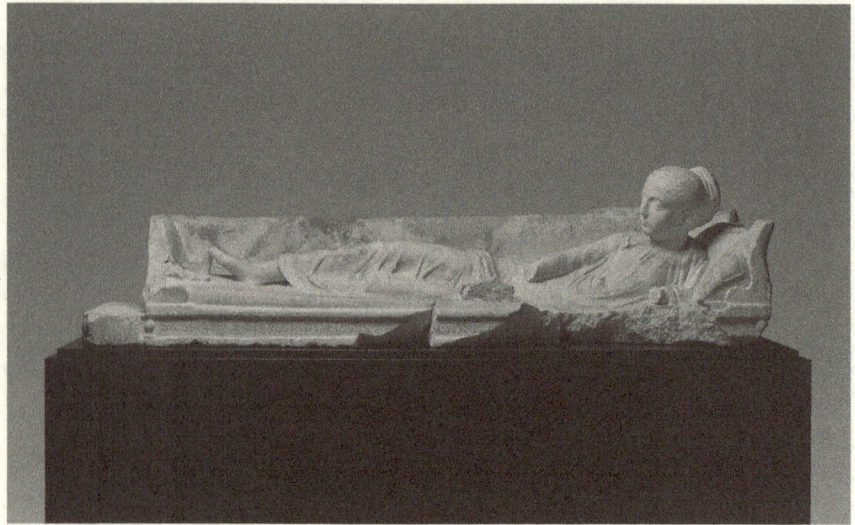

Fig. 7 *Kline* Monument with a Reclining Girl (J. Paul Getty Museum).

presided over the turning points of a woman's life, and/or Venus, the goddess of sexuality.[37]

In essence, dolls modeled to the upper class Roman girlchild the feminine ideals of "elegance," "adornment," and "refinement," which taken together implicitly prescribed the attainments of the adult Roman "woman's world"—a highly refined and artificial state that demanded ongoing attention to the cultivation of all aspects of one's appearance.[38] These feminine ideals are of special relevance to Sulpicia because the cycle of poetry by and about her opens with a celebration of her exquisitely polished appearance (3.8.1–2, 7–20). Sulpicia enters the collection as a young woman of extraordinary cultivation and refinement, elegantly turned out in the most expensive dress, scents, and jewelry available to the Roman upper classes. In her costly dress and accoutrements, she seems the very incarnation of elite Roman elegance, adornment, and refinement, attired as she is in the expensive luxuries with which antique dolls came equipped in miniature. Thus, the purple mantle that Sulpicia sports (3.8.11) was characteristically worn by married women outdoors,[39] and its rich purple dye would have marked her as a privileged member of the upper classes. The ancient city of Tyre in the Levant was famous for the production of costly purple dye from local shellfish,[40] and the double-dyed cloth was rare and valuable in classical Rome. Likewise, perfumes and unguents from the middle east were expensive luxury items, imported into Rome for the use and enjoyment of the elite.[41] Indian pearls were another highly prized commodity in ancient Rome, where their luster and distant provenance were emblematic of their value.[42] The intense focus on Sulpicia's hairstyle in the opening poem (3.8.9–10) is also characteristic of both contemporary elegiac poetry and upper-class households, in which the slave hairdresser enjoyed privileged access to the mistress' person and her boudoir.[43] In this context, the third-person speaker's emphasis on the god Vertumnus' "thousand" outfits and adornments (3.8.13–14) also seems significant, as it suggests the extent of Sulpicia's wardrobe and costly accessories, all of which would have required a large staff of (mostly) slaves and (a few) freed personnel to maintain.[44] Sulpicia evidently learned very successfully the implicit lessons imparted by doll-play in her childhood.

Daughters of the Roman elite thus seem to have been schooled in the conventions of married life from an early age. Since public life was not open to women, the expectation was that they would marry and bear children— sons to fill the ranks of the military, as well as legal and political offices, and daughters to continue the family line. By the Augustan period, citizen women enjoyed the legal capacity for marriage when they reached the age of twelve,[45] an age associated with the onset of puberty (if not always of menarche) in the medical writers.[46] We hear of girls married even before the age of twelve: Sulpicia's grandfather, the jurist Ser. Sulpicius Rufus, apparently clarified the rules about the dispensation of the underage girl's dowry in his treatise on the subject (Ch. 2).[47] Daughters of the upper classes seem normally to have married in their teens, after a betrothal that could (but need not) have been arranged in childhood.[48] Conventional criteria applied to the choice of husband for an elite Roman girl included birth, wealth, good looks, and virtuous character.[49] The quality of paramount importance in the girl's own character was *pudicitia*, "chastity"—i.e., an unblemished reputation.[50] Susan Treggiari conjectures that a virtuous adolescent girl's female relatives and friends—her aunts, married sisters, and family connections—could bring her to the attention of other respectable women and recommend her to potential suitors.[51] Sulpicia undoubtedly enjoyed access to such women's channels through her numerous female relatives (Chs. 2, 3). From Cicero's correspondence about his daughter Tullia's third marriage, when Sulpicia's father was identified as a potential candidate (Ch. 2), we glean the outlines of upper-class women's networks in the selection of a groom, and Valeria was surely intimately involved in the search for her daughter's husband. We may conjecture that she might have looked as high as she pleased for a son-in-law in the 20s BCE, given her brother's elevated military, political, and social standing (Ch. 3).

After informal inquiries had narrowed the field, negotiations confirmed the groom's identity through a series of increasingly formal stages: agreement, promise, and betrothal.[52] The girl's parents and/or guardian—in Sulpicia's case, presumably her mother Valeria and uncle Messala—came to an agreement in principle, perhaps at a meeting with the groom and his father (if still alive). Sulpicia will then have found herself "promised" in a "solemn agreement" made by her uncle and mother with her intended bridegroom and perhaps his father. The agreement (*pactio*) was less formal than, but by Sulpicia's day notionally equivalent to, the legal betrothal itself (*sponsio*), which was officially marked by a ceremony called the *sponsalia*. The bridegroom seems to have sent his betrothed a ring as well. Strictly speaking, all that was legally necessary for both engagement and marriage was the consent of the bride and groom, and their fathers (if alive) or guardians (if the principals were underage); but a party to celebrate the happy occasion publicly was normally given by the bride's guardian for the prospective groom. Relatives and friends of both families would have attended the festivities to witness the public announcement of their formal intention to unite in marriage, and the bride and groom seem to have clasped hands and kissed to formalize their betrothal. There may also have been an exchange of gifts between the betrothed couple and/or their families at the start of the engagement.

The length of the engagement itself will have depended on the ages of the bride and groom at betrothal and the circumstances of their families. Among the Roman elite in this period, we hear of both short and long engagements and also of first marriage for women as early as at fourteen years of age (Augustus' daughter Julia, b. 39 BCE) and as late as at nineteen or twenty (Augustus' niece, the younger Antonia, b. 36 BCE). Augustus' daughter Julia was Sulpicia's close, perhaps slightly younger, coeval, but she seems to have embarked on her first marriage at the unusually young age of fourteen for dynastic reasons. Married three times, on each occasion she wed her father's designated successor: in 25, her cousin Marcellus (d. 23); in 21, her father's best friend, the general Agrippa (d. 12); and in 12 or 11, her stepbrother Tiberius.[53] Other attested upper-class engagements were of longer duration, however, and Sulpicia may well have been in her mid-teens at betrothal and her late teens at marriage, as her mother seems to have been (Ch. 3). An interval between the two ceremonies, moreover, will have allowed her the opportunity to get to know her future husband.

Inevitably, we would like to know just how well it was possible for a betrothed couple to come to know one another before marriage. Susan Treggiari, author of the standard work on Roman marriage, notes that Christianity imposed a new anxiety across the Roman Mediterranean about pre-marital sex with a young woman's fiancé.[54] Indeed, she argues that there was some expectation in our period that the bride-to-be should have feelings for her future husband—and contemporary Latin love elegy offers ample evidence of the potential for amatory trysts among the upper classes of Augustan Rome (Ch. 5).[55] Thus, the elegist Propertius (ca. 54–ca. 15 BCE), writing in the mid-20s BCE, at roughly the same time as Sulpicia's presumed engagement and marriage, expects his erotic verse to ignite love in both girls and youths (3.9.45–46): "Let my writings kindle passion in boys and maidens, let them acclaim me a god and make sacrifices to me."[56] Propertius' slightly younger contemporary, the poet Ovid (43 BCE–16/17 CE), also writing amatory elegy in this period, invites girls and youths to read his poems and think of their beloved (*Am.* 2.1.5–6): "Let them read me—the maiden who warms to see her betrothed, and the inexperienced boy, touched by an unknown love."[57] Ovid even describes the amatory intrigue of the mythical teenagers Acontius and Cydippe in terms that may approximate contemporary Roman courtship: Cydippe claims (*Her.* 21.195–96) that Acontius "whispers sweet nothings, seeks a few kisses, and calls me his own in a timid voice."[58] Similarly suggestive are the sensual frescoes adorning the walls of upper-class Roman bedrooms in this period, including imagery that evokes a bride on her wedding night (Fig. 8, erotic scene from *cubiculum* D, Villa della Farnesina, 20s BCE, Museo Nazionale Romano, Palazzo Massimo alle Terme) and a pair of youthful lovers (Fig. 9, erotic scene from *cubiculum* B, Villa della Farnesina, 20s BCE, Museo Nazionale Romano, Palazzo Massimo alle Terme).[59] Of particular salience is the emergence of this rich body of erotic elegy and domestic fresco in the decade preceding the passage of Augustus' marriage and adultery legislation (18–16 BCE), which seriously restricted extra-marital erotic opportunities for elite women and men.[60]

While we lack evidence for Sulpicia's engagement and marriage, the elegiac poetry by and about her bears witness to the social conventions of erotic awakening, elite betrothal, and marriage. Indeed, Susan Treggiari has interpreted the amatory relationship commemorated in the Sulpicia cycle

Fig. 8 Matrimonial scene, couple in bed. Erotic Fresco, Cubiculum D (right wall), Villa della Farnesina (Museo Nazionale Romano).

Fig. 9 Erotic scene, couple in bed. Erotic Fresco, Cubiculum B, Villa della Farnesina (Museo Nazionale Romano).

as a stylized version of upper-class courtship at Rome, between an eligible young man and a nubile teenager.[61] It is particularly instructive that Sulpicia enters the poetry sequence as the object of our collective gaze, sumptuously attired in the mantle (3.8.11) of a married woman on the first day (Kalends) of March. The month took its name from the Roman war-god Mars, who is expressly invoked by the third-person speaker (3.8.1) and invited to admire Sulpicia's beauty (3.8.2–4).[62] But the Kalends of every month were sacred to the Roman goddess of marriage, Juno, who was especially venerated as Juno Lucina ("the light-bringer")[63] on the first day of March, the birthday of her temple on the Esquiline hill.[64] An ancient commentary on Horace's *Odes* explains that "the Kalends of March used to be called the *Matronalia* for the reason that husbands used to pray for the conservation of their marriages, and that day was appropriately observed by matrons."[65] The festival was publicly celebrated by families and their neighbors in the Field of Mars and was marked by role reversal in the provision both of gifts, by husbands to their wives, and of food, by married women to their slaves.[66] Introducing Sulpicia in the context of the *Matronalia*, under the auspices of Juno Lucina, implies that she has successfully negotiated the passage from betrothal to wedding, perhaps very recently, and invites the reader to interpret the elegies that follow under the reassuring sign of marriage—whatever the implied settings of the poems (Ch. 6) and their actual circumstances of composition (Ch. 7).

In the second elegy of the sequence, the admired *matrona* of the preceding poem speaks for herself (*ipsa ego*, 3.9.12, 13) in the voice of a young woman passionately in love; she is well versed in the elegiac conventions of amatory servitude (*seruitium amoris*; cf. 3.11.4), on display in her offer to accompany her beloved on the hunt.[67] Throughout the classical period, the hunt was an upper-class pastime reserved for adult citizen males (no doubt supported by a retinue of slaves and freedmen), and so the poem's concluding couplet intimates (3.9.23–24): "But you, leave the pursuit of hunting to your father, and run swiftly back into my embrace." The servile Greek name Cerinthus[68] thus appears to conceal an elite Roman man's identity.

In calling her beloved by a Greek name, Sulpicia conforms to Latin elegiac practice, insofar as this can be established from a passage in Apuleius, the mid-second-century CE rhetorician and philosopher. He details the Greek pseudonyms chosen by the Latin amatory poets for their Roman mistresses: "C. Catullus…names Lesbia for Clodia; and Ticidas, similarly… wrote Perilla when she was Metella; and Propertius…says Cynthia to conceal Hostia; and Tibullus...loved Plania in his heart, Delia in his verse."[69] Apuleius' evidence is further illuminated by one of Horace's ancient commentators, who explains that that poet's literary pseudonyms have the same number of syllables as the name for which they substitute.[70] On the basis of this onomastic convention, Renaissance humanists connected Sulpicia's "Cerinthus" with the Cornutus of Tibullus' elegies 2.2 (Appendix) and 2.3,[71] and the identification has seemed attractive to many scholars because the two names share not only the same scansion (i.e., the same metrical pattern of long and short syllables) and number of syllables, but also a proposed semantic parallel between the Greek *kéras* ("horn") and Latin *cornu* ("horn"),[72] as well as the same sequence of consonants (c-r-n-t): Cērĭnthŭs: Cōrnūtŭs.[73]

The Cornutus of Tibullus' elegies 2.2 and 2.3 has been identified as M. Caecilius Cornutus, a political adherent of Messalla and lesser patron of his poet Tibullus.[74] Cornutus came from a wealthy family of praetorian rank, whose membership in the senatorial aristocracy dated at least from the period of the social war (91–87 BCE), in which his (probable) grandfather, an ex-praetor of the same name, served as a legate.[75] This man's (probable) homonymous son, our Cornutus' father, was urban praetor in 43 BCE, when the senate dispatched both consuls against Antony after the failed embassy on which Sulpicia's grandfather died (Ch. 2). In charge of the city in the absence of the consuls, Cornutus committed suicide upon the troops' transfer of allegiance to Octavian. His son, Tibullus' addressee, seems to have been associated with Messalla by the late 40s, when they seem to have served together in the republican forces of Brutus and Cassius (Ch. 3).[76] Inscriptions recording dedications at Pergamum to both Messalla and Cornutus have been taken to imply that Cornutus was attached to Messalla's force (like Tibullus), during his eastern mission a decade later, after the battle of Actium (Ch. 3).[77] Scholars have therefore accepted the surmise that this Cornutus was the same as the historical writer Cornutus (otherwise all but unknown),[78] and even that he was also responsible for the posthumous publication of his father's work on legendary catasterisms.[79] The two men's shared literary interests will have further cemented their friendship.[80]

Cornutus is also attested as a member of the Augustan college of Arval Brethren, along with his patron Messalla, in an inscription from 21–20 BCE— surely, closely contemporary with the composition of Tibullus' elegies 2.2 and 2.3.[81] Whether or not Tibullus himself arranged his second poetry collection before his death in 19 BCE, the inclusion of two elegies for Cornutus (2.2, 2.3), between two lengthy elegies in honor of his patron Messalla (2.1) and his patron's elder son Messallinus (2.5), confirms Messalla's strong support of Cornutus.[82] The first of Tibullus' two elegies for Cornutus has engendered particular interest because it takes the form of a wedding song with an embedded birthday poem, a structure highly reminiscent of Tibullus' elegy 1.7 for Messalla, a birthday poem with an embedded panegyric of his triumph (Ch. 6).[83] It has therefore been surmised that the elegist was recruited by Messalla to compose elegy 2.2 for the occasion of Cornutus' wedding-cum-birthday celebration.[84] Under the circumstances, it is not unreasonable to suppose that Cornutus' bride must have been related to Messalla, and Syme (1986, 47), among others, concludes that "she might even be the poetess Sulpicia."[85] Commentators have been reluctant to see Messalla's friend Cornutus, who was in his early 40s in the mid- to late 20s BCE, as the inspiration for Sulpicia's handsome young beloved, Cerinthus,[86] but the presumed age difference between the two is commensurate in this period with that between Augustus' daughter Julia and his best friend Agrippa (m. 21 BCE), while anyone who has ever written or received love poetry will know how far such verses diverge from the mundane details of quotidian life in their inflection of generic convention.

The state of our evidence must preclude ultimate certainty as to the identification of either Cerinthus or Sulpicia's bridegroom.[87] Still, the marriage context of 3.8, along with the hints elsewhere in the sequence of her guardians' matrimonial ambitions (3.11, 3.16), may encourage the reader to supply a marital outcome for the lovers,[88] especially in the light of the opening sequence of the Tibullan appendix, in which the elegist "Lygdamus" laments the loss of a quasi-marital relationship with Neaera, his beloved "wife."[89] The one thing we can say for certain is that marriage was the ineluctable destiny of the upper class Roman girlchild, and Sulpicia's initiation into love (and love-poetry) surely confirms her fate.

In this context, the opening allusion to Adonis' death in the hunt invites further speculation about Sulpicia's upcoming nuptials. Fearing Adonis' fate, gored by a boar (3.9.1–4), for her lover, Sulpicia implicitly likens herself to Adonis' divine lover, Venus (cf. 3.9.19, "now let there be no Venus/love/sex without me"). But as the poem progresses the goddess of love vies with the goddess of the hunt, Diana, for Cerinthus' attention. Diana—"the Delian" (3.9.5) because born on the island of Delos—leads him away from the city to hunt in the countryside (3.9.6), in an evocation of the plot of the

Euripidean tragedy *Hippolytus*, where the titular character is punished by Aphrodite, the Greek goddess of love, because he rejects her pursuits in favor of those of Artemis, the Greek goddess of wild nature.[90] By associating Cerinthus with Adonis and Hippolytus, Sulpicia assumes the *personae* alternately of Venus and Diana. Both goddesses were appropriately educed at the time of a Roman girl's wedding, moreover, since Diana presided not only over the hunt, but also over the turning points or transitional stages of a female life (puberty, marriage, childbirth, and death), while Venus held sway over the erotic life such as Sulpicia vividly imagines in 3.9.15–16 (cf. 3.13, Ch. 6). In addition, we have seen that before her marriage a Roman girl customarily dedicated her dolls to one or both of these goddesses. The god of love, Amor (3.9.4), was also regularly invoked in the context of the Roman wedding (cf. 3.8.6, 3.12.12, 3.13.1).[91]

The sequence of elegies thereby lends support to Treggiari's view that this poetry reflects "the preliminaries to a marriage which was socially a *digna condicio*"—i.e., a "suitable match."[92] Thus, the third-person speaker of elegy 3.10, which treats Sulpicia's illness, exhorts Cerinthus to lay aside his anxious fear and commit wholeheartedly to loving her (3.10.11–16), since "god does not harm lovers" (3.10.15). In 3.11, the second elegy voiced in the first-person feminine, Sulpicia (apparently recovered) promotes Cerinthus' birthday to a personal festival (3.11.1–2) and asks his birth-spirit (*Genius*, 3.11.9; cf. *natalis*, 3.11.19)[93] to grant her wish that he "warm" to her (3.11.9–10; cf. Ov. *Am.* 2.1.5, quoted above) as she has to him (3.11.5). Unlike the male elegists (Ch. 5), however, she consistently prays for a "mutual love" (3.11.7; cf. 3.11.6, 13–20; 3.12.8), figuring it in the reciprocal terms of equal service (cf. 3.11.13), and asking that each be bound by the same indissoluble chains of love (3.11.14–16). Whether or not we conceive of the elegy as reflecting a time before the pair's nuptials, it seems clear that the female speaker has some expectation of marriage.

Particularly striking, in this context, is her appeal (in her prayer to her youth's birth-spirit) not only "by [her] beloved's fine eyes" (3.11.8) but also by their "very sweet trysts" (3.11.7). The third-person speaker of elegy 3.12, next in the sequence, elaborates on the lovers' assignations: s/he notes the inability of Sulpicia's "watchful guardian to catch the desirous lovers" (3.12.11) and attributes to Amor the management of "a thousand paths of deception" (3.12.12). The unnamed third-person poet may even gesture to the passage of time from betrothal to marriage implicit in the cycle in the request that Sulpicia's tutelary divinity, *Natalis Juno* (her "female birth-spirit"), favor the pair's "mutual bond" of love (3.12.8) and confirm it on her next birthday as "now of long standing" (3.12.20). The hints of Sulpicia's forthcoming marriage led Treggiari (1991, 122) to describe this poetry as limning "the private preliminaries to marriage, the kisses once concealed and the subject of rumour, which then become licit."

Sulpicia herself proclaims the suitability not just of her match but also of her lovemaking (3.13.10): "a worthy/noble woman I shall be said to have been/lain with a worthy/noble man."[94] Other poems in the sequence similarly hint at the lovers' assignations. In elegy 3.18, for example, Sulpicia apologizes to her beloved for gauchely retiring from his company the evening before out of a modest desire to conceal her passion (3.18.5–6), while in 3.16 she rebukes him for preferring an enslaved prostitute to herself (3.16.3–4). Her reproach seems motivated by the amatory passion on display throughout this poetry. Particularly interesting in this regard is the hope she expresses in elegy 3.17 that Cerinthus may feel "due concern" (*pia cura*, 3.17.1) for her, as she suffers from an "unhealthy heat" or "fever" (*calor*, 3.17.2). The *pia cura* she hopes to inspire in Cerinthus encompasses both the lover's solicitude for his beloved (*OLD* s.v. *cura* 5) and the husband's dutiful devotion to his spouse (*OLD* s.v. *pius* 3),[95] and contrasts pointedly with Cerinthus' sexual interest in the slave-prostitute of the preceding elegy (3.16.3). Her own fever (*OLD* s.v. *calor* 4), moreover, is readily interpreted figuratively in the sense of the heat of "love" or "passion" (*OLD* s.v. 6), as the word so often means in contemporary erotic verse (Ch. 6).[96] Following directly on from Sulpicia's suspicion of Cerinthus' sexual interest in a slave-prostitute, elegy 3.17 articulates her anxiety that her own ardor may not be reciprocated.

Sulpicia's rebuke of Cerinthus in elegy 3.16 is informed by class privilege in the stark contrast she draws between her patrician filiation and her rival's servile dress and occupation (3.16.3–4): "Be concerned for your toga and a prostitute, weighed down by a wool-basket, rather than Servius' daughter Sulpicia." The patrician poet juxtaposes her own aristocratic lineage with the wool-working slave-prostitute's anonymity,[97] and invites her lover to reflect on her family's august social standing in their devoted promotion of an advantageous marriage for her (3.16.5–6): "they're solicitous for my interests, whose greatest cause for grief is that I might fall to an ignoble bed." Her phrasing implies that, by bedding a slave, Cerinthus assimilates himself to the servile classes and thereby makes himself socially unworthy of marriage with a woman of her patrician birth. Two other poems in the cycle bear witness to the special interest close family members were expected to take in arranging a suitable match. The third-person elegiac speaker of 3.12 portrays Sulpicia's mother as ambitiously promoting the wrong prospective bridegroom to her daughter, who secretly desires some-one else (3.12.15–16), while in elegy 3.14, Sulpicia herself remonstrates with her guardian Messalla because the birthday treat he plans—a trip to her family's estate near Arezzo—would separate her from her beloved on the festal day. In ancient Rome, as we have seen, a daughter's mother and father or guardian were the very family members traditionally responsible for arranging her wedding, and it is precisely in this role that they enter the cycle. By contrast, contemporary male-authored elegy abjures not only any reference to the poet-lover's parents but also any suggestion that the elegist and his mistress might hope to marry.[98]

In this context, Sulpicia's reference to her uncle's proposal that she stay at the family estate near Arezzo for her birthday is particularly interesting (3.14.1–4). Epigraphic evidence for Sulpicii in this part of Tuscany suggests that the estate belonged to Sulpicia's paternal family rather than the Valerii.[99] At the death of her father, the property will have passed into his heirs' patri-mony and was presumably managed by his widow Valeria and her brother Messalla, perhaps in the legal role of his sister's "financial trustee" (*OLD* s.v. *tutor* 1). The epigrapher Alberto Fatucchi has therefore conjectured that Messalla proposed the visit to the farm precisely in order to administer the property, and I would suggest that it may have formed a part of Sulpicia's dowry. Certainly, she speaks of it with both familiarity (3.14.3–4) and dis-like (*rure molesto*, 3.14.1). Her evident reluctance to spend time in a rustic villa situated on a cold stream suggests, in Fatucchi's words, that "her sojourns there will have been neither infrequent nor short." The conven-tional elegiac espousal of urbanity, and concomitant rejection of rusticity, that Sulpicia articulates in this poem (Ch. 6) also reflects the circumstances of her elite privilege. For a city-girl accustomed to a life of urban elegance, visits to a rustic farm without coastal access cannot have held the same appeal as holidays at a seaside villa. Moreover, while luxury villas are well attested at this period on the Bay of Naples in the south, the same was not true of Tuscany.[100]

Several poems in the sequence reflect the importance of the annual birthday celebration in ancient Roman culture. We have seen Sulpicia pro-mote Cerinthus' birthday to a personal holiday in 3.11, and in 3.14 she complains of having to celebrate her own birthday in the country without

Cerinthus. Elegy 3.15 in turn proclaims her delight (3.15.3–4) that she will not have to travel after all (3.15.1) and can observe her birthday at Rome (3.15.2), presumably with her beloved. These elegies belong to the genre of *genethliakon*, "birthday poem" (*OLD* s.v. *genethliacon*), popular with the members of Messalla's circle (Ch. 6). But the Sulpicia cycle also provides important evidence for the existence of a female counterpart to the male *Genius*, a man's presiding deity or personal spirit, which we considered above in connection with elegy 3.11. In elegy 3.12, *natalis Juno* ("birthday Juno") is invoked to preside over Sulpicia's anniversary rites.[101] Exquisitely attired for the occasion (3.12.3–5), the birthday-girl burns incense to her Juno (3.12.1–2) and makes offerings of sacrificial cake and wine at the family altar (3.12.13–14). The Roman *materfamilias* ("mother of the household"), presumably Valeria on this occasion, was responsible for the provision of a type of grain, coarsely ground (doubtless by her slave-women), for the porridge (*puls*) that traditionally accompanied the cake and wine offered at birthday celebrations.[102]

Another god mentioned in the cycle, Vertumnus, is adduced by the speaker of the first elegy as a model for Sulpicia's extensive wardrobe and rich accessories (3.8.13–14), though women are not recorded as celebrating his cult.[103] Sulpicia's older contemporary, the elegist Propertius, refers to him as an Etruscan god who deserted the town of Volsinii before Rome conquered it and who subsequently moved to Rome, where he had a temple on the Aventine (Prop. 4.2.3–6). He also had a statue in the *Vicus Tuscus*, "Tuscan Row" (Prop. 4.2.1–2; cf. 4.2.50), at which shopkeepers frequently left offerings (Prop. 4.2.13).[104] Varro describes him as the "leading god of Etruria" (*L.* 5.46). Associating the god with seasonal change, the Augustan poets connect his name etymologically with the Latin verb *uerto*, "turn, change" (*OLD* s.v. 1, 10).[105] As a former Etruscan transplanted to Rome, Vertumnus mirrors in his divine person the geographical relocation of Sulpicia's family, landholders in Tuscan Arezzo, to the imperial metropolis. His association with alteration, visible in his wardrobe changes in [Tib.] 3.8.13–14, has also been seen as an allusion to the alternation of third- and first-person speakers in the opening elegies of the cycle.[106]

The prominent position assumed by Phoebus (Apollo) and the Muses in the Sulpicia elegies is also noticeable and must be related to their role as the tutelary divinities of poetry and poets in Augustan Rome.[107] Although the first elegy in the sequence opens with an invocation of Mars, it closes with an address to Apollo and the Pierian Muses, who are invited to venerate

Sulpicia on the occasion of the *Matronalia* (3.8.21–22). In this regard, the elegy's close mirrors its beginning, where Mars is invited to admire Sulpicia (3.8.1–4), rather than Sulpicia to worship Mars and/or Juno on their festal day, the Kalends of March. The elegy thereby upends the conventions of both Latin elegy and Roman ritual to make Sulpicia, elsewhere in the sequence the elegiac poet-speaker, the object not only of these verses but also, figuratively, of cult worship.[108] Apollo and the Muses, moreover, are expressly addressed in their capacities as musician (3.8.22) and poet/singers (3.8.21) respectively.[109] Their invocation as the divine patrons of poetry at the conclusion of the inaugural elegy in the Sulpicia cycle establishes them as the presiding deities of the sequence and anticipates Sulpicia's emergence as a poet herself in the next elegy. The third-person speaker in the sequence shows a special devotion to Phoebus, repeatedly addressing him again in elegy 3.10 (vv. 2, 3, 19), where, however, he is invoked as a healing god, whose songs (*cantus*, 3.10.10) and skills (*artes*, 3.10.26) can restore Sulpicia's health and thereby save both lovers (3.10.19–20). In the first-person elegies, by contrast, Sulpicia favors Venus (3.9.18–19, 3.11.13, 3.13.5) and the Muses, whom she calls by their Roman name of *Camenae* (3.13.3),[110] over Apollo, whom she never invokes. Indeed, in elegy 3.13, her Camenae—understood as both her Muses and her poems (*OLD* s.v. *Camena* 2)—are instrumental in securing Venus' active support in her love affair with Cerinthus (3.13.3–5). Perhaps it is time, therefore, to consider in more detail the Latin vogue for love-poetry that appears to have inspired her father and uncle, as well as Sulpicia herself.

Sulpicia: Life, Love, and Literature in Ancient Rome. Alison Keith, Oxford University Press.
© Oxford University Press 2026. DOI: 10.1093/9780197607008.003.0005

III

LITERARY CONTEXTS

5

Pretexts

Sulpicia's Literary Precursors

Sulpicia passed her youth in the literary firmament of which her father and uncle were leading critics and practitioners. The poet Horace moved in their circle in his youth and judged both men discriminating critics, including them in his roster of the most eminent literary men of the mid-30s BCE:[1]

> Without being accused of flattery, I can mention you
> **Pollio**, you **Messalla**, along with your brother, and also
> you **Bibulus** and **Servius**, and together with these you, lucid
>   **Furnius**;
> many others too, whom I purposely pass over, though they are
> learned men and my friends—whom I should wish these satires,
> such as they are, to please, as I should also regret it if they should
>   please
> less than my hope.

The men Horace names here belonged to the highest rungs of the senatorial elite—sons of the leading statesmen of the late republic, and/or already themselves engaged in political careers during the triumviral period. They were also prominent patrons of literature and celebrated authors themselves. Pollio, for example, knew Catullus in his youth and, as an adult in the late 40s, "discovered" the poet Vergil and acted as his earliest patron, the addressee of three of Vergil's eclogues as also of a Horatian ode.[2] He established the first public library at Rome in 39 and authored well-regarded tragedies, orations, and a history of the civil wars.[3] Messalla too wrote in almost every genre—history, oratory, poetry, philosophy, and works on grammar and style—and was a prominent patron of letters during the reign of Augustus (Ch. 3).[4] He counted among his protégés not only the elegists Tibullus and Ovid, but also an unknown author of a hexameter panegyric on his exploits.[5] His half-brother Gellius Publicola was the son of the homonymous consul of 72 BCE and consul himself in 36, the year before Horace published his first book of satires. Like Pollio, Gellius moved in Catullus' literary circle in his youth, and was the target of several of that poet's abusive epigrams.[6] He, too, may have dabbled in epigram, and in adulthood he acted as a literary patron as well as a statesman. Bibulus and Furnius also seem to have had literary pretensions.[7] Plutarch consulted the memoir Bibulus composed about his stepfather, the tyrannicide M. Junius Brutus, for his biography of Brutus,[8] and in his life of Mark Antony he preserves the information that Furnius was a skilled orator.[9]

The inclusion in Horace's roster of Sulpicia's father—he is the Servius named along with Bibulus—implies that he likewise participated in the literary debates of the mid-30s, and we have seen that he made his name as an orator (Ch. 2). Quintilian reports the more idiosyncratic details of the oratorical training and practice of Servius and his brother-in-law Messalla: while the latter used translation exercises in his oratorical training, the only such exercise the former employed was the translation of poetry.[10] Far from relying on notes when he spoke at trial, Quintilian comments, Servius improvised in court and only wrote up the speeches afterwards for publication.[11]

The ancient sources also preserve traces of Servius Sulpicius' interest in, and talent for, erotic poetry, both Greek and Latin. In *Tristia* 2, Ovid bears witness specifically to his poetic gifts at the end of his catalogue of Roman authors of erotic verse:[12]

> So was his woman often celebrated by sexy Catullus,
>   to whom the name Lesbia was falsely given;
> nor content with her, he published abroad many love affairs,
>   in which he himself confessed his own adultery.
> Equal and similar was the license of small Calvus,
>   who laid bare his own amatory thefts in various measures.
> Cinna too was their colleague, and Anser more frivolous than Cinna,
>   and the slight work of Cornificius and the equal work of
>   [Valerius] Cato.
> Why should I mention the verse of Ticida or Memmius,
>   among whom
>   all sense of modesty is lacking in their themes and words,

and in whose works we read of a woman at one time concealed
> under the name of Perilla,
at another called by your name, Metellus?
He too [Varro of Atax], who led the Argo into Phasis' waves,
> was unable to keep silent about his own erotic dalliances.
Neither are Hortensius' poems less indecent, nor **Servius**.
Who could hesitate to follow such great names?

Ovid's catalogue begins with Catullus (ca. 85–55 BCE) and encompasses a host of literary men and up-and-coming politicians who lived at the end of the republic and into the triumviral period, such as Catullus' friends Calvus (?82–?54/3 BCE),[13] Cinna (?90–44 BCE),[14] and Cornificius (d. 42 BCE),[15] whose verse survives only in scattered fragments. The roster also includes Memmius, the corrupt governor of Bithynia under whom Catullus and Cinna served in 57–56 BCE[16] and dedicatee of Lucretius' Epicurean master-piece *De rerum natura*.[17] Other poets named in the passage were also roughly contemporary with Catullus, working in the same meters and/or mentioned in his verse: Valerius Cato,[18] Ticida (d. 46 BCE),[19] and Varro Atacinus (b. 82 BCE).[20] The names Hortensius and Servius (i.e., Sulpicius) at the end of Ovid's catalogue, belonged both to prominent late republican politicians (Cicero's rival in the courts and his friend the jurist, respectively) and to their sons, and Roman conventions of nomenclature inevitably pre-clude certainty about whether father or son is meant.[21] Yet given the gener-ally chronological trend of Ovid's lines, moving from the heyday of Catullus and his friends in the 50s and 40s BCE toward his own generation, it is surely preferable to view Ovid's Hortensius and Servius as slightly younger contemporaries of Catullus and his friends, born around 80 BCE as has been conjectured for our poet's father.[22] The younger Pliny may support the evi-dence of Horace and Ovid, with his inclusion of Servius Sulpicius in his own list of Roman authors of erotic poetry.[23]

If only faint traces of the younger Servius' literary interests are preserved in our sources, overshadowed as he was by his father the jurist, there is ample testimony to his brother-in-law Messalla's literary attainments (Ch. 3). Moreover, it seems that Messalla wrote poetry in addition to his treatises on Latin letters and orthography, his speeches,[24] declamations, and transla-tion exercises. The younger Pliny includes Messalla too in his list of Roman authors of erotic poetry,[25] and the poet of *Catalepton* 9 specifies the form of his poetic efforts as bucolic verse in Greek.[26] This poet praises the "pure Attic language and wit" of Messalla's poems (*Cat.* 9.14) and implies that they had an amatory profile (9.23–38). Boris Kayachev has therefore suggested that Messalla composed Greek bucolic verse as a youth, during his stay in Athens in the mid-40s BCE (Ch. 3).[27]

A long-standing interest in poetry is also implied by Messalla's receipt (or the fiction of his receipt) of three panegyrics[28] in the decade from 36 to 26 BCE during the acme of his military-political career: *Catalepton* 9, preserved in the *Appendix Vergiliana* and datable to the mid-30s;[29] the *Panegyric of Messalla*, preserved in the *Appendix Tibulliana* as [Tibullus] 3.7 and composed in honor of his consulship in 31;[30] and Tibullus' elegy 1.7, commemorating his celebration of a triumph on his birthday, September 25, 27 BCE.[31] Syme has suggested that the author of the panegyric was a young nobleman on Messalla's staff during his command in Illyricum,[32] like the elegist Tibullus who, in elegy 1.3, depicts himself as a member of Messalla's entourage on campaign in the east, presumably after Actium.[33] Ceri Davies compares the encomiastic cast of the poetry in the Tibullan corpus to an earlier republican tradition, which saw Roman generals include poets on their staff,[34] though we might also recall the custom for Roman provincial governors to include aristocratic youths embarking on political careers in their entourages abroad.[35]

In addition to these three encomiasts, the poet of the *Panegyric of Messalla* identifies a certain Valgius, already in the patronage of Messalla, as another potential panegyrist:[36] "You have Valgius, who could gird himself for your great feats [i.e., to celebrate them in his verse]: none other is closer to immortal Homer." The poet and politician Valgius Rufus may have been the earliest member of the literary circle that subsequently formed around Messalla. In the mid-30s BCE, Horace mentions Valgius in the same list of discerning critics that included Messalla and Sulpicia's father,[37] and by the late 30s (on the evidence of the *Panegyric of Messalla*) he was closely associated with Messalla. Like his noble patron, Valgius worked in a wide variety of literary genres. His extant prose fragments address questions of grammar and philology,[38] while the elder Pliny cites an unfinished treatise on herbal medicine.[39] Quintilian attests to Valgius' rhetorical interests as well in his notice that he was "the most scholarly exponent" in Latin of the training of the rhetorician Apollodorus of Pergamum (Augustus' rhetoric teacher).[40] In addition to these prose writings, the younger Seneca ascribes to Valgius a work on the Sicilian volcano Etna.[41] This has been conjectured to be a didactic poem in hexameters,[42] in part because the *Panegyric of Messalla* associates Valgius with Homeric epic and in part because another of Messalla's client poets, the Augustan epicist Cornelius Severus, included a set piece on Etna in his hexameter epic, which apparently treated the Sicilian war of the early 30s BCE.[43] Valgius' other extant fragments include a variety of different verse forms: hexameters of a bucolic cast, epigram, and especially elegiac and amatory poetry.[44] Horace confirms Valgius' erotic elegiac focus in his *Ode* 2.9 (datable to ca. 27 BCE),[45] where he decries his friend's unceasing production of plaintive elegies for his deceased beloved, whom Horace dubs Mystes.

Valgius' composition of elegiac verses also seems to have encompassed praise of Messalla, as the poet of the *Panegyric of Messallae* proposed—though in the event, Valgius seems to have lauded his patron's poetic talent, rather than his military exploits. Vergil's commentator Servius Danielis, in a note on the seventh eclogue, mentions that Valgius in his elegies praised Codrus—a poet lauded by the victorious pastoral singer Corydon and criticized by his defeated rival Thyrsis.[46] This encomium is preserved in a Verona palimpsest, which explicitly names Valgius as the author of four fragmentary elegiac distichs celebrating Codrus' soft voice, learned breast, and sweet poems composed in the style of Catullus' friend Cinna.[47] The form Codrus is a Latinization of the name of the ancient Athenian king Kodros, a byword for noble birth.[48] Augusto Rostagni therefore suggested that Messalla Corvinus, the author of "Cecropian" (i.e., Attic) poems and scion of an ancient patrician line, circulated his Greek bucolic poetry under that pseudonym.[49] Valgius' portrayal of Codrus' poetry as learned, along with his explicit comparison of Codrus' poems to those of Cinna, the last surviving member of Catullus' circle (d. 44 BCE), is in keeping with Messalla's presumed composition of bucolic verse during his stay in Athens in 44 BCE, while the sweetness of Codrus' voice in recitation coheres with the characterization of Messalla's oratory by Tacitus, who describes him as a speaker both "softer and sweeter" than Cicero.[50]

The preponderance of elegiac distichs in Valgius' extant fragments is also consistent with Messalla's well-attested patronage of elegiac poets. His friendship with Albius Tibullus, for example, antedated the latter's first book of elegies (put into circulation as a collection in late 27 or early 26 BCE) and endured until the poet's untimely death in 19.[51] Under Messalla's aegis, Tibullus composed two books of elegies, explicitly naming his patron in several of his poems,[52] as well as celebrating his triumph of 27 BCE in elegy 1.7, and the appointment of his elder son Messallinus to the Board of

Fifteen Men who oversaw the sacred books in elegy 2.5.[53] The poets of the *Appendix Tibulliana* must also have been in some way associated with Messalla, though we cannot now discern the precise relationship in every case. Thus, the hexameter poet whose panegyric is preserved in the *Appendix Tibulliana* supplies valuable evidence of Messalla's early interest in Latin verse, as well as details of his military career,[54] while our poet Sulpicia names Messalla as her kinsman and implies that he stood in the relation of a guardian to her (3.14; cf. Ch. 3). The elegist Lygdamus is the outlier in the collection, for he never mentions Messalla.[55] If scholars are correct in their ascription to Messalla of the *nom de plume* "Codrus" for his composition of bucolic verse, however, he shares with Lygdamus the concealment of his Roman identity beneath a Greek pseudonym.

Ovid too, in his exile poetry, testifies to an early association with Messalla, calling him the "encourager, cause and fire of [his literary] pursuits,"[56] and attributing to him the suggestion that he follow the path of poetry rather than politics:[57] "your famous father, whose eloquence in the Latin language was no less than his noble birth, first urged me to dare to entrust my poems to Fame: he was the guide of my talent." Born in 43 BCE and thus perhaps coeval with Sulpicia, Ovid came to Rome to complete his studies at a young age and claims to have begun composing poetry shortly after he assumed the adult toga, perhaps in the mid-20s BCE.[58] He recalls his welcome at Messalla's house in his youth[59] and, in an elegy addressed to his patron's younger son, trades on their lifelong friendship to plead for recall from exile.[60]

Sulpicia must therefore have passed much of her youth in an intensely literary environment (Ch. 6). Indeed, her family's cultural attainments, and especially their enthusiastic practice and patronage of contemporary poetry and poets, support the suggestion advanced in the previous chapter that the female slave reader Petale, whose death is commemorated in an inscribed verse epitaph (*Appendix*), belonged to her family, perhaps even to her (cf. Ch. 7). And another important context for Sulpicia's literary interests and poetic experimentation can be seen in the vogue for amatory lyric and elegiac poetry at Rome from the end of the republic to the early years of Augustus' reign.

From Catullus (ca. 84–54 BCE) to Horace (69–8 BCE) and Gallus (70/69–27/26 BCE) to Ovid (43 BCE–16/17 CE), the most popular genres of the period were love-lyric and erotic elegy. Catullus' compositional heyday in the mid-50s preceded Horace's poetic career (ca. 35–8) by a generation, but the poet-politician Gallus bridged the lifetimes of both lyric poets, as well as inaugurating the tradition of elegiac love poetry in Latin (ca. 45–33).[61] Gallus composed four books of *amores*, "love-elegies," before his death by suicide in 27 or 26 BCE, on Augustus' renunciation of his friendship. He was also an intimate of the young Vergil, who in his earliest collection lauds his friend's poetic talent even as he censures his erotic obsession with his mistress "Lycoris."[62] Although we have lost most of Gallus' verse and so remain ill informed about his amatory elegies, it is clear that the genre he founded, basically an expansion of erotic epigram, was still flourishing in the 20s BCE.[63] This was the decade that saw the publication not only of Horace's three-book collection of lyric poetry (ca. 23), but also of Propertius' first three books of elegies (ca. 29, 25, 21), Tibullus' first book of elegies (ca. 27–26) and the composition of the elegies of his second book (apparently published posthumously after his death in 19), along with Ovid's earliest elegiac compositions, later collected among his *Amores*.

The efflorescence of Latin amatory poetry across the genres of lyric, epigram, and elegy was undoubtedly sparked by the publication of Meleager's *Garland*, a collection of Hellenistic Greek epigrams compiled about 95 BCE and very popular with educated Roman readers as well as Greek audiences.[64] Meleager included in his *Garland* not only short epigrams but also longer elegies by the most famous poets of the Greek literary tradition. The formal constraints imposed on epigram in the Hellenistic period and memorialized in Meleager's anthology are equally telling for Sulpicia's poetic practice, especially the metrical restriction of the genre to elegiac distichs (rather than the hexameters of the earliest inscribed epigrams),[65] and the preference for "epigrammatic" brevity over "elegiac" length.[66] Thus, four- and six-line epigrams prevail in Meleagrian sequences of the Greek anthology. Nonetheless, Meleager's modern editors A. S. F. Gow and D. L. Page attribute seventy-one epigrams of over eight lines to his *Garland*, including one by Theocritus of eighteen lines, another by Antipater of Sidon of twenty-four, and one by Meleager of twenty, in addition to his fifty-eight-line preface.[67] These "long" epigrams in elegiac distichs illustrate the difficulty of distinguishing the genres of epigram and elegy when Meleager compiled his *Garland* around 95 BCE.

By the time Ovid was writing elegiac couplets in Latin rather than Greek a century later, however, the two genres had apparently been decisively distinguished from one another. Thus, Ovid repeatedly limits the Latin elegiac canon to Gallus, Propertius, Tibullus, and himself,[68] and Quintilian reifies this canon a century later.[69] Although Ovid recognizes Catullus and Calvus as amatory poets,[70] he always omits them from his canon of Latin elegists. Yet Gallus and Propertius, at least, seem to have followed Catullus' practice in composing shorter poems, which we would now call epigrams, alongside longer poems, which we would now call elegies.[71] Moreover, Propertius' own statement of the elegiac canon includes both Catullus and Calvus, alongside Varro of Atax, Gallus, and himself.[72] Sulpicia's verse output in elegiac distichs of four to twenty-four lines thus seems highly comparable to that of the earliest practitioners of Latin elegy, who composed both elegy and epigram in the wake of Meleager's influential anthology.

Meleager's inclusion of female authors in his *Garland* is another factor that will have informed Sulpicia's composition of erotic verse. In the preface to his anthology, Meleager lists the poets whose verses he includes:[73]

> "To whom, dear Muse, do you bring these varied fruits of song, or who was it who also wrought this garland of poets?"
>
> "The work was Meleager's; he produced this gift as a keepsake for the illustrious Diocles. He wove in many red lilies of **Anyte,** and many white lilies of **Moero**; a few of **Sappho,** but they are roses; a narcissus, pregnant with piercing songs of Melanippides; and a young twig of Simonides' grapevine. Mingled with these he wove in the sweet-scented blossoming iris of **Nossis** (the wax of her tablets Love himself melted) and with it marjoram from fragrant Rhianus; **Erinna's** sweet saffron, with a maiden's blush. . . ."

Sappho herself, dubbed "the tenth Muse" in Hellenistic epigram,[74] enjoyed renewed acclaim and popularity at Rome in the aftermath of Meleager's inclusion of a few of her "roses" in his collection (Fig. 10).[75] Catullus' lyric *libellus* opens with an allusion to Meleager's preface,[76] and his surviving lyrics, elegies, and epigrams testify to the currency of Sappho's poetry in late republican Rome—in his application of the poetic pseudonym "Lesbia" (after Sappho's provenance) to his mistress, in his translation of one of Sappho's poems,[77] and in his introduction of her eponymous meter, the Sapphic stanza, into Latin poetry.[78] Horace too pays explicit homage to Sappho in his poetry and employs the Sapphic stanza across his four lyric collections as well as in the *carmen saeculare* of 17 BCE.[79] Both Latin lyric poets thereby attest to the archaic Greek poet's continuing acclaim across

Fig. 10 Bust of Sappho. Roman copy of an original from the early fifth century BCE (Palazzo dei Conservatori. PD-US).

the half-century spanning the end of the republic and establishment of the principate.[80] The special focus of Sappho's poetry on love, moreover, made her especially congenial to the amatory elegists, the Latin lyric poets' younger contemporaries, who name her as a model for their girlfriends' music-making and verse-composition, recommend her poems to amorous youth, especially female readers, and imitate her verses in their own.[81] Ovid even ventriloquizes Sappho in *Heroides* 15,[82] and we will see that Sulpicia too evokes Sappho's poetry in her own (Ch. 6).

In the mid-50s, moreover, when Catullus and his friends Calvus and Cinna were composing their newly fashionable love lyric and dabbling in elegy and epigram, Pompey the Great began construction of an entertainment complex in the heart of Rome that included a temple to Venus, a theater, and a shaded colonnade surrounding a public park.[83] Financed by, and adorned with, the spoils of his eastern wars, Pompey's Portico was dedicated in 55 BCE and displayed a statue of Sappho by the early Hellenistic sculptor Silanion in the company of statues of other notable Greek female poets.[84] Catullus refers to the portico as "the Great man's garden path" in one of his lyric poems, and he implies its popularity as a promenade for Roman women and love-struck youths.[85] Octavian rededicated the complex a generation later, in 32 BCE,[86] and both Propertius and Ovid attest to the portico's continuing popularity as a site for amatory trysts in the early principate, as does Martial over a century later.[87]

Writing in the third quarter of the second century CE, the Christian apologist Tatian catalogued the statues of female poets he saw there:[88]

> For Lysippos cast a bronze statue of **Praxilla**, even though she said nothing useful in her poems; Menestratos made a statue of **Learchis**, Silanion of **Sappho** the courtesan, Naukydes of **Erinna** from Lesbos, Boiskos of **Myrtis**, Kephisodotos of **Myro** from Byzantium, Gomphos of **Praxagoris**, and Amphistratos of **Kleito**. And what can I say about **Anyte**, **Telesilla**, and **Nossis**? The first was created by Euthykrates and Kephisodotos, the second by Nikeratos, the third by Aristodotos. Euthykrates made a statue of **Mnesarchis** from Ephesos, Silanion the **Korinna**, Euthykrates the **Thalarchis** from Argos.

While Tatian here denounces Sappho as a "courtesan" (*hetaira*), it is clear from the company she keeps, as well as from the name of her statue's sculptor (independently attested by Cicero),[89] that she is the acclaimed poet. Moreover, she appears here with thirteen women who were also remembered as illustrious female poets in ancient Greece,[90] and we have already seen that Meleager included selections from the poetry of several of these women in his *Garland*.

In addition, Sappho and eight of her statuary companions reappear together by name in an epigram by the Greek poet Antipater of Thessaloniki, who lived and worked in Rome during Augustus' reign, in the patronage of Piso Pontifex.[91] Antipater celebrates these authors as a canon of nine Greek female poets by reference to the nine Muses:[92]

> These are the immortal-tongued women that Helicon fed
>   with songs,
> and the rock of Macedonian Pieria:
> Praxilla, Moero, the mouth of Anyte, the female Homer,
> Sappho, glory of the beautiful-haired Lesbian women,

Erinna, renowned Telesilla, and you, Korinna,
who sang the onrushing shield of Athena,
female-tongued Nossis, and sweet-sounding Myrtis,
all craftswomen of eternal pages.
Great Ouranos gave birth to nine Muses, and these nine
Gaia bore, deathless delight for mortals.

All nine of Antipater's "immortal-tongued women" reappear in Tatian's later catalogue, and so it has been plausibly argued that his epigram speaks to the Augustan currency of the statuary display of female poets in Pompey's portico.[93] In this artistic milieu, where Greek poetry and sculpture were celebrated together in the Latin-speaking capital of the Roman empire, we can see compelling evidence for the continuing popularity of the ancient Greek female poets in Sulpicia's day.[94] Indeed, Antipater's epigram underlines the tight correlation between the literary fame of these Greek women and their artistic commemoration in Augustan Rome.

The earliest of these poets, after Sappho, were Myrtis of Anthedon and Korinna of Tanagra, both of whom composed choral lyric like their younger Boeotian contemporary Pindar (518–ca. 438 BCE), though apparently with a focus on local myths and heroic genealogies, perhaps from a gynocentric perspective.[95] Of Myrtis' verse, nothing survives beyond a prose summary by Plutarch of a lyric poem explaining the etiology of a Tanagran hero's worship.[96] Korinna, however, seems to have been much more widely read in antiquity. The author of five books of poetry in the Alexandrian edition (to Sappho's nine),[97] she was reputed to have bested Pindar in a poetry contest which a series of Pompeian frescoes has been thought to represent.[98] Both Propertius and Ovid bear witness to her contemporary currency among Latin speakers in Augustan Rome, the former by naming her as a model of poetic composition for his mistress Cynthia, the latter by giving her name to his own elegiac mistress Corinna.[99] Moreover, a Roman-era miniature copy of Silanion's fourth-century BCE bronze portrait statue of Korinna survives in marble (Fig. 11), showing her unrolling a scroll (presumably a volume of her poetry), with a book box containing her four other scrolls by her left foot.[100]

"Renowned" Telesilla, from Argos, also composed lyric poetry. Active in the first half of the fifth century BCE, she emerges in the sources as a poet of strikingly similar profile to Korinna. Just as Korinna's fame was measured against that of her Boeotian contemporary, the epinician poet Pindar, so

Fig. 11 Roman miniature copy of Silanion's original bronze statue of Corinna (ca. 320 BCE). Marble. Late second or third century (Musée Vivenel, Compiègne. PD-US).

Telesilla's was compared favorably with that of Bacchylides (ca. 518–ca. 451 BCE), another epinician poet. Like Korinna, Telesilla too seems to have composed poetry for a female audience: an address to "maidens," in one of the extant fragments has suggested to scholars that she wrote *partheneia*, choral lyric songs performed by young women of marriageable age.[101] Again like Korinna, she seems for the most part to have treated mythological subjects in her verse, if the surviving fragments of her poetry are representative. Like Sappho, moreover, she gave her name to a lyric meter, the Telesillan. Her continuing fame in the Hellenistic period can be discerned in her receipt of a portrait statue sculpted by the first-century BCE Greek artist Nikeratos, on display in Pompey's Portico. In the imperial period, moreover, both Plutarch (ca. 40–after 119 CE) and Pausanias (ca. 110–180 CE) report that she was admired "by/among women" for her poetry.[102]

Praxilla of Sicyon, who heads Antipater's canon, composed lyric poetry in the middle of the fifth century BCE.[103] She too imparted her name to a lyric meter, the Praxilleion, a rhythm associated with drinking songs. Her five extant fragments include three such drinking songs, a dithyramb, and a hymn to the dying Adonis,[104] Venus' youthful lover, in whose image we have seen Sulpicia figure her beloved Cerinthus on the hunt (Ch. 4; cf. Ch. 6).[105] Like Sappho, Praxilla earned early fame for her poetry. By the end of the fifth century BCE, the Athenian comic poet Aristophanes had parodied her verse in two of his extant plays, *Wasps* (422 BCE) and *Thesmophoriazousae* (411 BCE), while in the fourth century BCE, the famous Greek sculptor Lysippus, also from Sicyon, cast a statue portrait of her in bronze. As Tatian attests, this was the statue which stood in Pompey's portico throughout the principate.

Erinna is reported by Eusebius to have lived around the middle of the fourth century BCE. She was especially famous for her poem the *Distaff*, a hexameter lament in three hundred lines about the death of her childhood friend Baucis. Supposedly composed when Erinna was only nineteen years of age,[106] her poem was favorably compared to the verse of Homer and Sappho in antiquity (cf. Ch. 6).[107] The biography of Erinna in the tenth-century CE *Suda* relates conflicting information about her life, reporting four different possible provenances; making her a contemporary of the archaic poet Sappho; and registering not only her composition of the *Distaff* at the age of nineteen but also her own death in the same year, at the same age as that of her friend. Unimpeachable evidence from the Hellenistic period confirms the wide circulation of, and great admiration for, her *Distaff*, among Greek audiences. As we have seen, Meleager excerpted some of her epigrams in his *Garland*, characterizing them as "sweet saffron, with a maiden's blush." Early Hellenistic epigrammatists too—among them Asclepiades (third century BCE) and either Leonidas (also third century BCE) or Meleager (writing at the end of the second century BCE)—commemorate her by name.[108] Three epigrams attributed to her survive: two about the death of Baucis, the subject of her celebrated *Distaff*, and a third praising the verisimilitude of a woman's portrait.[109] Like Sappho, Korinna, and Telesilla, Erinna seems to have composed poetry primarily about women and their characteristic pursuits (weaving, friendship, and lament). Like Sappho and Korinna, moreover, her work appears to have been collected and studied by male scholars and teachers in the Hellenistic period, for the epigrammatist Antiphanes—writing during the reign of Augustus' successor, the emperor Tiberius—implies that Erinna's poetry garnered the attention of literary critics and scholars in his day.[110] We thus have further evidence from the early principate of the contemporary currency of her poetry.

Meleager's *Garland* contained not only the poetic "roses" of Sappho and "sweet saffron" of Erinna, but also verse "lilies" by two early Hellenistic female authors of epigram, the "white lilies" of Moero/Myro and "red lilies" of Anyte. Both women are mentioned by Antipater and Tatian as well, so we can be confident that statues of these women too stood in Pompey's portico. The *Suda* reports Moero's provenance as Byzantium and preserves the information that her father or son (both named Homerus) was a tragic poet.[111] Modern scholars date her poetry early in the Hellenistic period, ca. 300 BCE.[112] Although she is reputed to have authored epic, elegy, and lyric poetry, only two short epigrams composed in elegiac couplets survive, both preserved in the Greek anthology,[113] along with ten hexameter lines about the Pleiades quoted by the second-century CE author Athenaeus.[114] Despite the paucity of her extant verses, we can be sure that she and her poetry were popular among Hellenistic Greek audiences and familiar to late republican and early imperial Roman readers since Meleager included some of her epigrams in his *Garland*. The late Hellenistic poet Parthenius of Nicaea also incorporated the tragic tale of Alcinoë, which he drew from Moero's poem *Curses*, in his mythographic handbook of *Erotic Sufferings* (§27). The last of the Hellenistic poets, Parthenius was captured in the Mithridatic wars and brought to Rome in 72 BCE by Catullus' friend Cinna, where he purportedly taught Greek to Vergil and became a friend and poetic mentor to the elegist Gallus. His literary friendship with Gallus is confirmed by the dedication of his *Erotic Sufferings* to the Roman elegist "as a storehouse from which to draw material, as may seem best to you, for either epic or elegiac verse." His inclusion of a tale drawn from Moero's verse in this work is important evidence of the circulation of her poetry among the elegiac poets of the Augustan age.

The poetry of Moero's contemporary Anyte (ca. 300 BCE)[115] survives in greater abundance than that of any other ancient female author except

Sappho and Erinna: the *Greek Anthology* ascribes twenty-five epigrams to her, of which modern scholars accept the authenticity of twenty or twenty-one.[116] Her provenance is reported as Tegea, in the mountainous back-country of Arcadia,[117] which seems to be reflected in the pastoral themes of her verse. Yet such was her fame that the sons of the two most famous Greek sculptors of classical antiquity cast the portrait statue of her that stood in Pompey's portico. She herself, moreover, seems to have played a "pivotal role in the history of epigram," as the first classical author to have collected her epigrams (funerary, dedicatory, and descriptive) and issued them in a book of verse.[118] The Augustan epigrammatist Antipater's praise of her as "the female Homer" testifies to her extraordinary and enduring popularity among readers in classical antiquity. Yet his phrase is also highly paradoxical, since she worked in the smallest of poetic forms, epigram, rather than in Homer's expansive genre of epic, at the apex of the literary hierarchy; and she reoriented her verse from the public-facing themes (martial and political) of her male predecessors to the domestic concerns of the feminine sphere (women, children, animals, the landscape). Indeed—like Sappho, Korinna, Telesilla, and Erinna—she is credited with bringing to her poetry a distinctively female perspective.[119]

Anyte's impact on the classical literary tradition reverberates beyond the genre of epigram. In an epigram long interpreted as a statement of poetic program, Anyte invites a passing traveler (i.e., her reader) to linger in the shade of a pastoral grotto (i.e., her pastoral epigram collection):[120]

> Stranger, rest your weary limbs under this rock
>   (**sweet** sounds the breeze in the green foliage)
>   and drink cool water from the spring, for this respite
>   from the summer's heat pleases travelers.

The sweetness of her verse is sounded by the adjective she applies to the breeze rustling the foliage, along with the coolness of the spring water and the shade afforded by the recessed grotto. This imagery delimits the ancient trope of the *locus amoenus*, a "pleasant place" or "pleasance," and its features are recuperated, both individually and as an ensemble, by later poets as a way of symbolizing their literary ambitions to compose poetry that is sweet, pure, and original.[121] Indeed, the sweetness of Anyte's poetry is programmatically integrated into the subsequent traditions of both epigram and bucolic. Her younger contemporary Asclepiades sounds the amatory focus of his epigram collection in a priamel that explicitly acknowledges, even as it rejects, Anyte's pastoral vision of the genre:[122]

> **Sweet** for the thirsty in the summer is snow as a drink, and **sweet**
>> for sailors
>>> after a storm is the sight of the spring constellation "Crown,"
>> but **sweeter** still is when a single cloak covers two lovers,
>>> and the Cyprian goddess is praised by both.

Adopting Anyte's programmatic imagery of sweetness, Asclepiades strategically reorients the genre of epigram from pastoral to erotic themes. Somewhat later, however, the bucolic poet Theocritus (ca. 300–ca. 250 BCE) reclaims her imagery for his own pastoral verse, echoing Anyte's parenthetical remark, extolling the sweetness of the breeze in the rural foliage, in Thyrsis' opening lines of the first idyll ("Sweet is the song of the whispering pine, goatherd, that one by the springs; and sweet is your piping"), to which his interlocutor, a goatherd, responds "Sweeter is your song, shepherd."[123] In Asclepiades' amatory epigram and Theocritus' bucolic poetry, as well as in Meleager's inclusion of her epigrams in his anthology of course, we can see Anyte's innovative and influential literary program appropriated by the male poetic tradition.

We can also see her impact on another slightly younger contemporary, "female-tongued" Nossis (ca. 300–275 BCE).[124] A native of Epizephyrian Locri in southern Italy, Nossis too was a composer of dedicatory, ekphrastic, and funerary epigrams with a distinctly gynocentric focus. Of her eleven extant epigrams, nine celebrate women and women's deities. Poetic composition is also an important subject of her epigrams, and she "signs" three of her quatrains with her own name.[125] The first of these signed epigrams has been interpreted as the prologue to her poetry collection because she there announces the primacy of love as the subject of her verse:[126]

> Nothing is **sweeter** than love. Everything desirable
>> is second to it. I spit even honey from my mouth.
> Nossis says this: The one who has never been loved by Aphrodite,
>> that woman does not know what sort of flowers roses are.

In her opening words, Nossis distills a double debt to earlier practitioners of epigram: to Anyte, for the sweetness of her gynocentric verse, and to

Asclepiades, for the innovative amatory focus of his epigrams.[127] Kathryn Gutzwiller has argued that Nossis' proemial epigram also engages with Erinna's verse, in her avowed preference for poetry about erotic experience over that by or about unmarried virgins (i.e., Erinna and her friend Baucis).[128] Such a concentration of literary allusion in the brief compass of a four-line epigram underlines the intensity of Nossis' gynocritical poetics. In another of her signed epigrams, moreover, she explicitly names Sappho as her literary "foremother":[129]

> If you, stranger, are sailing to Mytilene where dances are lovely,
>   in order to borrow the flower of Sappho's graces,
> announce that a Locrian woman bore one dear to the Muses
>   and to her. You should know that my name is Nossis. Now go.

Formally a funerary epigram, the poem has been identified as the epilogue to Nossis' poetry book.[130] Here she explicitly sets her verse in relation to that of Sappho, the fountainhead of female poetic production in ancient Greece, and seals her literary descent from the Lesbian poet.

Particularly noteworthy are the female perspective and amatory focus of the surviving poems by Greek women from Sappho to Nossis, and this is clearly another crucial context in which to set Sulpicia's own innovative foray into Latin elegy. The amatory tradition of classical literature in which the Greek female poets participated, moreover, was amplified not only by their inclusion in Pompey's portico but also in Meleager's *Garland*, the first book of which seems to have contained exclusively erotic epigrams.[131] Given the novel visibility of Greek female authors at Rome in this period, we must also inquire into the possibility of female precedent for Sulpicia's foray into Latin letters. Here too, I suggest, we can see some important models for her innovative verse.

The earliest Roman woman whose authorship is uncontested in the ancient sources was Cornelia, "the mother of the Gracchi" (ca. 190–ca. 102 BCE),[132] though the authenticity of the two extant excerpts from her correspondence cited by the late Roman republican biographer and historian Nepos (ca. 110–ca. 25 BCE) is debated.[133] Women's composition of Latin verse, however, seems to have begun in the generation after the compilation of Meleager's *Garland*. The historian Sallust (ca. 86–35 BCE), writing in the triumviral period, introduces a woman sympathetic to the Roman revolutionary Catiline in his account of the conspiracy of 63 BCE:[134]

Among the conspirators was Sempronia, who had committed many crimes of masculine recklessness. This woman was fortunate in birth and beauty, as also in husband and children; she was skilled in Greek and Latin literature, in playing the cithara and dancing more elegantly than is necessary for a virtuous woman, and many other things which are the requirements for luxury....But her character was by no means uncivilized: she could write verses, make a joke, use language modestly, gently, or provocatively; in short she had much wit and charm.

Sallust's character sketch of Sempronia clearly reflects on the dissolute character of his anti-hero Catiline, whose attempt to overthrow the Roman republic in 63 BCE was prompted by recklessness, debt, and the desperation arising from a lack of electoral success.[135] But his casual attribution of literary interests and poetic talent to a Roman woman in the late 60s BCE, even before the efflorescence of Latin lyric and elegy among Catullus and his friends in the mid-50s, is intriguing and may offer further evidence of the impact of Meleager's anthology of Hellenistic epigram on Roman readers.

Better attested than either Cornelia's letters or Sempronia's verses, are the literary works of two Roman women whose compositions date to the late 40s BCE, at the very beginning of the triumviral era: Hortensia and Cornificia. The former came to prominence in 42 BCE when the triumvirs Octavian, Mark Antony, and Lepidus—after compiling a register of men for proscription (Ch. 2)—drew up another list of the wealthiest 1,400 Roman matrons, whom they proposed to tax in order to finance their preparations for war against the republican forces.[136] The matrons pleaded with the triumvirs' womenfolk to intercede with them for the remission of the tax but were refused by Antony's wife Fulvia. As a result, Hortensia—the daughter of Cicero's rival Hortensius Hortalus and sister of his eponymous son, mentioned as the author of erotic verse by Ovid (quoted above)—led a delegation of Roman matrons to the forum, where she delivered a speech against the tax and succeeded in inducing the triumvirs to reduce the number of matrons subject to the levy from 1,400 to 400.[137] Quintilian says that her speech was still read in his day, and "not only in honor of her sex" (i.e., because by a woman).[138] Fifty years or more later, the historian Appian paraphrases her Latin text in his (Greek-language) history of the civil wars, thereby confirming that it was still in circulation in his day.[139]

The single most important Latin female model for Sulpicia, however, must have been the Cornificia whose "famous epigrams" Jerome mentions under the year 41 BCE in his death notice for her brother Cornificius: "The poet Cornificius perished, deserted by his soldiers, whom he had called 'helmeted hares' because they often fled. His sister was Cornificia, whose famous epigrams survive."[140] Brother and sister were commemorated together on an inscription, now lost, from a funerary monument in ancient Rome:[141] "Cornificia, Quintus' daughter, wife of Camerius / Quintus Cornificius, Quintus' son, her brother / Praetor and Augur."[142] Cornificius was the recipient of the poet Catullus' request for a consolatory dirge in the style of the Greek lyric poet Simonides of Ceos and the addressee of a series of letters from Cicero.[143] Catullus admired his poetic skill, Cicero his Atticist oratory, and we have seen that Ovid included Cornificius in his roster of Latin erotic poets (quoted above).[144] Like Catullus' friends Calvus and Cinna (and Sulpicia's uncle and brother), moreover, he enjoyed a successful political career, at least until he was finally deserted by his soldiers and killed on the battlefield. As a young man in 50 BCE, he was engaged to the daughter of Catiline's widow.[145] A supporter of Caesar, he served as quaestor (in place of a praetor) in Illyricum in 48[146] and became augur shortly afterwards, perhaps in 47.[147] He then governed Cilicia, saw military action in Syria, and was elected praetor in 45.[148] After Caesar's murder, however, the senate appointed him to the command of the province of Africa Vetus and he resisted the triumvir Antony's efforts to reinstate the previous governor.[149] Proscribed by the triumvirs, he was attacked by the governor of Africa Nova, Octavian's appointee, and killed near Utica in late 42 BCE.[150]

Since Cornificius belonged to Catullus' literary circle, his sister Cornificia's husband Camerius has often been identified with the addressee of Catullus' poems 55 and 58b.[151] Especially intriguing is Catullus' search for Camerius and his inamorata in Pompey's portico in the former poem:[152]

I beg you, if it isn't any trouble, to show where your lurking-place is. I sought you in the lesser Campus, in the Circus Maximus, in all the bookshops, in the temple consecrated to highest Jove; in the Great man's garden walk, my friend, I stopped all the little ladies, but I saw they looked blank. I kept on calling to them, demanding an answer, "Give me Camerius, you wicked women!" One of them, baring her bosom, replied "Look! Here he is, hiding in my rosy breasts." But to endure you now is a labor of Hercules; in such great arrogance do you deny me, my friend. Tell us where you'll be, publish it boldly, give it up, trust the light. Do the milk-white maidens detain you? If you keep your tongue still within your closed mouth, you will lose all the fruits of love. Venus rejoices in a wordy declaration. Or if you want, you can lock up your speech, provided I may share in your love.

It is tempting to believe that Cornificia found inspiration for her famous epigrams among the statues of the illustrious female poets in Pompey's portico as much as in the contemporary composition of epigrams and elegies by her brother and perhaps her husband, as well as by Catullus and his friends. Whatever the inspiration for her epigrams, however, it is striking that our disparate sources, both material and textual, when gathered together reveal the outsize influence of Hellenistic epigram on Catullus and his friends' experimentation with love lyric, elegy and epigram; their impact, in turn, on Sulpicia's father and uncle, as well as on the elegiac poets of early Augustan Rome; and the lingering allure of the famous Greek female poets whose statues adorned Pompey's portico. These are the multifaceted literary contexts in which Sulpicia came of age, and we turn in the next chapter to her poetry, to explore its debts to the Greek female poets, Hellenistic epigram, and the Latin love poets.

Sulpicia: Life, Love, and Literature in Ancient Rome. Alison Keith, Oxford University Press.
© Oxford University Press 2026. DOI: 10.1093/9780197607008.003.0006

6

Intertexts

Sulpicia and Her Literary Interlocutors

Sulpicia writes exultantly about her amatory success in 3.13, a poem that has been interpreted as offering programmatic reflection on her poetic achievement (3.13.1):[1] "At last (*tandem*) has come love/love-poetry (*amor*)."[2] Her opening words imply the further novelty of a woman's entry into the hitherto normatively male genre of Latin love elegy.[3] For Sulpicia strikes a distinctively female posture in relation to contemporary male-authored elegy with her very first word, which echoes the opening word of Propertius' mistress Cynthia in her first elegiac speech:[4] "At last (*tandem*), has another woman's affront returned you to our bed and shut you out from her closed doors?" From one perspective, the situation that Cynthia laments in Propertius' elegy is precisely the opposite of that which Sulpicia celebrates in 3.13:[5]

> For where did you waste the long hours of a night that was mine,
> returning exhausted—ah, wretched me!—once the stars were
> driven away?
> Oh! Would that you might spend such nights, you shameless man,
> as you always bid me, poor wretch (*me miseram*), suffer!
> For sometimes I staved off sleep by spinning a purple thread,
> and again, though tired, by singing a poem on Orpheus' lyre;
> sometimes, abandoned, I complained softly to myself
> of your frequent long delays in another's arms:
> until Sleep overcame me with his soft wings.
> That was the last concern for my tears.

Only at the end of a long night, misspent dancing attendance on her rival—Cynthia complains—does her reprobate of a lover return to her, having abandoned her to a lonely evening of weaving and song (i.e., poetry). By contrast, Sulpicia records the triumphant consummation of her love affair (and her elegiac poetry) in almost the same number of couplets that the Propertian Cynthia devotes to her erotic frustration (five: six).

Yet both Sulpicia and Propertius' Cynthia draw closely on contemporary Latin love poetry to fashion themselves as elegiac poets. Thus, Propertius represents Cynthia's first-person feminine elegiac discourse (the earliest words attributed to a woman in extant Latin love elegy) as an adaptation of the genre's conventional lexicon in her reversal of the gendered roles of love-poet and elegiac mistress. In her self-characterization as a "poor wretch," for example, Cynthia echoes Propertius' self-portrait at the outset of his first collection, as well that of his model Catullus.[6] When she "complains softly to herself" about her lover's "long delays in another's embrace,"[7] the abandoned Cynthia adopts the characteristic posture of her poet-lover, who continually complains of her inconstancy and unavailability.[8] In her efforts to solace her unhappy love too, by spinning and singing snatches of verse to the accompaniment of "Orpheus' lyre," she recalls both Catullus' depiction of the Fates singing a wedding song to the accompaniment of their spinning,[9] and Propertius' comparison (echoing Gallus?) of his elegiac verse to Orpheus' song.[10] Moreover, the tears Cynthia sheds over her love[11] likewise evoke her elegiac poet-lover's lachrymose plaints about his faithless mistress:[12]

> Against me, Venus provokes bitter nights
> and at no time does idle Amor desert us.
> Avoid this evil, I warn you: let his own love (*cura*) occupy each man,
> nor let him change place from his accustomed love.
> But if anyone turns slow ears to my warnings,
> alas! With what great grief will he recall my words.

The Propertian Cynthia thereby casts *herself* as the devoted poet of love and her poet as the faithless beloved.

Sulpicia too draws at length on the literary metaphor of text as textile in her program poem. But where Cynthia models exemplary Roman female modesty in her housebound spinning, Sulpicia boasts of exposing her sexual joys for all to read. Instead of modestly "cloaking" her passion, she "strips it bare" in her verse (3.13.1–2),[13] playing on the conventional image of the love god *Amor* (Gk. *Erôs*) as "naked" in Hellenistic epigram and Latin elegy.[14] She credits Venus for her amatory success (cf. 3.13.5), in the vivid image of the Cytherean goddess placing her beloved in her embrace (3.13.3–4) or, more literally, in "the cavity or fold produced by the looping of [her] garment."[15] With this expression, she continues the sartorial imagery of her opening couplet but eschews the rhetoric of spinning and weaving pervasive in male-authored Latin love poetry.[16] The word she uses for her embrace at the end of her second couplet (*sinum*, 3.13.4), echoes an earlier occurrence of the word in the cycle, along with its metrical position, when Sulpicia asks her beloved to "run swiftly back into [her] embraces" (*sinus*, 3.9.24). The echo hints at the effectiveness of her earlier verses, not only in 3.9 but also in 3.11 where Sulpicia asks Venus for a mutual love (3.11.13–16).[17] The intratextual verbal reminiscence skillfully knits her small corpus tightly together and throws into relief the programmatic nature of 3.13.

Venus' fulfillment of Sulpicia's prayers (3.13.3–5) evokes a range of early Greek intertextual models, starting with Sappho's famous poetic prayer to Aphrodite, the poem that stood at the head of her first book in the Alexandrian edition of her corpus:[18]

Richly enthroned deathless Aphrodite,
child of Zeus, wile-weaver, I pray to you:
break not my spirit, Mistress, with heartache
of anguish;

but come here, if ever at some other time 5
you heard my cry from afar, and marked it,
and came, leaving your father's house,
having yoked

your golden chariot: beautiful and swift
sparrows conveyed you, on rapidly whirling
wings 10
above the dark earth from heaven
through the mid-air;

and swiftly they arrived; but you, blessed
goddess,
with a smile on your deathless face,

asked why I'm suffering again, and why 15
I summon you again,

and what I most desire to happen, frenzied
in my heart. "Whom am I to persuade
to join your friendship again? Who
wrongs you,
Sappho? 20

For even if she flees, she will soon pursue;
and if she won't receive gifts, yet shall
she give;
and if she loves not, she shall soon love
even though unwilling."

Come to me now too and release
me from 25
cruel cares; fulfil all that my heart
desires to fulfil and you yourself be
my ally.

Sappho bases her renewed prayer to the goddess on Aphrodite's pattern of past aid, and the love-goddess' consistent promotion of Sappho's amorous affairs and tutelary role in her amatory verse underlie Sulpicia's portrait of Venus in 3.13. Sulpicia implies that her prayers too take the form of poems, since she has entreated the goddess "with the Camenae" (3.13.3)—i.e., her muses.[19] She too has successfully engaged the goddess' attention, moreover, for "Venus has fulfilled her promises" (3.13.5) just as Sappho asks the goddess to do at the end of her prayer.[20] While Sappho does not address Aphrodite with the epithet *Cytherêa* in this poem, she uses it elsewhere of the goddess and it may bear a particularly Sapphic resonance in the context of Sulpicia's "Sapphic" prayers.[21]

Venus aids Sulpicia by bringing her lover to her in a fashion similar to the way in which Aphrodite engineers the amatory union of Paris and Helen in *Iliad* 3.[22] There the Homeric goddess snatches Paris from his battlefield duel with Helen's former husband Menelaus and wafts him to his bedchamber (*Il.* 3.373–82), bidding Helen join him (*Il.* 3.410–12). The Iliadic passage, which culminates in the couple's lovemaking (*Il.* 3.447), well illustrates Aphrodite's coercive sexual power and illuminates the erotic currents of Sulpicia's poem. Where her first distich promises to "strip her love bare" (3.13.2), the second brings her lover directly into her embrace (3.13.4). Given the dynamics of the Iliadic scene, it is only to be expected that erotic "joys" (*gaudia*, 3.13.5)[23] result from Sulpicia's congress with her lover (cf. 3.9.18, Ch. 4). Indeed, at the end of the poem she proudly proclaims the suitability not just of their match (Ch. 4)[24] but also of their lovemaking (3.13.10): "a worthy/noble woman I shall be said to have been/lain with a worthy/noble man." For the idiom "to be 'with' someone" was a euphemism for sexual intercourse.[25]

Sulpicia bolsters an invitation to her readership to publicize her joys (3.13.5–6), specifically directed to anyone lacking an erotic relationship of their own, with a reference to the material means of literary dissemination (3.13.7–8): "I would not wish to entrust anything to sealed tablets (*signatis tabellis*), / so that none might read it before my lover (*meum*)."[26] Elsewhere in Latin amatory elegy, writing-tablets carry love letters or invitations to erotic assignations between poet-lover and mistress: in the paired poems *Amores* 1.11–12, for example, Ovid asks Corinna's hairdresser Nape to take her mistress his proposal for an amatory tryst on sealed tablets.[27] But the diversity of uses for ancient writing tablets invites slippage between the lover's private correspondence with his beloved and the poet's circulation of his love poems to a wider audience. Thus, Catullus asks his lyrics to hound

a woman into returning his writing-tablets:[28] "Come here, my hendecasyl-
lables, as many as you are / all of you everywhere, however many you all
are. / A shameless hussy thinks I'm a joke / and denies she'll return to me /
my writing-tablets, if you please." Catullus implies that his hendecasyllabic
poems are inter-changeable with his writing-tablets—i.e., that they circulated in that medium.[29]

Propertius too plays on the relationship between the lover's sealed and
the poet's unsealed tablets at the end of his third book of elegies, where he
figures the circulation of his seductive verse in the loss of his tablets:[30] "And
so our tablets of such learning have perished, / and along with them so
many good pieces of writing." In his absence, the public's familiarity with
his characteristically seductive eloquence confirms his authorship of the
writings contained in his tablets.[31] The conceit of the poem lies in
Propertius' offer of a reward for the return of his tablets,[32] but we can read
the elegy, in metaliterary terms, as an announcement of the circulation of
his new collection of elegies. Sulpicia's open invitation in 3.13 to read her
verse before her lover has therefore been interpreted as a similar claim to
literary publication.[33]

The poem concludes with Sulpicia's proud assertion of her disdain for
scandal (3.13.9–10): "But sin (peccasse) is pleasing; to compose my features
(uultus componere) for reputation (famae) / is a bore." The Latin love poets
characteristically employ the verb pecco, "blunder," in the sense of "commit
a moral offence, do wrong," especially in the context "of offenses against the
sexual code."[34] In this period, Horace uses the word of young men's costly
extra-marital affairs as also of a liaison with a harmless courtesan where
"the word suggests naughtiness rather than sin,"[35] while the elegists apply
the term to their mistresses' violation of their exclusive erotic commitment.[36] Sulpicia's use of the word implies her recognition of the potential
impropriety not only of her prosecution of an amatory affair but also of her
composition of erotic verse. For with the circulation of her poetry, she
renounces any desire to save face (uultus componere, 3.13.9)—i.e., to protect
her sexual reputation (fama, 3.13.10; cf. pudor, 3.13.1).[37] Rather, she
embraces the prospect of earning poetic renown (fama) through her risqué
verses.[38]

The literary distinction Sulpicia seeks from her poetry's circulation is
instantiated in the poem in her repeated recourse to verbs of speaking and
their cognate nouns, of which she and her verse are the objects rather than

the subjects. In the first distich, she anticipates the greater "disgrace" (3.13.2)[39] that would redound upon her[40] for concealing her love out of shame rather than for baring it to someone.[41] The syntax of the Latin is difficult, but I accept the interpretation of Tränkle and Lyne, among others, that the infinitives "conceal" and "bare" should be construed as subjects with the predicate nominative *fama*, a noun cognate with the verb *fari*, "to speak."[42] On this interpretation, Sulpicia highlights the transgressive force of female discourse already in her first couplet, both in the sentiment of the verse ("baring" her love in poetry when it should rather be "cloaked out of feminine modesty") and in the sense of *fama* as, precisely, "notoriety" or "disgrace."

She pursues this risqué course still more overtly in the third couplet, by inviting anyone without a love of their own to disclose hers (3.13.5–6).[43] Particularly arresting is the collocation *narret*/*dicetur* at the pivot of the distich. Both verbs of speech, they are strikingly juxtaposed to one another, the first in the active voice and the second in the passive, thereby constructing an echo chamber in which the very person who is to recount Sulpicia's erotic joys "is themselves reported" (*dicetur*, 3.13.6) not to have their own.[44] This strained use of *dicetur* calls attention to the thematic valence of speech in the poem, and underlines Sulpicia's concern with reputation in the sense of both gossip and literary renown.[45]

Sulpicia has been interpreted as implying "let the old fogies talk, I don't care," along the lines of Catullus' dismissal of censorious old men's prurient interest in his scandalous liaison with Lesbia or Propertius' disdain for such critics' censure of elegiac carousing.[46] Sulpicia's indifference to her sexual reputation is confirmed in the following couplet, where she invites anyone to read her sealed tablets before her lover (3.13.7–8), an indifference given ringing endorsement in the proud assertion of her sexual "sin" in the final distich (3.13.9–10). The last word of the poem (*ferar*, 3.13.10)—whether construed as future indicative ("I shall be said") or present subjunctive ("let me be said")[47]—both enacts the notoriety for which she expresses enthusiasm throughout the poem and transmutes it into literary renown. The poet thereby transforms what might have been deemed scandalous into the poetic currency of fame.[48]

This interpretation of 3.13, broadly indebted to feminist criticism and current trends in Latin literary scholarship,[49] emphasizes the double valence of sexual and poetic license propounded in the epigram and proposes it as characteristic of Sulpicia's small corpus. Such a double vision of the elegy is facilitated by the language of covering and baring in the opening couplet (3.13.1–2); by the invocations of Venus (3.30.3, 5) and by the goddess' gift of the desired youth (3.13.3); by the very site of Supicia's receipt of her beloved, *viz.* in her lap or embrace (3.13.4); by her sexual joys (3.13.5); and even by those sealed tablets (3.13.7), which elsewhere in Latin amatory elegy carry verse invitations to erotic assignations. Perhaps the single most telling lexical marker of Sulpicia's interlinked thematics and poetics, however, is the noun *amor* in the first line, which authors from Terence to Gellius employ in the sense of "a love affair" or "sexual intercourse,"[50] but which becomes, in our period, a quasi-technical term for love poetry. Indeed, the noun frequently appears in the plural, *Amores*, as a title for elegiac collections from Gallus—perhaps on the model of the Hellenistic Greek poet Phanocles' *Erôtes*—through Propertius and Valgius to Ovid.[51]

In addition to the amatory content and literary craft of Sulpicia's poetry, commentators often stress the difficulty of her grammar and syntax, especially in 3.13.[52] Gruppe attributed the idiosyncrasy of her Latin expression to "feminine Latin," which he characterized as "impervious to analysis by rigorous linguistic method."[53] More recently, however, scholars have eschewed speculation about gendered Latin and concentrated on identifying a suite of stylistic traits that recur in Sulpicia's poetry and can therefore be used to confirm her authorship of the eight first-person poems.[54] Many of these syntactical peculiarities are illustrated in 3.13: multiple subordinate clauses ("hypotaxis") and sub-subordination (3.13.1–2, 7–8; cf. 3.9.15–18); a proliferation of subjunctives, both jussive (3.13.5, 10; cf. 3.14.5; 3.15.3; 3.16.3) and characteristic or potential (3.13.2; cf. 3.14.3; 3.17.4, 5); a predilection for infinitives, especially perfect infinitives (3.13.1, 2, 6, 9, 10), particularly as the penultimate word in a pentameter (fourteen in her full corpus of forty-two distichs)[55] but also as the penultimate word in the hexameter (six more instances);[56] "the highly idiosyncratic predilection for comparative constructions" (3.13.1–2; cf. 3.16.3–4, 3.17.3–4);[57] elaborate conditionals (3.13.6; cf. 3.9.15–18; 3.17.4, 5); and the postponement of the relative pronoun to the first position of the second half of the pentameter (3.13.8; cf. 3.11.16).[58] Other notable features of her verse include rhetorical questions (3.9.7–8, 9–10; 3.11.15–16; 3.14.3, 4; 3.15.1; 3.16.1–2, 5–6); the use of noun clauses with *quod* to introduce a poem's central situation (3.11.5–6; 3.16.1; 3.17.1–2); the "focusing" *iam* (3.14.5, 3.15.2, 3.16.1) and comparable force of *nunc* (3.9.19, 3.17.2); and the periphrastic use of the gerundive with *erit* (3.11.16; 3.14.2).[59]

In contrast to the difficulty of Sulpicia's syntax, her metrical technique is remarkable for its anticipation of an Ovidian standard of ease and fluidity in the regular closure of the pentameter line of the distich with an iambic disyllable (i.e., a two-syllable word in the metrical shape of an iamb, ⌣⌣). This rhythm is consistent across the first-person poems with a single exception at 3.16.4, a pentameter line concluding with the poet's signature "Servius' daughter Sulpicia" (*Serui filia Sulpicia*). This, the sole non-disyllabic ending in the first-person poems, as has often been observed, proves the rule: in a metrical tour de force, Sulpicia integrates her filiation into a pentameter that ends with her own quadrisyllabic name.[60]

On the basis of Sulpicia's lexicon, syntax, and metrical technique, Hermann Tränkle dated the short poems (3.13–18) to the years 25–20 BCE. This dating has been accepted by most scholars because it is consistent with both the timelines of the genealogical stemma that has been painstakingly constructed for Sulpicia and also the linguistic standards of late republican/ early imperial Latin verse during the heyday of elegiac composition at Rome.[61] I accept the same dating for the two first-person elegies in the Sulpicia cycle (3.9 and 3.11) as well, because their lexicon, grammar, syntax, and meter have been shown to overlap extensively with 3.13–18; indeed, as we shall see, they are also fully consistent with contemporary elegiac verse in respect to their conventional characters, settings, and themes.[62] Yet they have often been attributed to another hand, writing at a later date, because of their slightly greater "elegiac" length and somewhat smoother "elegiac" flow, and it is certainly true that they lack the compression of the epigrams along with their occasionally strained expression. In my view, however, the stylistic differences between Sulpicia's longer elegies and shorter epigrams have been overstated in the critical literature,[63] for they are in no way as great as those that distinguish Catullus' polymetrics (1–60) and long elegies (65–68) from his short epigrams (69–116) and occasioned the classic study of D. O. Ross, Jr.[64] Indeed, in most respects the differences in form and content between Sulpicia's two longer elegies and six shorter epigrams are slight, closer to the minor variation in style and theme that distinguish the first twenty elegies of Propertius' earliest collection from the two epigrams that close it.[65] For that reason, I attribute the first-person elegies 3.9 and 3.11 to Sulpicia and discuss them alongside the epigrams.

The mid- to late 20s are also the years to which the Sulpicia Petale epitaph (Ch. 4) must belong because of certain features of its lexicon, orthography, and meter:[66] the old spelling of *quoi* for *cui*, "to whom" (*AE* 1928.73.2); the ante-classical adverb *longinquom*, "at length" (*AE* 1928.73.7), which does not appear elsewhere in the Augustan period and features a similarly archaic orthography of *qu* for *c* and *o* for *u*; the masculine gender of the word for "distaff," *colus* (*AE* 1928.73.8), used by Catullus and Propertius alone among Latin authors, who otherwise treat it as feminine;[67] and the metrical diversity of the epitaph's pentameter line-endings,[68] as was characteristic of Catullus, Gallus, and early Propertius (Sulpicia's admired models: see below). Since we know that Servius' daughter Sulpicia was writing elegiac verse at precisely this time, Jérome Carcopino proposed that our poet composed Sulpicia Petale's funerary inscription.[69] As he noted, the deceased is commemorated under the Roman gentilician name of Sulpicia, which stands at the head of the first line of the epitaph and thereby communicates her status as a freedwoman. Scholars have surmised that she was manumitted on her deathbed, since a full line is devoted to her servile name Petale (*AE* 1928.73.2) and her son Aglaos also bears a Greek name (*AE* 1928.73.4), which was a marker of enslaved status in ancient Rome. Taken together, her gentilician and servile names confirm her enslavement to a Sulpicius or Sulpicia, though we cannot determine their identity with any further precision.[70]

As with Petale's epitaph, so with the cycle: the name Sulpicia stands at the start of the opening poem (3.8.1), giving the title *Sulpicia* to the collection (Ch. 7).[71] Introduced in the third person as an admired elegiac *puella* (3.8.15, 24; cf. 3.10.1, 11, 16; 3.12.2, 9), the poet herself irrupts into elegiac discourse in 3.9, the second poem in the sequence. First-person pronouns and pronominal adjectives proliferate from the outset (3.9.1, 4, 12, 13, 15 [*bis*], 19, 21, 24),[72] marking the shift from third-person object of the verse to first-person speaking subject. Opening with a direct address to a fierce boar in the rustic wilds, the speaker requests that the beast spare her young man (3.9.1–4), identified by the Greek servile name Cerinthus (3.9.2), and decries her beloved's enthusiasm for the hunt (3.9.5–10), before proposing to join him in the countryside, even on the chase (3.11–18). Caught in the toils of love, Sulpicia envisages serving her beloved like a slave by carrying his nets and tracking his prey (3.9.11–14). In this way, she literalizes two of the elegiac genre's most common structural metaphors: "the slavery of love" (*seruitium amoris*) and "the nets of love . . . and strong bonds of Venus."[73] Yet Sulpicia overturns the gendered conventions of both metaphors by applying to her own situation the erotic slavery and amatory hunting characteristic of the male poet-lover in Latin amatory verse. Thus, the metaphor of *seruitium amoris* conventionally casts the poet-lover as a slave to his mistress—on the basis of the class status implicit in the Latin word *domina* ("mistress of the house[hold]" = *materfamilias*—i.e., female slave-owner)—as if to overturn normative gender hierarchies, only to reassert the masculine authority of poet over his material, lover over his mistress, Roman over Greek, etc.[74] Likewise, the metaphor of the amatory chase conventionally casts the male poet-lover as a hunter of women as Ovid instructs his male pupils in the first book of his *Art of Love*:[75] "The hunter knows well where to spread his nets for deer; / he knows well in what valley the boar, gnashing his teeth, lies in waiting . . . / You too, who seek material for a long love-affair [or love-poem], / learn in what place a girlfriend can be before you haunt it."

Gallus seems to have been the originator of the trope of love as a hunt, if Propertius' Milanion *exemplum* is correctly traced back to him.[76] Jacqueline Fabre-Serris has therefore proposed that a Gallan model lies behind Sulpicia's lines, noting the words Vergil sets in Gallus' mouth in the tenth eclogue ("or I shall hunt fierce boars")[77] and triangulating back to Gallus from hunt scenes in Propertius and Ovid that share situational and lexical similarities.[78] But service in the hunt also appears in Tibullan elegy, where it is a strategy to woo the good-looking youth, Marathus.[79] Sulpicia's description of "her young man" (3.9.1), Cerinthus (named at 3.9.11), as the handsome possessor of both "tender hands" (3.9.8) and "gleaming shins" (3.9.10) assimilates him to the enslaved "boy-toy" (*puer delicatus*) of Latin love elegy—a figure familiar not only from Tibullus' Marathus, but also from Catullus' Iuuentius and Gallus' "Hylas" in Propertius' elegy 1.20.[80]

Like both Marathus and Hylas (but in striking contradistinction to Iuuentius),[81] Cerinthus is attested as a Greek servile name, borne by slaves and freedmen at Rome in the early principate.[82] In this regard, as we have seen (Ch. 4), Sulpicia conforms to established Latin elegiac practice regarding the pseudonyms given to elegiac beloveds as attested by Apuleius.[83] As with the names of the other elegists' mistresses,[84] the name Cerinthus carries multiple literary resonances. Transliterated into Latin from the Greek word *kêrinthos* meaning "beebread"—"a compound of honey and pollen,"[85] which was the fodder of bee larvae[86]—the name is closely connected with two other apian substances, honey (Gk *meli*) and wax (Gk *kêros*, from which *kêrinthos* was derived) that, like bees themselves, bore poetic associations in classical literature.[87] Sulpicia's reference to sealed writing tablets in

3.13 (*signatis tabellis*, 3.13.7) is especially suggestive in this regard, since writing tablets were not only lined with wax for ease of both composition and erasure but also customarily sealed with wax.[88] Cerinthus' very name, which we might translate "Honey,"[89] thus bespeaks the material form (*qua* "beeswax") of the tablets in which he is memorialized.

The tradition of Hellenistic epigram furnishes several pertinent examples of the programmatic correlation of poets with bees, honey, and/or wax.[90] But it is notable that the association is particularly sustained in the case of the early Hellenistic author Erinna (Ch. 5). Asclepiades characterizes her poetry as "sweet," while an unattributed Hellenistic epigram celebrates her verses as "bee-born" and an epigram of uncertain authorship (composed by either Leonidas or Meleager) commemorates her as a "maiden honeybee… gathering the flowers of the Muses."[91] Another anonymous epigram elaborates the metaphor at even greater length:[92] "From Lesbos is this honeycomb of Erinna. If it is small, yet it is wholly suffused with honey from the Muses."[93] As a bee-maiden, Erinna composes verse imbued with the Muses' honey, and so the epigram likens the repository of her honeyed speech to a honeycomb (*kêrion*), styled "Lesbian" because her poetry was modeled on Sappho's (Ch. 5). It has therefore been suggested that these evocations of Erinna's beelike nature imply that the symbolism of bees and honey were especially appropriate for the young female poet, perhaps because she drew on the image in her *Distaff*.[94] Indeed, the name Cerinthus concisely translates the same sort of dual allusion as Erinna's honeycomb, which itself alludes to and is etymologically derived from the wax on the tablets on which poetry was written down.[95] We can be certain, moreover, that the precedents of Erinna, Asclepiades, Leonidas, and Meleager, would have been available to Sulpicia when she came to decide on a pseudonym for her beloved.[96]

The metapoetic valence of the name Cerinthus is further enhanced by two contemporary Latin literary intertexts. Horace applies the name to the low-born suitor of a wealthy *matrona* in his first book of satires, put into circulation in 35 BCE, a decade before Sulpicia composed her elegies and epigrams:[97]

> … Therefore, lest you regret it,
> stop pursuing matrons, whence there's more bad
> trouble to derive than fruit to harvest from the affair.
> Nor, though she be laden with pearls and emeralds,

> is her thigh more tender than yours, Cerinthus, or her leg
> straighter, and very often a toga-clad prostitute has an even
> better one.

Sulpicia's appropriation of the name Cerinthus from Horatian satire for her elegiac "Honey" implies both his good looks and his modest social standing, at least by comparison with her own proud patrician lineage (Chs. 2–4; cf. 3.16.4–6, discussed below).[98] The same implication may be felt in the resonance of Vergil's commendation in the *Georgics* of the "lowly plant honeywort" as fodder for the farmer's bees.[99]

Sulpicia thus exhibits consummate control of the generic characters, metaphors, and themes of Latin amatory verse even as her innovative feminine voicing of elegy radically destabilizes both Latin literary conventions and Roman social codes. This gender trouble is fully realized in her decision to join Cerinthus on the hunt (3.9.12–13): "I myself (*ipsa ego*) would carry the twisted nets over the mountains / I myself (*ipsa ego*) would seek the tracks of a fleet deer." On the one hand, these lines articulate a truly shocking statement of female subjectivity, unmasked (or "laid bare") in the gender of the intensive pronoun *ipsa* (3.9.12, 13), whereby Sulpicia differentiates her female perspective from the hitherto resolutely masculine outlook of Latin love elegy. On the other hand, the speaker's female standpoint is muted (or "cloaked"): first in the elision of *ipsa ego* to *ips' ego*, where the feminine ending -*a* is lost to the initial vowel of the following word, with the result that feminine *ipsa* becomes virtually indistinguishable aurally from the masculine *ipse*; and then in an intertextual reminiscence of Propertius' self-same statement of personal agency in elegy 2.19, where he renounces love for hunting: "I myself shall hunt" (*ipse ego*).[100]

Sulpicia thereby cues Propertius' uncharacteristic rejection of elegiac urbanity for the rustic hunt in 2.19 as an important intertextual model for her own elegy, which takes up the lexicon, setting, and themes of his.[101] The boar's remote mountain haunts of Sulpicia's opening lines look remarkably like the remote country fields to which Cynthia has retired in Propertius' elegy:[102]

> Though you're leaving Rome, Cynthia, against my wishes,
>   I'm happy that you'll frequent the remote countryside (*deuia*
>   *rura coles*) without me.
> There will be no youthful seducer in the chaste fields,
>   who might lure you from being virtuous by his flattery:

> neither will any quarrel arise before your windows,
>> nor your sleep become bitter because you're called for outside.
> You'll be alone, Cynthia, and you'll look upon the lonely
>> mountains (*montis*)
>> and herds and fields of a poor farmer.
> There no games or shrines will be able to corrupt you,
>> the most frequent cause of your sins (*peccatis*).

Like Cynthia in Prop. 2.19, Sulpicia imagines her removal to a distant rural landscape marked by good pastureland, hills, and woods.[103] We may also note the overlap in the two poets' second-person address to Cynthia and the boar, respectively, who are imagined to "frequent the remote" countryside in the opening distichs of their respective poems.[104] Although Sulpicia describes her young man (3.9.1) as a "chaste boy" (3.9.20), with "chaste hands" that she hopes will touch only his hunting nets (3.9.20), Cerinthus brings to life Propertius' "youthful seducer in the chaste fields"[105]—an urban swain transplanted to the remote countryside that Propertius was so sure he would not visit even "to lure Cynthia from probity by his flattery."[106] Indeed, Propertius rejoices that in the countryside Cynthia must forego the corrupting influence of the urban "games or shrines," which he sees as "the most frequent cause" of her "sins"—i.e., her sexual infidelity to him. The sexual valence of Cynthia's "sins"[107] is also worth highlighting, given Sulpicia's employment of the same verbal root in her program poem (3.13.9), especially as she foresees Cerinthus' hunt ending in their sexual tryst (3.9.15–18). While Propertius plans to go hunting himself (quoted above) and take charge of the hounds,[108] Sulpicia offers to attend her young man on his wanderings in the back country (3.9.11–14) and serve him by carrying his nets over the mountains, tracking his prey, and releasing the hounds. Like Propertius,[109] moreover, Sulpicia worries that she might have a rival in the countryside (3.9.21).

As we have seen (Ch. 4), Sulpicia opens 3.9 with an allusion to the myth of Venus and Adonis (vv. 1–4), in a scenario that implicitly likens the female speaker to the goddess of love (cf. 3.9.19, "now let there be no Venus [i.e., "love" or even "sex"] without me"). Throughout the elegy, however, Venus vies with Diana, goddess of the hunt, for Cerinthus' attention. Diana enters in the third couplet (3.9.5), where she is identified as "the Delian mistress" (because born on the island of Delos). In the Latin literary context, the epithet functions as a double allusion: to Vergil's use of the name for Diana in the seventh eclogue, where the goddess receives a wild boar in sacrifice, on

the one hand;[110] and to Tibullus' application of the name to the mistress of
his first book, with whom he desires to live in an idealized countryside, on
the other.[111] In Sulpicia's elegy 3.9, Diana (perhaps in company with a mor-
tal rival, 3.9.21) keeps Cerinthus away from the city, hunting in her woods
(3.9.6), as the Euripidean Hippolytus does in his eponymous tragedy. By
associating Cerinthus with Adonis and Hippolytus, Sulpicia assumes the
personae alternately of Venus and Diana (Ch. 4),[112] the twin deities who
preside over Propertius' elegy 2.19, in which he imagines himself taking up
the rustic hunt of Tibullus' elegy 1.4, in place of his own characteristic pursuit of Gallus' urban elegy.[113] Propertius sets his rural scene in elegy 2.19 on
the banks of the river Clitumnus in Umbria, where his family owned property,[114] while Sulpicia emphasizes the hills (3.9.2, 7, 12) of her family's
Tuscan farm (Ch. 4).[115]

Sulpicia's evocation of the myth of Venus and Adonis in elegy 3.9 invites
comparison with several other writers, in the first instance Sappho, whom
we have already identified as an important model for our poet.[116] The
Hellenistic poet Dioscorides, in a funerary epigram lauding Sappho's poetic
achievement, pictures her "mourning in company with Aphrodite, while
the goddess laments for the fair young son of Cinyras"—i.e., Adonis.[117] Two
extant fragments confirm that Sappho composed at least one lament for
Adonis, presumably for performance at the Adonia, a festival for the dead
youth celebrated by women across ancient Greece.[118] The longer of the two
fragments seems to have featured responsion between a chorus of female
mourners and the goddess Aphrodite:[119] "'Delicate Adonis is dying,
Cytherêa; what shall we do?'/ 'Beat your breasts, maidens, and tear your
clothes.'" Sappho names both the youth and the goddess, the latter precisely
by the epithet *Cytherêa*, which we have seen Sulpicia adapt into Latin in
application to Venus at 3.13.3 (discussed above). While treatments of the
myth of Adonis occur sporadically in Greek literature after Sappho,[120] perhaps the most famous was Praxilla's hymn to Adonis, which includes a
speech set in the mouth of the dying youth:[121] "'The most beautiful thing
I leave is the light of the sun, / second the shining stars and face of the moon,
/ and also ripe cucumbers, apples and pears.'"[122] Several critics have seen in
Praxilla's lines sustained allusion to Sappho's poetry,[123] and it is attractive to
read Sulpicia's evocation of the myth of Adonis in 3.9 as a gesture toward a
tradition of women's poetry, since the myth is not widely disseminated in
extant Latin literature until after Ovid treats it in his *Metamorphoses*,
around thirty years later.[124]

The state of our evidence does not allow us to know whether the myth was broached by an earlier generation of Latin love poets, though both Cinna and Gallus are plausible candidates.[125] Propertius certainly handled the myth in his elegy 2.13, however, in couplets addressed to Cynthia which have been viewed as Gallan in inspiration:[126]

> Yet you will sometimes weep over your lost lover:
>> it's right always to love dead husbands.
> She is my witness, whose snow-white Adonis was gored once upon
>> a time
>> while out hunting on Idalion's summit by a harsh boar;
> in those waters there you, Venus, are said to have bathed your
>> beautiful lover,
>> and to have gone with your hair disheveled.
> But in vain will you summon my mute Shade back, Cynthia:
>> for what could my fragmented bones say?

In these couplets, the longest extant Latin treatment of Adonis before Ovid, Propertius sets out the same relationship of mourning female lover and prostrate male beloved as Sulpicia implies in 3.9.1–4. Propertius emphasizes the amatory nature of the relationship,[127] directly addressing his beloved Cynthia, just as Sulpicia addresses her beloved Cerinthus (3.9.11). Venus, moreover, bears witness to the truth of Propertius' exemplum for Cynthia's benefit, just as Sulpicia asks that her beloved Cerinthus enjoy no Venus (i.e., love/sex) without her (3.9.19). Both authors even seem to pun on a false (i.e., poetic) etymology linking Venus with the hunt.[128] Yet Sulpicia offers a novel gyno-centric perspective on the mythic *mise-en-scène* in 3.9 by actively joining Cerinthus on the hunt to keep him safe from boars rather than rehearsing the traditional contours of the myth such as we find in Propertius' elegy 2.13, where the *exemplum* constitutes a final lachrymose meditation on the poet's own death in the conventional context of elegy's funereal associations. The Propertian Venus thereby assumes the profile of his elegiac mistress Cynthia that we saw in his elegy 1.3 (discussed above), disconsolate in her plaint for her absent lover. Where Propertius chides Cynthia in the final distich of his poem for thinking she can call back his mute shade, however, Sulpicia sounds a note of confidence in the efficacy of her verse when she invites her lover to run quickly back into her embrace (3.9.24), anticipating her triumphant receipt of him in her lap at 3.13.4 (discussed above).

As in 3.13, moreover, the speaker of 3.9 openly avows sexual desire for her beloved (3.9.15–16): "Then the woods would please me, then my love, if with you / I could be proven (*arguar*) to have lain (*concubuisse*) [with you] before the nets themselves." The syntactical construction of the distich displays Sulpicia's characteristic predilection for the perfect infinitive at the start of the second half of the pentameter (*concubuisse*, 3.9.16) in a conditional clause (3.9.15–16), as well as the self-conscious portrayal of her sex life as the object of other people's discourse (*arguar . . . concubuisse*, 3.16) familiar from 3.13.5–10. The verb *concubuisse* ("to have lain," 3.9.16), moreover, makes explicit the euphemism of her phrase "to have been with" in 3.13 (v. 10),[129] while the sexual valence of Sulpicia's hoped-for "joys" (*gaudia*, 3.9.18) is emphasized in its collocation with the phrase "of passionate love" (3.9.17–18): "then though the boar approach the hunting-nets, he will go away unharmed, / so as not to disturb the joys of passionate love" (*ueneris cupidae gaudia*).

The succeeding couplets continue the focus on Sulpicia's sexual desire for Cerinthus, but her concern that there be "no Venus" (i.e., love or sexual congress) without her (3.9.19), opposes Venus to Diana, whose "law" of chastity governs the hunt (3.9.19–20), and newly broaches the possibility of a rival for his affections. Sulpicia emphasizes her Honey's sexual "purity" in the repetition of the adjective "chaste" at beginning and end of the first half of the pentameter 3.9.20, in application both to him ("chaste youth") and his hand ("with a chaste hand"). The stress on his chastity, however, is a striking departure not only from Roman social standards, in which it was the freeborn *woman*'s most highly valued attribute (Ch. 4),[130] but also from Latin elegiac convention, in which the male poet-lover either prosecutes an adulterous affair with a married woman or pursues a socially disreputable liaison with an unmarriageable woman.[131] The shadowy outline of a rival then appears in the following couplet, where Sulpicia voices the fear that another woman "stealthily approaches [her] love" (*furtim subrepit amori*, 3.9.21). Here, as often, the verbal prefix *sub-* implies furtiveness and intensifies the suggestion of her rival's devious conduct, while the adverb *furtim* ("stealthily") echoes the question she earlier posed to her lover about his "pleasure in entering the haunts of wild beasts by stealth" (3.9.9) and may retrospectively imply a connection between Cerinthus' interest in the hunt and amatory duplicity.[132]

Sulpicia consigns her rival to wild beasts (3.9.22), perhaps in an evocation of the staged hunts of the amphitheater,[133] to end the poem with the self-serving proposal that her young man "run swiftly" back into her embrace (3.9.24). It has been observed that Sulpicia's phrasing turns the would-be hunter Cerinthus into her hunted prey, as the alliterative Latin phrasing implies he ought to make tracks.[134] In her valedictory distich, Sulpicia thus upends the gendered norms of elegiac hunting to cast herself, *qua* elegiac speaker, as huntress, Cerinthus as her prey.[135]

The metaphors of erotic slavery and the chains of love recur in 3.11, a birthday poem (*genethliakon*) for Cerinthus (3.11.1–2): "The day that has given you to me, Cerinthus, I must always / hold sacred and celebrate amid the festivals."[136] As in 3.9, the first-person perspective (absent from 3.10) is enunciated in the second word of the poem (*mihi*, 3.11.1; cf. *meo*, 3.9.1). The poet implies a return to the female perspective by merging her voice with those of the three Fates, who sing as they weave the destiny of the new-born Cerinthus (3.11.3–4): "At your birth the Fates foretold (*cecinere*) for girls (*puellis*) a new / slavery (*seruitium*) and gave proud realms to you." Sulpicia eschews weaving metaphors in her characterization of the Fates' work as poetic song (cf. 3.13.5), but her phrase *Parcae cecinere* (3.11.3) echoes the Fates' celebrated singing in Tibullus' panegyric for Messalla and in Catullus' epyllion *Peleus and Thetis*, where they sing an *epithalamium* (64.323–81) that accompanies their weaving (64.303–22).[137] Sulpicia thereby invests her birthday poem for Cerinthus with panegyric overtones and implies the couple's future marriage. Such a socially respectable outcome for the affair can only be hinted at in elegy, however, since the genre conventionally explores amatory passion in the context of an extra- or non-marital relationship. Indeed, Sulpicia reverts to elegiac convention in the next line, where she figures the relationship in the elegiac commonplace of "the slavery of love" (*seruitium amoris*) and suggests multiple rivals for her beloved in her reference to plural "girls," underscored in the next line where she herself "burns before the rest of them" (3.11.5).

Scholars have remarked a pun on Sulpicia's filiation (*Serui filia Sulpicia*, 3.16.4) in her explicit reference here to amatory slavery (*seruitium*, 3.11.4),[138] and the pun offers tacit confirmation of her authorship of the poem. The phrase "proud realms" is Tibullan,[139] but Sulpicia's reuse of it in the context of her unorthodox love-affair unmasks the artificiality of the trope of the male poet-lover's subordination to his mistress in contemporary elegy through her reassertion of masculine authority in her own. Her ostensible restoration of the hierarchy of the sexes, however, entails further gender trouble in the disruption of the class order through the problematic

elevation of the Greek slave, "Cerinthus," above the Roman aristocrat, "Sulpicia."
In her strict application of elegiac onomastic conventions to herself and
her beloved, Sulpicia lays bare both the class and gender hierarchies of her
genre while potentially exposing herself not only to gossip (cf. 3.13), but
even—after Augustus' marriage and adultery legislation of 18/16 BCE—to
legal penalties (Ch. 7).

Sulpicia embraces the fire of love that consumes her (3.11.5, a conventional elegiac image),[140] as long as her beloved feels a "reciprocal fire" (3.11.6)
and "heats up" (3.11.10) at the thought of her (cf. Ch. 4).[141] In her express
desire for a "mutual love" (3.11.7; cf. 3.11.6, 13–20; 3.12.8), she adheres to
an amatory paradigm proposed for others by Catullus and recommended
to his mistress by Tibullus, but that is otherwise rare in contemporary elegy,
which conventionally articulates a model of erotic domination.[142] She figures the mutual love she would share with Cerinthus in the reciprocal terms
of equal service (3.11.13), retrofitting the trope of *seruitium amoris* to both
lovers equally in her prayer that each be bound by the same indissoluble
chains of love (3.11.14–16). While her appeal to her lover's eyes (3.11.8) is
conventional,[143] she innovates in her vow "by the very sweet trysts" (3.11.7)
she has shared with Cerinthus. These are the "stolen pleasures" celebrated
by the male love poets and denounced by Vergil in the *Aeneid*,[144] here,
unprecedentedly, appropriated by a female speaker.

Sulpicia's appeal to Cerinthus by his birth-spirit can be paralleled elsewhere in Latin verse, but a direct prayer to someone else's—as with her invocation of her Honey's "great birth-spirit" (3.11.9)—is otherwise unattested
and suggests a confidence in her elevated birth and class standing not usually on display in male-authored elegy. This may also explain the vehemence of
her jealous wish for Cerinthus' birth-spirit to desert him "should he perhaps
sigh over other loves" (3.11.11).[145] She retreats from this extreme in the next
couplet, however, with her request that Venus either inspire her beloved to
experience equal bondage or lighten her own chains. The wish for her lover
to "serve [the goddess of love], equally bound" (3.11.13–14) constitutes a
"radical reinterpretation of the usual understanding of *seruitium amoris*, in
which the trope represents not hierarchy but intimacy."[146] Indeed, the rare
use of the adverb "equally" emphatically underscores the unconventional
mutuality of the love Sulpicia proposes. Her reference to lover's chains, however, is standard elegiac fare, as is their etymological connection with Venus
(implicit in the collocation *Venus.../uinctus...uincla*, 3.11.13–14)[147] and her
wish that their erotic bond (3.11.15) endure (3.11.16).[148]

The elegy concludes with two couplets that underscore the generic disruption and gender trouble entailed by a woman's expression of desire in Latin elegy (3.11.17–18, 20): "my young man desires the same as I, but he desires more secretly; / for he's ashamed to say these words openly. / . . . what does it matter whether he asks secretly or openly?" Sulpicia's lexicon here overlaps extensively with that of 3.13, where she "bares" her love by revealing all rather than modestly "cloaking" her passion: in both poems, a proliferation of nouns and verbs connoting speaking and reputation (3.11.17–18, 20; 3.13.1, 5 (*bis*), 6, 9, 10) thematizes the gender trouble occasioned by immodest female speech in the obstinately male genre of elegy. The gender inversion is underscored in 3.11 by Sulpicia's attribution to Cerinthus of the modesty and silence conventionally expected of Roman women but rejected by the poet herself in 3.13. Thus, the adverb Sulpicia uses of Cerinthus "secretly" (*tectius*, 3.11.17) desiring the same outcome as she hopes for is formed from the past participle of the verb she employs to express her rejection of the idea of "concealing" her passion in 3.13 (*texisse*, 3.13.1).[149] Similarly, Cerinthus' embrace of discretion (*pudet*, 3.11.18) mirrors on the verbal plane her rejection of modesty (*pudore* 3.13.1). Although Cerinthus is reluctant to speak openly (*dicere uerba palam*, 3.11.18), the poet herself brazenly invites her readers to publish her affair abroad (*mea gaudia narret / dicetur*. . . , 3.13.5–6).

There are few models in contemporary male-authored Latin amatory verse for such explicit statements of erotic passion as Sulpicia authors in 3.9, 3.11, and 3.13: nothing in Tibullus or Lygdamus; nothing extant in Gallus; and in Catullus, verses both cruder (*c.* 16, 32, 37, 41) and more veiled (*c.* 68). It is Propertius, rather, who offers the closest parallel in extant Latin love poetry for Sulpicia's elevated lexicon and sexually explicit themes in a pair of poems in the second book that revel in the elegist's amatory conquest of Cynthia in terms applicable to both sex and poetry. Thus, in his elegy 2.14, Propertius claims a night of triumph with his mistress in language, similar to Sulpicia's in 3.13, that puns on his literary and sexual success.[150] He explicitly proclaims his carnal joys[151] and dedicates gifts to the goddess Venus, whom he invokes by her epithet *Cytherêa*[152] (the very epithet used by Sulpicia at 3.13.3), in recognition of his admission to his mistress' bed.[153] He directly addresses his mistress with the endearment "my light" (*mea lux*), a phrase familiar from Catullus to be sure, but taken up particularly widely across Propertius' second collection and distinctive in the Tibullan corpus to the first-person Sulpicia elegies (3.9.15; 3.18.1).[154]

Propertius' elegy 2.15 is still more explicit about his carnal pleasures and the nudity that is the hallmark of his lovemaking:[155] "For sometimes she tussled with me, with her breasts bared (*nudatis*), / and sometimes she introduced a delay by covering herself with her tunic." Propertius is especially eloquent about the sight of Cynthia's naked beauty, which he compares to that of the most famous women of classical myth:[156]

> Paris himself is said to have perished for love of nude Helen,
>   when she rose from Menelaus' bed:
> and nude Endymion is said to have captivated Phoebus'
>   sister and to have lain with the nude goddess.

His repetition of forms of the root *nud-* ("nude, naked, bare")[157] seems to have impressed Sulpicia, who employs the verb *nudasse* ("bare") herself at 3.13.2 in an exploration of the themes of poetic reputation and publication figured as the consummation of a love affair. Moreover, she deploys precisely the same diction (of speaking) and syntax (indirect discourse) as that which Propertius uses in 2.15 to emphasize the publication and circulation of her verse. But where Propertius emphasizes the lovers' pillow talk, Sulpicia invites anyone who lacks erotic success to narrate her own carnal joys (3.13.5).[158] Her repeated recourse to indirect discourse in the passive voice may also derive from Propertius, who reports Paris' love for Helen and Endymion's impact on Diana not only in the same syntactical structure but even in the same lexicon that Sulpicia employs to publish her own love affair.[159] In lexicon, syntax, and theme, Sulpicia reveals herself a close and careful reader of Propertius' amatory elegy.

The fame that Sulpicia courts with the publication of her elegiac affair therefore invites particular scrutiny in relation to the notoriety Propertius won with the publication of his *Cynthia*—both the name of his girlfriend and, as the first word of his opening elegy, the title of his first collection.[160] Of particular note, in this connection, is Propertius' emphasis, throughout his second book of *amores*, on both the material form of his elegies in a book-roll, and the verbal circulation of the narrative of his erotic liaison. We can see this double emphasis already in the opening couplet of his elegy 2.1, where he addresses an enthralled public inquiring into the source of his literary inspiration: "You ask whence comes my inspiration for composing so many 'loves' / whence comes my soft book to my lips." Elegy 2.3 opens with an unnamed interlocutor rebuking the poet/lover for his incessant writing/loving, which he predicts will result in a second book within a month:[161] "Scarcely can you rest a month, unhappy man, / and already there will be a second shameful book about you!" Propertius varies the pattern in elegy 2.5 by charging his mistress Cynthia with responsibility for the scandal of his notoriety:[162] "Is this true, Cynthia, that your name is a byword in the whole of Rome / and you live a life of notorious depravity?" His opening couplet sounds a similar note to Sulpicia's expression of pleasure in sin and disinclination to consider her reputation in 3.13.9, and he concludes the elegy by threatening to write what Cynthia could never live down.[163] Propertius thereby imputes to Cynthia the same kind of contempt for her reputation that Sulpicia asserts in 3.13.[164]

A particularly suggestive example of Propertius' use of the trope appears at the beginning of elegy 2.24:[165]

> 'Can you talk, when you're already a byword because of your
> notorious book
> and your *Cynthia* is read all over the Forum?'
> Whose temples would sweat *not* drench at these words?
> Gentlemen must maintain their discretion (*pudor*) or hide
> their love (*amor*).
> But if Cynthia now were compliant and inspired me,
> I would not be said to be the source of depravity (*nequitiae*).
> Nor would I be infamously traduced throughout the whole city,
> and though I be burned, I would not have the name of deceiver.

In these difficult couplets, we see the same disjunction between the poet's literary fame and the lover's sordid reputation set out in the same amatory lexicon that Sulpicia employs in 3.13: Propertius' "book" *Cynthia*, "read" all over the forum, corresponds to Sulpicia's "writing tablets" (3.13.7), left unsealed so that anyone "might read" them (3.13.8) before her lover. Like Propertius, moreover, who contrasts love or love poetry (*amor*) with gentlemanly discretion, Sulpicia juxtaposes her love and love poetry (*amor*) with the expectation of womanly modesty (3.13.1).[166] Both poets embrace "sin"[167] but are also acutely conscious of being talked about by others.[168] They have become "gossip" and "disgrace" (*fama*, 3.13.2, 9)[169] as their elegiac affairs circulate on the lips of others (3.13.10).[170]

If Sulpicia's commemoration of her erotic joys in 3.9, 11, and 13 is indebted to the elegies of Propertius, her interest in the form of the "birthday poem," *genethliakon*,[171] in 3.11 looks closer to home, to the circle of poets around her uncle Messalla. The earliest birthday poem in extant classical literature is Tibullus' panegyric of Messalla in elegy 1.7, a celebration of his patron's receipt of a triumph for his military success in Aquitania and the east, celebrated on his birthday.[172] Here too, the celebrant's "birth-spirit" is invoked[173] and reference is made to offerings of incense, cake, wine, perfumes, and garlands.[174] In the following book, Tibullus' birthday-poem for Cornutus in his elegy 2.2 furnishes another example of the form (Ch. 4):[175] with a request for silence, the poet as master of ceremonies initiates the birthday prayer by invoking the celebrant's birth-spirit and describing the ritual offerings of incense, unguents, garlands, cake, and wine. The poet's augury of his friend's birthday wish for a happy marriage, in preference to land and wealth, constitutes the focus of the elegy and shares with Sulpicia's elegy 3.11 a conventional lexicon and normative system of imagery that includes Venus and Amor, the birth-spirit, ritual sanctity and divine assent, ceremonial offerings, the flames of love and the pyre, and the chains of long-lasting love. Tibullus' *genethliakon* may be distinguished from Sulpicia's by the augural language in which he expresses his good wishes for the marriage of his addressee Cornutus,[176] especially in contrast to our poet's unusual articulation of female desire; but in most respects the two elegies take up the conventional themes of the classical birthday poem in a closely overlapping lexicon. The two elegies are also almost exactly the same length at Tibullus' twenty-two and Sulpicia's twenty verses respectively. It has therefore been suggested that Tibullus' poem was a major influence not only on 3.11, but on all the poems (voiced in both first- and third-person) collected in the Sulpicia cycle.[177]

The Sulpicia cycle also includes two more *genethliaka* in the form of a pair of epigrams on the strikingly original theme of the poet's own birthday (3.14–15)—"a nice twist on the tradition of celebrating girlfriends' birthdays."[178] In the first and longer of the two (discussed earlier in Ch. 4), Sulpicia disavows any celebratory aspect to the day, on the grounds that she will be parted from her beloved Cerinthus (3.14.1–2), unwillingly dragged off to her family villa by her uncle (3.14.3–8). Her characterization of this traditionally happiest of days as "hateful" (3.14.1) in the first word of the elegy, and "unhappy" (3.14.2) in the next line, marks an extraordinary departure from the conventional Roman worldview. Her description of the family estate near Arezzo as "tiresome" (3.1.4.1), likewise in the opening line of the elegy, also departs from the traditional Roman idealization of the farming life, as articulated in this period by Varro in his *De re rustica* ("On Rural Themes") of 37 BCE and Vergil in the *Georgics* (29 BCE). The sentiment is entirely at home in Roman elegy, however, which is conventionally set in the imperial metropole and characteristically adopts the urbane outlook of the worldly (male) poet-lover.[179] Sulpicia's embrace of urban life, and concomitant rejection of her family's rural property, thus bears the stamp of her genre (3.14.3): "What is sweeter (*dulcius*) than the city?" The elegiac *puella* is an urban creature by generic convention and so Sulpicia, *qua* elegiac *puella* (3.14.3, 3.15.1, 3.17.1; cf. 3.8.14, 24; 10.1, 11, 16; 12.2, 9) belongs in the city rather than in a country-villa on a river in the countryside around Arezzo (3.14.3–4).

Sulpicia's rhetorical questions in this distich (3.14.3–4) imply not only her generic commitment to the urban settings of Roman elegy but also her rejection of the rustic landscape of pastoral verse newly introduced into Latin poetry by Vergil in his *Bucolics* of 37 BCE: we may compare the "sweet fields," from which Meliboeus laments his exile in the first eclogue.[180] Indeed, as we have seen (Ch. 5), sweetness had become a critical convention of Hellenistic pastoral, used programmatically by Anyte of her rustic epigrams and applied subsequently by Theocritus to his bucolic idylls.[181] Yet sweetness was not the exclusive property of pastoral verse. Already in the Hellenistic period, epigrammatists from Asclepiades to Meleager reasserted a claim to the quality as characteristic of erotic epigram (Ch. 5). Thus, while Asclepiades acknowledges the "sweet" setting of Anyte's pastoral epigrams, he proposes his own erotic focus as "sweeter still" and Nossis agrees with him that "nothing is sweeter than love."[182] Meleager too prioritizes the erotic profile of verse epigram by devoting the first book of his *Garland* to amatory themes (Ch. 5). Sulpicia's question "what is sweeter than the city" thus intervenes in a Hellenistic literary debate over which genre—pastoral or epigram—was "sweeter" and asserts the primacy of epigram.

Sulpicia also seems to engage with the ethical tenets of Epicurean philosophy in her epigram.[183] A philosophy of hedonism, Epicureanism proposed "pleasure" (Greek *hêdonê*, cognate with the adjective *hêdus/hâdus*, "sweet") as the goal of human life and counseled the avoidance of "trouble" in its pursuit.[184] In the last generation of the Roman republic, Epicurean philosophy found a masterful exponent in Lucretius, whose *On the Nature of the Universe* adapts Epicurus' thirty-seven books "On Nature" into six books of Latin hexameters, while in the triumviral period Vergil and Horace composed poetry with a markedly Epicurean ethical perspective.[185] Sulpicia's vocabulary in 3.14 engages with contemporary expressions of Epicurean sentiment in Latin literature. For example, her characterization of the countryside as "tiresome" or "troublesome" (3.14.1) reverses the conventional view of the attractions of rural life in Epicurean thought on display across Vergil's pastoral collection and Horace's satires,[186] to portray the idealized setting of Epicurean philosophy as "tiresome." Moreover, her cheeky request that her uncle "give it a rest" (3.14.5), by foregoing the planned trip to the Tuscan estate, mischievously draws on the lexicon of Epicurean philosophy, in which "relief from toil or exertion, rest, repose"[187] sums up the sect's ideal of "freedom from disturbance"—i.e., quietude, the state of true pleasure envisaged as the goal of the philosophical life. Her characterization of her uncle as "too solicitous" (3.14.5) also seems indebted to Epicurean disavowals of troublesome labor.

In the final couplet of the epigram, Sulpicia returns to the conventional Latin lexicon of amatory verse (3.14.7): "carried off (*abducta*), I leave my heart (*animum*) and senses (*sensus*) here." With these words, Sulpicia disavows the Epicurean principal of avoiding mental perturbation, especially that caused by erotic obsession. In elegy, the *animus* is the part of the mind where the emotions reside,[188] while *sensus* is synonymous with "the mind's emotions."[189] At Rome, elegy was conceived as the genre of affect, and Sulpicia's language in this line asserts the centrality of subjective emotion to her genre. In her self-characterization as "carried off," moreover, she implicitly likens herself to the Homeric heroines proposed as paradigms of Latin elegiac love: Helen, Briseis, and Andromache.[190] While mythological heroines characteristically weep in male-authored elegy,[191] Sulpicia eschews elegiac tears to protest her subjection to her uncle's authority (3.14.8): "since you do not permit me to be under my own control." Sulpicia voices a rare protest against the legal constraints on female agency intrinsic to both her genre and her society, even as her phraseology subverts the elegiac convention of the domineering mistress' power over the male poet-lover to restore normative Roman hierarchies of age and gender.[192]

Sulpicia's elegiac "plaint" apparently had its desired effect, for the next epigram gleefully reports that her birthday will be celebrated at Rome after all (3.15). The quatrain is clearly a companion piece to the preceding epigram and implies the efficacy of that poem. Verbal echoes between the two confirm the pair's responsion.[193] Of particular interest is Sulpicia's circulation of the news that her birthday "should be celebrated by us all" (3.15.3), which recalls her invitation to those without their own love to "tell her joys" (3.13.5–6). Throughout the cycle, Sulpicia consistently "exposes" her amatory affairs beyond the purview of family and household.

Such literary and erotic daring is on full display in 3.16, where Sulpicia acidly decries her lover's amatory interest in a lowborn bedmate. Jealousy is "the elegiac passion" par excellence,[194] and that emotion seems to motivate the poet's proud statement of her patrician lineage (*Serui filia Sulpicia*) in contrast to her rival's servile status (3.16.3–4). The figure of the rival pervades contemporary male-authored elegy, but in male-authored elegy the challenger is not only wealthier than the poet-lover but also often socially more prominent and/or already pursuing a politically career: we may compare Propertius' elegies 1.8 and 2.16, where a wealthy praetor is represented, first, as nearly successful in his efforts to detach Cynthia from Rome (and her elegist) in order to keep him company on his provincial posting and then, on his return, briefly seduces her with his gifts. Sulpicia, by contrast, portrays her rival as an enslaved sex-worker, whose class position at the bottom of the Roman social hierarchy is marked by the basket of wool she carries (3.16.3–4), which exposes her to male sexual depredation. Her servile wool-working distinguishes her from the patrician poet, who wears the products of slave labor (cf. 3.8) and removes them at her own discretion (cf. 3.13). Cerinthus himself appears careless (*securus*, 3.16.1)[195] not only of his sanctioned girlfriend, the poet, but also of the political career, symbolized in Sulpicia's reference to the *toga*, which he owes to his birth (3.16.3; cf. 3.9.23, Ch. 4). Yet her reference to the toga is bitterly ironic, for it was the characteristic garb not only of the Roman male citizen ("be concerned for your toga," 3.16.3) but also of the enslaved prostitute ("be concerned for your toga-clad prostitute"), and so she glosses the item of dress in the next line with the synonym "prostitute" (3.16.4).[196] Contact with the servile sex-worker transmutes Cerinthus' social standing into that of "an unknown bed" (3.16.6), with the result that Sulpicia fears both ceding her lover to a slave and falling to a baseborn lover.

Sulpicia strains the conventional lexicon and syntax of Latin erotic poetry in this difficult epigram, as she condenses the clash between male sexual privilege and female sexual agency into a series of pointed wordplays. The movement from the first distich, where she fears that she "may take a sudden fall into disgrace" (*subito ne male inepta cadam*, 3.16.2), to the last, where her relatives worry that she "may yield to an ignoble bedmate" (*ne cedam ignoto . . . toro*, 3.16.6), turns on the roughly synonymous, near homonyms *cadam* and *cedam*. Cerinthus' lack of concern for her (he is *securus*, sure of himself, 3.16.1) is juxtaposed not only with his care (*cura*, 3.16.3) for an enslaved prostitute but also with her relatives' solicitous attention to her welfare (3.16.5–6). In the wordplay *securus...cura* (3.16.1–3), Sulpicia may even play on the sound of Cerinthus' name (suppressed in this epigram). Her potential folly, or ineptitude (*subito ne male inepta cadam*, 3.16.2), is reflected in Cerinthus' ignoble (both unknown and unworthy) bed/mate (*ignoto toro*, 3.16.6). Although unparalleled in contemporary Latin elegy, the sentiments Sulpicia expresses in 3.16 are consistent with the other first-person poems in the cycle—as, for example, when she notes how much Cerinthus "permits" himself (3.16.2; cf. 3.14.8; 3.15.2), the sudden reversal in her own fortunes (3.16.2; cf. 3.15.4), or her beloved's wandering "concern" (*cura*, 3.16.3; cf. 3.9.5, 3.17.1, 3.18.1).

The two epigrams that conclude the cycle return to more familiar *topoi* in their exploration of the erotic commonplace of lovesickness, another structural metaphor of Latin elegy.[197] Catullus ventriloquizes Sappho fr. 31 in his poem 51 to portray the physical symptoms of love that overcome him as he watches his beloved Lesbia with a rival,[198] while the elegists' girlfriends regularly fall sick.[199] In 3.17, however, Sulpicia herself assumes the role of the sick girlfriend (cf. 3.10, Ch. 7), specifying her illness (*morbos*, 3.17.3, 5) as a "fever" (*calor*, 3.17.2), which scholars have long interpreted as a metaphor for her erotic ardor.[200] While Catullus establishes the trope of lovesickness in Latin love poetry, among Sulpicia's Augustan contemporaries it is Propertius who most frequently employs the figure, and her vocabulary is indebted to both. The "faithful concern" (*pia cura*, 3.17.1) she hopes Cerinthus will show her in her fevered state, bears a marked Catullan resonance, for it recalls the late republican poet's request that the gods return him to health in recognition of his "devotion":[201] "I myself wish to be well and to lay down this foul disease (*morbum*). / O gods, repay this to me for my faithfulness" (*pro pietate mea*).[202] Her use of the interjection *a!* (3.17.3) is also characteristically Catullan in both emotional intensity and feminine application.[203]

At the same time, however, Sulpicia's self-characterization as an elegiac *puella* (3.17.1)[204] and her use of the verb "buffets" (*uexat*, 3.17.2) are indebted to Propertius' amatory lexicon:[205] "Jupiter, at last you will pity my afflicted mistress (*puellae*): / such a beautiful corpse will be a crime laid at your door . . . / But for you [*sc.* Cynthia], buffeted (*uexatae*) through life's many dangers / a gentler hour will come at the end of the day." Propertius introduces the metaphor of the "fever" of love (*calor*) into extant Latin elegy,[206] aligning Catullus' metaphor of "lovesickness"[207] with the conventional metaphor of the "flame" of love. Propertius also initiates the elegiac use of the adjective *lentus*, meaning "both pliable and slow,"[208] the latter especially of the unenthusiastic lover.[209] The unusual cadence of the hexameter of the final distich, which ends with two monosyllables (*si tu*, 3.17.5), is likewise resonant of Propertius' handling of the hexameter in his first three books, perhaps indebted to Gallus.[210]

The last epigram in the cycle continues the febrile imagery of 3.17 in the phrase "fevered care" (*feruida cura*, 3.18.1). The repetition of *cura* ("concern, care, love") across Sulpicia's small corpus (3.9.5, 3.16.3, 3.17.1, 3.18.1; not in 3.8, 10 or 12), and especially in the final three poems of the cycle, is a significant index of her generic allegiances, for the noun is a hallmark of the earliest Latin elegiac verse.[211] Catullus employs the word programmatically in the long elegies that stand at the head of his elegiac collection while Gallus seems to have extended the amatory usage of the term to include the sense of "girl(friend)," punning on Greek *kôrê*, "girl."[212] In his earliest collections, Propertius too employs the word across the full range of its meaning, and from there the term is taken up by Tibullus and Ovid, both of whom use it more sparingly.[213]

Sulpicia addresses her beloved as "my light" in the first line of the epigram (*mea lux*, 3.18.1), using the phrase in the same way as she had earlier in the cycle (3.9.15), *viz.* adapting to a male addressee the terminology employed of their girlfriends by Catullus and Propertius (and later Ovid).[214] Also recurring here is the adverb "equally" (3.18.1), which may yet bear a trace of Sulpicia's earlier emphasis on the mutuality of the lovers' bonds and service (3.11.13–14). Lyne attributes the difficulty of Sulpicia's syntax in this epigram, which consists of a single sentence with multiple subordination unrolling over three distichs, to her use of colloquial constructions.[215] He also highlights the "Catullan affiliations" that the epigram displays, from the structural framework of one long sentence,[216] to the specific subordinating phrase at the opening of 3.17.3, *si quicquam*, with which two of Catullus' epigrams begin, poems 96 and 102. Fulkerson also sees a Catullan resonance in Sulpicia's temporal phrase "yesterday night" (*hesterna nocte*, 3.18.5), which echoes, as it also reverses, the time specified at the opening of Catullus' poem 50 ("yesterday, Licinius"). By contrast, Lyne attributes Sulpicia's inspiration to the opening words of Propertius' elegy 2.29: "yesterday night, my love, when I wandered drunk. . . ."[217]

Sulpicia particularly regrets her "foolish" (3.18.3) decision to "leave her lover alone" (3.18.5), the latter another phrase reminiscent of both Catullus and Propertius.[218] Yet Sulpicia radically reorients the conventional gender roles of abandoning and abandoned lovers, for it is the woman who is traditionally deserted by her lover in neoteric and elegiac verse.[219] We might explain the gender inversion as a restoration of the lovers' respective class positions, but in the epigram's concluding expression of a desire to dissimulate her passion (3.18.6), Sulpicia also seemingly gestures to the restoration of normative feminine codes of conduct.[220] In her final line, Sulpicia continues to espouse late republican linguistic standards: *ardor* is used of the passion of love by both Catullus and Lucretius and employed by Propertius exclusively in his first book.[221]

The Sulpicia cycle has been much studied in relation to the poetry of Tibullus and Ovid, as is both understandable and appropriate, given the poems' manuscript transmission in company with Tibullus' elegies and Sulpicia's familial association with their shared patron Messalla.[222] Beyond elegy and epigram, moreover, I have argued elsewhere for Sulpicia's engagement with Vergil's contemporary epic project of the *Aeneid*, taking shape over the decade of the 20s BCE,[223] and others have explored Sulpicia's employment of legal terminology in her poems as befits a granddaughter of the jurist Ser. Sulpicius Rufus.[224] In this chapter, by contrast, I have focused on Sulpicia's intertextual relations with the classical tradition of female writers and early Latin elegy and epigram from Catullus, via Gallus, to Propertius, whose contemporary compositions seems to have inspired her own poetic ambitions.

Another index of her engagement precisely with these latter literary models can be seen in her paired epigrams, 3.14–15 and 3.17–18. Almost fifty years ago, there was published a monograph devoted to "dramatic pairings in the elegies of Propertius and Ovid," in which the author showed that the principle for pairing poems in these elegists was precisely their shared theme.[225] We have no extant evidence for Gallus' practice in this regard, but Catullus seems to have borrowed the principle from the epigrams collected in Meleager's *Garland*,[226] and so it is not unlikely that Gallus may also have employed it.[227] However, this structural device is not normally seen as an organizing feature of Tibullan elegy, which looks to the model of Vergil's *Bucolics*,[228] though Tibullus' elegies 1.8–9 may constitute just such a pair. Nonetheless, Sulpicia also looks to Propertius for her inspiration in this regard, inasmuch as the most famous of the paired poems in the Latin elegiac dossier are found in his first two collections,[229] and dramatically paired poems also span Propertius' books.[230] In every case, dramatically paired poems must be interpreted as having been composed *in medias res*, even though such pairs also require, almost by definition, a pause between their action.[231] This is clearly the case not only within Propertius' elegies 1.8a and 1.8b, where Propertius' poetry persuades Cynthia to stay in Rome rather than accompany the elegist's praetorian rival abroad,[232] but also between Propertius' elegy 1.8b (where Cynthia stays in Rome) and his elegy 2.16, where the praetor returns from his province, flush with cash, to tempt Cynthia to stray once again. The Propertian pair of elegies 1.8a and 1.8b even seems to have influenced Sulpicia's birthday poems, which moot the lovers' separation (3.14) but likewise foreclose the possibility (3.15).[233] We can trace a similarly responsive relationship between Sulpicia's fever in the paired poems 3.17–18 and Cynthia's illness in Propertius' two-part elegy 2.28.[234]

The recent spate of commentaries on the Tibullan *Appendix*—from Tränkle's masterful 1990 synthesis of the German tradition through Lyne's posthumously published notes on 3.13–18 and Fulkerson's 2017 commentary on the elegies of the Tibullan Appendix to Maltby's 2021 commentary on the entire book—collects a wealth of literary comparanda against which to contextualize Sulpicia's verse, and my own discussion of her poetic inspiration and multifaceted achievement is heavily indebted to their findings. The weight of the textual evidence they have collected supports the dating of her poems to the mid- to late 20s BCE, after Gallus' death in 27/26, when Propertius and Tibullus dominated the elegiac field at Rome and Ovid was just beginning to emulate their verse in his *Amores*. Sulpicia puts into play the characters (the beloved, the rival, the blocking figure of her uncle), themes (the amatory hunt, birthdays, erotic trysts, and illness), and poetics (fame and urbanity at any cost) familiar from the elegiac collections of her male contemporaries. There are few models in male-authored Latin amatory poetry for women's statement of erotic passion or poetic principle, however, and so we have also traced the inspiration of Sulpicia's gynocentric themes and gynocritical poetics back through the Greek tradition of female-authored verse. Sulpicia's critical intervention into the discourse of Latin elegy and classical epigram consistently troubles the gendered codes of these popular genres and disrupts social hierarchies (of male over female, freeborn over enslaved, and Roman over foreigner) long normalized in republican Rome. Who might have responded to Sulpicia's poetry, and how, are the subjects of the next chapter.

Sulpicia: Life, Love, and Literature in Ancient Rome. Alison Keith, Oxford University Press.
© Oxford University Press 2026. DOI: 10.1093/9780197607008.003.0007

7

Rescripts

Sulpicia's Artistic Reception

The poems by and about Sulpicia are preserved together in the *Appendix Tibulliana* (Ch. 1), in what appears to be no random sequence but a carefully ordered poetic "garland."[1] Her name stands as the first word in the first poem of the cycle (3.8.1) and thereby confers the title of *Sulpicia* on the sequence in a fashion reminiscent of Propertius' use of his girlfriend's name Cynthia as the title (inasmuch as the first word) of his first elegiac collection.[2] Near the end of the cycle, moreover, Sulpicia signs one of the first-person poems with her patrician name and filiation, "Servius' daughter Sulpicia" (3.16.4), thereby claiming the collection (or at least the first-person poems) as her own. The recurrence of her beloved Cerinthus' name from 3.9.11 to 3.17.1, and across poems couched in both the first person (3.9.11; 3.11.1, 5; 3.14.2; 3.17.1) and the third person (3.10.15), also unifies the collection and confirms the first-person authorial voice as Sulpicia's. What are we to make, however, of the third-person poet's commentary on the couple's relationship in 3.8, 10, and 12, or of the alternation of third- and first-person poems in the so-called "Garland of Sulpicia," as 3.8–12 have been dubbed (Ch. 1)?[3] This chapter considers Sulpicia's literary afterlife and argues that her earliest readership included the third-person author of 3.8, 10, and 12.

The age in which Sulpicia lived and composed poetry was one of intense literary discussion and experimentation, and we have abundant evidence of contemporary poets' passionate interest in one another's compositional practice at the levels of both form and content (Ch. 5). Catullus, for example, writes of his outrage upon receiving from his friend Calvus—fellow poet, successful orator, and aspiring politician (Ch. 5)—a collection of bad poetry as a Saturnalia gift, and he threatens to reciprocate with poems by the worst poets of the day.[4] Elsewhere, however he testifies to his admiration of his friends' verse in requests to see poems by Caecilius and Cornificius;[5] records his friend Hortensius' entreaty for a translation of

Callimachus;[6] and recalls with pleasure a day devoted to poetic experimentation and compositional rivalry with his friend Calvus:[7] "Yesterday Licinius, at our leisure / we sported much in my tablets, / as we had agreed to be self-indulgent: / each of us, writing little verses, / was playing now with this meter, now that, / giving and taking while joking and drinking." The strongly homosocial aspect of literary composition in this period is also attested by Cicero, whose letters to his friend Atticus document the collegial activity of elite male authors in "the Roman republic of letters."[8]

Literary composition in the following generation was no less socially inflected. Vergil, in his *Bucolics*, registers his literary admiration for the contemporary poets, generals, and politicians Pollio and Gallus,[9] while Horace in his satires quotes from a series of epigrams by the Epicurean poet and teacher Philodemos and expresses the hope that the most distinguished Roman men of letters, whose ranks included generals and politicians, would approve his own verse.[10] The Latin elegists too seem to have circulated their poems to friends both before and after publication. In his poetic autobiography, Ovid claims that "Propertius was accustomed to recite his 'flames' [i.e., his love poems], by virtue of the close association in which he was bound to me."[11] In their published poems, moreover, the elegists directly address literary associates and rivals: thus, Propertius invokes Bassus, Gallus, Ponticus, "Lynceus" (i.e., L. Varius Rufus; cf. Ch. 5n49), and Maecenas;[12] Tibullus addresses Messalla, Cornutus, and Macer;[13] and Ovid names his friends Atticus (*Am.* 1.9) and Graecinus (*Am.* 2.10).[14]

We gain vivid insight into the intensely social dynamics of Latin literary culture from Ovid in *Amores* 2.18, addressed to his friend Macer—an epic poet, perhaps the same man as Tibullus' addressee in his elegy 2.6[15]—whose martial poetry Ovid invokes as a foil to his own poetic projects of love elegy (i.e., the *Amores*); tragedy, presumably his lost *Medea*; didactic elegy (i.e., the *Art of Love*); and elegiac epistles from the abandoned heroines of classical myth (i.e., the *Heroides*, "letters from mythological heroines"). In reference to his *Heroides*, moreover, Ovid records the tantalizing information that Sabinus, another of his friends, had composed replies to the heroines' plaints:[16] "How swiftly my dear friend Sabinus has returned from all over the world / and himself brought back written communications from different places!" Sabinus' putative "letters from the mythological heroes" Ulysses, Hippolytus, Aeneas, Demophoon, Jason, and Phaon must have corresponded very directly to Ovid's single *Heroides*;[17] and, indeed, it has been suggested that his friend's compilation may even have given Ovid the idea for his later collection of "double Heroides," letters between the lovers Paris and Helen, Hero and Leander, and Acontius and Cydippe.[18] Ovid's poetry collections from exile further document the literary fellowship he had participated in at Rome in his youth and missed so much in Tomis.[19]

Scholars have recently suggested that the "Garland of Sulpicia" also took shape in the context of literary fellowship, though they typically see Sulpicia's gender as precluding any opportunity for her to associate with the elite male poets in Messalla's patronage—Valgius, Tibullus, "Lygdamus," and Ovid, among others (Ch. 5).[20] Instead, it has been suggested that a literary amanuensis like Sulpicia Petale (Ch. 4) could have had a hand in shaping the "garland" of Sulpicia.[21] This is an attractive suggestion, as scholars have documented the presence in Roman grandees' townhouses not only of female slave readers, secretaries, and clerks, but also of female slave writers and scribes in this period.[22] Their male counterparts are widely attested in the correspondence of both Cicero and Pliny as the close collaborators of elite men of letters, in addition to the distinguished friends of their own class to whom elite Roman writers dedicated their works.[23] Indeed, it is difficult to imagine any other context for the preservation of Sulpicia's poetry than the literary duties associated with the secretaries and librarians of an elite household,[24] and it is by no means unlikely that she was assisted in her poetic endeavors by such slave and/or freed personnel as Sulpicia Petale.

Skepticism about Roman women's access to elite male literary coteries, however, is not supported by the evidence feminist scholars have amassed for female participation in the male poetic culture of the first century BCE.[25] Although well founded for the provincial sensibilities of the younger Pliny writing a century and more after the entrenchment of Augustus' marriage and adultery legislation in Roman imperial law, scholarly hesitation seems overly cautious for the very different social context of the upheavals of the late republic and early principate. We have already considered Cornificia's publication of "famous epigrams" at the end of the republic in connection with the literary experimentation of Catullus and his friends, including her brother Cornificius and her husband Camerius (Ch. 5), and Caecilia Attica's closeness to the grammarian, Q. Caecilius Epirota, with whom she continued her literary studies in the early years of her marriage to Augustus' friend Agrippa (Ch. 4). In the same period, Catullus certainly implies a female readership for the poetry that he and his friends composed.[26] A generation later, moreover, the elegist Propertius characterizes his mistress Cynthia as a poet as talented as Sappho, Corinna, and Erinna (ca. 25 BCE),[27] and Ovid addresses the third book of his *Art of Love* (ca. 1 CE) to "Penthesileia's Amazons"—i.e., the women of his contemporary Rome.[28]

Toward the end of Augustus' reign, moreover, Ovid claims to have advised a young female protégée, whose name he conceals under the pseudonym "Perilla," in the composition of poetry.[29] In a poem addressed to her from exile, Ovid asks if she remains "devoted to our common pursuits of composing learned poems"[30] and reminds her that he served as her earliest poetic mentor: "I was the first to perceive this talent in the tender years of your youth, / and as a father to his daughter I was your leader and comrade."[31] Ovid's description of their relationship has been taken to imply a familial dimension, not only because of their association from her early youth, but also because he elsewhere mentions a stepdaughter in a poem addressed to her husband Suillius, his "almost" son-in-law.[32] In *Tristia* 3.7, he even describes his poetic tutelage of the young "Perilla":[33]

> While it was permitted, I often used to read your verse to myself
>   and mine to you;
>   often I was your critic, often your teacher:
> at times I offered my ears to the verses you'd composed,
>   and when you were idle, I was the cause of your blushes.

Ovid depicts their interactions in the same lexicon that earlier poets use to characterize literary composition as a collective activity in the late republican and triumviral periods. Thus, Ovid's picture here of the pair reciting their poetry to one another is reminiscent of Catullus' portrait of his idle day with Calvus, tossing off impromptu verses to one another (partially quoted above), while his self-representation as a "critic" of "Perilla's" verse recalls the use of the term by both Vergil and Gallus in discussions of poetry contests,[34] as well as the wish that Horace expresses that the distinguished men of letters of his day might give critical "approval" to his poems.[35]

The evidence for elite Roman women's access to masculine literary culture[36] in the late republic and early principate is thus primarily focused on domestic channels. Cornificia's family ties through blood and marriage with Catullus' friends Cornificius and Camerius no doubt facilitated her access to the exclusive literary circles in which her menfolk moved and smoothed the path to poetic publication. Similarly, Ovid's cultivation of Perilla's poetic talent may have arisen in the context of his marriage to her mother. Sulpicia, too, enjoyed the closest of blood ties to prominent men of letters: her father Servius and her uncle (and likely guardian) Messalla are recorded among the most discerning critics and poets of the triumviral period, while Messalla himself was celebrated for his patronage of literature across many different genres of both prose and poetry (Ch. 5).[37] It has therefore seemed plausible to many to identify Tibullus or Ovid as the author of the third-person poems in the cycle or even of all five of the poems in the "Garland of Sulpicia" (3.8–12).[38] Other elite names, mostly male, have also been proposed as the author of 3.8, 3.10, and 3.12, including Sulpicia's brother Servius Sulpicius Postumius;[39] Sulpicia herself;[40] Cornutus (Ch. 5);[41] Cerinthus and Sulpicia in alternation (across 3.8–3.12);[42] or even a later Neronian or Flavian author.[43]

Given the communal and familial dynamics of Roman literary culture, some model of distributed authorship certainly seems warranted for the third-person elegies about Sulpicia and perhaps even her first-person compositions—whether across class lines, gender hierarchies, or both. In this regard, scholars have pointed to several instances of "intratextuality" within the Sulpicia cycle.[44] For example, the three third-person poems (3.8, 10, 12) have been thought to take up the invitation, expressed in the first person at 3.13.5–6, for anyone who lacks their own amatory joys to relate Sulpicia's.[45] Thus, 3.8 introduces Sulpicia as an elegiac *puella* (3.8.15, 24; cf. 3.10.1, 11, 16; 3.12.2, 9), amplifying her own self-presentation in that guise in the epigrams (3.14.3, 3.15.1, 3.17.1).[46] Similarly, 3.10 treats the theme of Sulpicia's illness, the subject of 3.17.[47] Poems 3.11–12, moreover, form a pair of birthday poems (*genethliaka*), apparently on the model of the paired first-person poems 3.14–15 about Sulpicia's birthday, with 3.12 commemorating Sulpicia's birthday in response to the preceding first-person poem's celebration of her beloved's birthday (3.11).[48] These thematic and generic interrelations are complemented by the striking verbal similarity of the phrase *corpora fessa* ("my exhausted body"), which occurs in poems couched in both third person (3.10.11) and first person (3.17.2),[49] and the shared lexical emphasis across the cycle on the "worthiness" of Sulpicia and her match (3.8.15, 24; 3.12.10; 3.13.10).[50]

Linking the third-person poems 3.8, 10, and 12, moreover, are the speaker's hymnic invocations of deities at the outset of each.[51] In elegy 3.8, the third-person speaker summons "Great Mars" at the outset (3.8.1–4) and invokes Apollo and the Camenae at the conclusion (3.8.21–4), while in 3.10 s/he addresses Apollo in his capacity as a god of the healing arts (3.10.1–11,

19–26), and in 3.12 s/he invokes *natalis Juno*, Sulpicia's "birth-spirit" (3.12.1–16). These three elegies are the only poems in the cycle formally cast as hymns, though Sulpicia herself draws on the form in 3.11, where she addresses Cerinthus (also addressed in 3.9 and 3.16–18) and vows to keep his birthday sacred (3.11.1–4) before modulating into a prayer to his Genius (3.11.7–20); and in 3.13, where she cites the efficacy of her poetic prayers to Venus Cytherea (3.13.3–5). The first and last of the third-person poems, moreover, are also linked by the theme of marriage: the occasion of elegy 3.8 is the *Matronalia*, a festival for married women in Sulpicia's day and long after (Ch. 4), while 3.12 sounds a hymeneal note in the introduction of Sulpicia's mother, with her marital ambitions for her daughter (3.12.15–16), and the concluding hope that the lovers' bonds endure (3.12.19–20).[52] The third-person poems thereby exert a studied matrimonial pressure on Sulpicia's expressions of erotic desire in 3.9, 11, 13–18, and seemingly attempt to foreclose a scandalous (i.e., non-marital) interpretation of her poetry (Ch. 4).[53]

There is thus considerable evidence to suggest that Sulpicia could not have composed her poetry in a literary vacuum, even if we can neither identify the author(s) of the third-person poems in the cycle nor assign a name to her servile amanuenses. The artistic patterning of recurrent themes, poetic styles, and interwoven voices across the full cycle of the poetry by and about her, moreover, lends further support to this conclusion.[54] The cycle opens with an elegiac title, *Sulpicia*, and the author (at least of the first-person poems) signs herself in a sphragis toward the end of the cycle as Servius' daughter Sulpicia (3.16.14). Following the earliest practitioners of Latin elegy and epigram (Catullus in his elegiac book;[55] perhaps Gallus, on the evidence of a papyrus from Qasr Ibrîm; and Propertius in his first collection), Sulpicia and/or her editor (who may or may not have been identical with the author of the third-person poems) differentiates her poetry into elegies (3.8–12) and epigrams (3.14–18), organized around the central lynchpin 3.13, a publication poem or "proem in the middle."[56] Another principle of arrangement of the cycle may simply have been the length of the poems.[57] Scholars have also observed the numerical symmetry of the line-counts of the longer poems, 3.8–12 (24, 24, 26, 20, 20),[58] to which we might add that on display in the epigrams 3.14–18 (8, 4, 6, 6, 6), with 3.13 (at 10 lines) midway between the longer and shorter pieces. The way that the closing line of 3.8 cues Sulpicia's own voice in 3.9 has also been noted (3.8.24): "no maiden is more worthy of your chorus" suggests that there is no girl worthier of inclusion among the Muses than Sulpicia herself *qua* poet.[59] Prayers alternate in the first- and third-person voices in the elegies, while the epigrams offer intimate reflections on strictly defined occasions. The genre of birthday poem (*genethliakon*) spans both elegies (3.11–12) and epigrams (3.14–15) in artfully juxtaposed paired poems, while the elegiac themes of the lover's rival and the girlfriend's sickness are treated in not only longer elegies (3.9, 11, 12; 3.10) but also shorter epigrams (3.16, 17), voiced both in third (3.10, 12) and first person (3.9, 11, 16, 17). Finally, the theme of the pair's erotic congress and "burning passion," so unabashedly sounded in the first-person elegies and epigrams (3.9.15–18; 3.11.5–8; 3.13.5–10; 3.17; 3.18), is transmuted into the hints of a marital happy-ending in the third-person elegies (3.8.1, 23–4; 3.12.19–20).

While we can observe the care with which the extant cycle of elegies and epigrams has been structured, we can only conjecture how the cycle came together and who, besides Sulpicia herself, might have contributed to and/or (co-)edited the sequence. It has been suggested that the third-person poems (or even the five longer elegies, 3.8–12) were "gifts" to Sulpicia, possibly in the context of her marriage.[60] All we can say for certain, however, is that her own writing was in all likelihood assisted by enslaved librarians, readers, and/or scribes in her uncle's (or her own marital) household. If she had the occasion to recite her poems publicly, moreover, the opportunity would undoubtedly have come through her uncle Messalla's literary network. Whether or not she was able to recite publicly, however, there is no reason why she should not have met many of the foremost elegists of the day, among them Tibullus, the leading exponent of elegy in the period, and Ovid, then just beginning his poetic career. Writing in the mid- to late 20s BCE, Sulpicia will have been keenly interested in Tibullus' elegies, as his first collection appeared in late 27 or 26 BCE and he continued to compose verse in honor of Messalla and his friends until his death in 19 (Ch. 5). From Tibullus, indeed, Sulpicia seems to have derived the theme of amatory hunting in 3.9; the literary form of the *genethliakon*, which she employs in 3.11, 14, and 15; the ideal of mutual love in 3.11; as well as much of the verbal texture of her amatory lexicon (Ch. 6).[61]

It was in this period too that Ovid began to recite his poems, "when [his] beard had been cut once or twice."[62] As a member of Messalla's circle it is highly likely that he attended readings at the great man's house. Ovid specifies that his earliest compositions were love poems about "Corinna,"[63] presumably early examples of the love elegies that he first collected into five, and then eventually re-edited into three, books of *Amores*.[64] From his allusions to his tragedy *Medea*, his didactic *Ars amatoria*, and his epistolary *Heroides* in *Amores* 2.18, moreover, we may infer that he embarked on those works after his earliest amatory compositions, when he was still pursuing a senatorial career,[65] and he likely worked on them over the next couple of decades. Sulpicia's poetic *floruit* will thus have overlapped with Ovid's entry into Roman literary circles and his earliest foray into the composition of erotic elegy. Several scholars have even proposed that Ovid had a hand in shaping the Sulpicia cycle, since it seems clear that he was familiar with her verses.[66]

Stephen Hinds, Jacqueline Fabre-Serris, and Judith P. Hallett have explored several possible intertextual connections between Sulpicia and Ovid. Fabre-Serris convincingly traces many of these interconnections back to Gallus, the founder of the genre of elegy in ancient Rome. Given the loss of most of Gallus' poetry, however, I restrict my focus here to the lexical and thematic overlap we can discern between Sulpicia and Ovid. Of particular interest is Fabre-Serris's interpretation of the Phaedra epistle in Ovid's collection of heroines' letters (*Heroides* 4), which she has shown exhibits a number of verbal and thematic features familiar from Sulpicia's poems.[67] The Ovidian Phaedra summarizes her experience of falling in love with her stepson Hippolytus in language that sounds a highly Sulpician note:[68] "Love has come (*uenit amor*) the more heavily, as it has come later. I burn (*urimur*) within; / I burn (*urimur*) and my breast holds an invisible wound." Phaedra's phrase "love has come" recalls Sulpicia's description of love's advent in 3.13.1: "at last has come love" (*tandem uenit amor*). Fabre-Serris traces the phrase back to Gallus via Propertius (1.7.26, 2.3.46) and argues that we must account for gender when trying to decide poetic priority (a notoriously difficult problem) between Sulpicia and Ovid in its usage. Similarly marked by gender, moreover, is Phaedra's repetition of "I burn" (*uror*) in her declaration of amatory passion, a geminated structure used only by Sulpicia ([Tib.] 3.11.5) elsewhere in Latin elegy.[69] Fabre-Serris therefore makes the attractive suggestion that Ovid has borrowed a real woman's words when he imagines how a fictional female character might declare her love.[70]

Heroides 4 contains a second cluster of shared Gallan allusions with Sulpicia in 3.9, in the evocation of the hunt.[71] Both Sulpicia and the Ovidian Phaedra love youths—Cerinthus and Hippolytus respectively—whose passion for the hunt inspires them to join the chase, literalizing the trope of love as a hunt (Ch. 6). The commonality of lexicon, setting, and theme in these verses is indeed striking: just as Sulpicia proposes to carry her beloved Cerinthus' nets over the mountains, track deer for him, and unchain his swift dogs (3.9.9–14), in a gendered twist on the motif of *seruitium amoris* (Ch. 6), so Phaedra in *Heroides* 4 imagines driving the deer Hippolytus hunts into his nets and urging on his swift hounds over the mountain-ridges.[72] Similarly, both would-be huntresses reveal *amor* as their motivation by concluding their imagined hunts with lovemaking.[73] The Ovidian Phaedra explicitly announces her ambition to enjoy the same erotic dalliances with her beloved hunter as those enjoyed by Cephalus and Aurora, Venus and Adonis, and Atalanta and Milanion,[74] while Sulpicia opens her elegy with an address to the beast she most fears, the wild boar, because he "has sharpened" his "hard tusks for battle," in an allusion to the death of Venus' beloved Adonis on the chase (3.9.1–3; cf. Ch. 6).[75] Yet the thought of the woods pleases her when she dreams of making love with Cerinthus before the hunting nets (3.9.15–16), and she imagines that even if the boar approached them he would go away unharmed (3.9.17–18), just as Phaedra promises Hippolytus that the woods please her as a site for their lovemaking and denies that she would fear "even the boar, terrifying because of his tusk's sideswipe."[76] Ovid thereby retrospectively imbues Sulpicia with a Phaedra-esque quality that suggests his recognition of, and admiration for, her evocation of (?Gallan) hunting myths in 3.9.

Scholars have also identified parallels in Ovid's *Metamorphoses* with Sulpicia's hunting poem.[77] For example, her opening half-line, "Spare my young man" (*parce meo iuuenis*, 3.9.1), recurs with different syntax but in a strikingly similar context, in an address by the goddess Venus to her young lover Adonis, warning him of the perils of the chase: "Forbear, youth, to be reckless at my hazard" (*parce meo, iuuenis temerarius esse periclo*).[78] We can be sure of a direct link between the two passages because in both passages, a female speaker is concerned about the danger the hunt poses for her beloved.[79] Other correspondences have been recognized between Sulpicia's rhetorical questions at 3.9.7–10 and Ovid's phrasing at strategic moments in his treatment of the myths of Daphne and Io, sequentially related in *Metamorphoses* 1. Ovid reworks Sulpicia's rhetorical question, "why does it please you to enter the haunts of wild beasts by stealth" (3.9.9), in a half-line he gives to Jupiter, solicitously (and lustfully) offering his company to Io should she "fear to enter alone the haunts of wild beasts."[80] Two of Sulpicia's couplets (3.9.8–10), moreover, are also remarkably close in lexicon and thought to the god Apollo's equally spurious expressions of concern for Daphne, who is also out hunting: "ah! wretched me, should you fall down or the brambles scratch your legs unworthy of being harmed."[81] Moreover, Sulpicia's concluding couplet ("but you, leave the pursuit of hunting to your father, / and yourself run swiftly back into my embrace," 3.9.23–4) resounds in Ovid's *Remedies for Love*:[82] "or you must cultivate the pursuit of the hunt: often Venus has withdrawn / shamefully, vanquished by Phoebus' sister." Ovid's couplet reproduces the first four words of Sulpicia's, "or you, the pursuit of hunting" (*uel tu uenandi studium* 3.9.23), just as he imports the antithesis between Venus and Diana on display throughout Sulpicia's elegy 3.9.

While scholars agree on the parallels, they have disagreed about lines of priority and reception in these passages. Esther Bréguet attributes originality to elegy 3.9, which she views as by the young Ovid and so she sees an older Ovid echoing himself in the *Metamorphoses* (and, by implication, in the *Remedies for Love*);[83] while Stephen Hinds and Robert Maltby view the author of 3.9—whom they call the "*amicus*"-poet—as writing after Ovid, either commenting on Sulpicia's own verse (Hinds) or composing the entire *Appendix Tibulliana* (Maltby) at a later remove.[84] Since I view 3.9 as authored by an early Augustan Sulpicia, I see Ovid as the imitator here, taking up Sulpician phrases remembered from his youth and neatly repurposing them in thematically apposite contexts that pointedly return Sulpicia's studied gender inversions to patriarchal norms. The same practice can be seen in Ovid's allusions to Sulpicia's amatory experiences in his Sappho epistle and in the penultimate elegy of his *Amores*.

Further allusions to Sulpicia can be traced in Ovid's ventriloquized Sappho letter, *Heroides* 15, especially in his reapplication of the motif of erotic "joys" (*gaudia*) from the Latin verses of his Roman contemporary to his representation of the ancient Greek lyric poet.[85] Just as Sulpicia invites those without sensual joys of their own to tell of hers (3.13.5–6), the Ovidian Sappho admits that "when someone said to [her], 'Your joys (*gaudia*) are fleeting,' / for a long time [she] could neither weep nor speak!"[86] Sulpicia's emphasis in 3.13 on the worthiness of her match with Cerinthus (3.13.10; Chs. 4, 6) reverberates in Ovid's Sappho epistle as well:[87] "If no woman will be yours, unless her beauty could seem worthy (*digna*) of you, no woman will be yours." The Ovidian Sappho goes on to hint that her poetry made her worthy of her lover Phaon:[88] "But when I read my poems, now I seemed sufficiently beautiful; you swore that I was the only woman whose speech was forever decorous." Indeed, like Sulpicia, whose poetic prayers bring Cerinthus to her (3.13.3–4), Sappho wins Phaon's love through her verses:[89]

> I used to sing to you, I recall—lovers remember everything—
> and you used to snatch kisses from me as I sang.
> My kisses too you praised, and I pleased you in every way—
> but then especially, when the work of love (*amoris opus*) was
> in train.

The Ovidian Sappho puns on lovemaking and love-poetry making in the phrase *amoris opus*, (*Her.* 15.46). Like Sulpicia in [Tib.] 3.13, Ovid's Sappho implies that love-poetry both leads, and corresponds, to sexual congress. Fabre-Serris (2009, 164) concludes that *Heroides* 15 alludes to Sulpicia throughout, since "S[ulpicia], after all, claims to have conquered her lover through her poetry [3.13], continues her conquest through the same means, and concludes the cycle of her poems by evoking a night of intense passion [3.18]." In her longing to reunite with Phaon, the Ovidian Sappho may even allude to Sulpicia's final words in her hunting poem, where she invites Cerinthus to leave hunting to his father "and run swiftly back into [her] embrace" (3.9.24), with her plea that he "come here and slip back again into [her] embrace."[90]

Several further possible allusions to Sulpicia's poetry in the Ovidian corpus have been proposed.[91] Especially compelling is the connection of Sulpicia's themes and vocabulary with those Ovid attributes to the unnamed elegiac "girlfriend" (*puella*) of the penultimate poem of his *Amores*, whom the Ovidian poet-lover rebukes for her "sins," employing in his first six couplets four different forms of the verb *peccare*, which Sulpicia employs of her sexual "sins" (3.13.9).[92] The disillusioned Ovidian poet-lover invites his shameless girlfriend to continue to indulge her sexual peccadilloes, but pleads with her "only [to] deny she's sinned, / nor be ashamed to speak modest words in public."[93] Ovid's lexicon and themes recuperate, even as they demand the reversal of, Sulpicia's, especially in her opening couplet (3.13.1–2), where she proclaims that her love is "such as would disgrace [her] more to cloak out of shame than to expose to someone," and in her emphasis on the publication of her erotic joys (3.13.5–10). It has been conjectured that Ovid wrote this poem shortly after Augustus promulgated his moral legislation of 18 BCE, in order to explain his evident censure of the unnamed elegiac girlfriend's sexual misbehavior, perhaps also in an oblique critique of Sulpicia's outspoken celebration of her own illicit love affair.[94] Ovid's poem must, indeed, date from after Augustus' marriage and adultery legislation of 18–16 BCE, though his allusions to Sulpicia also further his literary plot of documenting the poet-lover's disillusionment with both his mistress (unnamed, but presumably Corinna) and his genre (erotic elegy), as he prepares to make his first break with love (and love-poetry) and move on to the composition of tragedy.[95]

Ovid went on writing elegiac poetry until his death in 16 or 17 CE, and while later poets and critics laud a shifting cannon of Latin elegists, Sulpicia (like Cornificia) is never named among the genre's practitioners (Ch. 5).[96] For that reason, it is difficult to document the circulation of her poems after the heyday of Latin elegy in the 20s BCE. The conjunction of her marriage (?in the mid- to late 20s BCE) with the promulgation of Augustus' moral legislation shortly thereafter (18–16 BCE) must account for the cessation of her literary activity and the silence of posterity. Especially if she went on to bear children, Sulpicia will have fulfilled her duty to family and fatherland (Chs. 2, 4),[97] and she may neither have survived nor continued to write afterwards.

It is particularly telling that until very recently no ancient author beyond the immediate circle of Messalla has ever been identified as even possibly alluding to Sulpicia. In a stimulating recent interpretation of Martial's epigrams 10.35 and 10.38, however, it has been argued that the Flavian epigrammatist (d. 103 CE) metamorphoses the Augustan elegist Sulpicia, poet of female passion, into a handbook for respectable Roman brides.[98] Martial opens *Epigram* 10.35 with Sulpicia's name at the head of an injunction to all monogamous brides and husbands to read her verse because she disavows the violence of women in Greco-Roman mythology—instantiated in Medea, Scylla, and Byblis—to focus instead on "chaste and modest loves."[99] Martial glosses the virtuous love Sulpicia teaches as "playfulness, luxuries, and clever witticisms," employing an erotic lexicon straight out of Catullus' playbook.[100] So attractive is Sulpicia—a latter-day Roman Sappho, according to Martial—that Phaon, "fresh from his starring role in Ovid,"[101] would have preferred her to Sappho herself! This Sulpicia is undeniably similar to our elegist—the author of playful erotic poetry couched in the style of Catullus and Propertius, and worthy of comparison to Sappho (Ch. 6).

But then the epigram ends with the genre's characteristic "sting in the tail"—the utterly unexpected information that this is not our Sulpicia, in love with her Cerinthus, but another Sulpicia in love with the Calenus

("Mr. Hottie") mentioned at the end of the poem.[102] The name of her beloved Calenus evokes *calor* ("heat" or "ardor") and elegiac passion,[103] and we have seen the importance of both these themes in our Sulpicia's verse (Ch. 6). Three poems later, however, it is revealed that Calenus is Sulpicia's husband:[104] "O gentle fifteen years, Calenus, / of marriage with your Sulpicia, / which god has granted and fulfilled!" In *Epigram* 10.38 too, Martial draws on motifs from Catullus' erotic lyric and Propertius' love elegy in their characteristic lexicon: love's "battles" and memorable nights, along with a happy little bed, and the lamp and perfumes of Hellenistic epigram;[105] all presented in one of Catullus' favorite meters, hendecasyllabics.

Martial's pervasive use of the vocabulary and themes of Sulpicia's favored elegiac models throughout these two epigrams, as well as the echo of her beloved's name "Cerinthus" in the later Sulpicia's "Calenus,"[106] certainly furnish food for thought, especially given the ancient poets' habit of drawing on another author's words and motifs when referring to them or their poetry.[107] The extant verses of Sulpicia the satirist, however, do not reveal any debt to our poet. Moreover, the late antique authors who drop the name "Sulpicia" clearly refer to the satirist rather than our elegist.[108]

The survival of our Sulpicia's poetry in antiquity cannot be traced, therefore, on the basis of the evidence available to us. If, however, as seems plausible, Sulpicia was assisted by a slave staff of her own (or her uncle's) readers, scribes, and librarians, there is no reason why her compositions should not have been included in the estate's library along with the poems celebrating her uncle (and husband?) by the greatest elegist of the day, Tibullus. The discovery of Philodemos' library at the Villa dei Papyri in Herculaneum provides material evidence for the value placed on their libraries by Rome's great families, who preserved and added to them over the decades and centuries.[109]

Sulpicia: Life, Love, and Literature in Ancient Rome. Alison Keith, Oxford University Press.
© Oxford University Press 2026. DOI: 10.1093/9780197607008.003.0008

8

Postscript

Servius' Daughter Sulpicia in Retrospect

The woman who emerges from this study is the Sulpicia of Heyne and
Haupt (Ch. 1): an Augustan-era poet, granddaughter of the great republican jurist Ser. Sulpicius Rufus (Ch. 2), and niece of Augustus' general
M. Valerius Messalla Corvinus (Ch. 3). Perhaps a close contemporary of
Ovid (b. 43 BCE) or Julia Augusti (b. 39 BCE), she came of age in the
mid-20s BCE (Ch. 4), at the height of the vogue for elegy at Rome (Ch. 5),
and experimented in the genre herself, on the model of the most admired
practitioners of the day—Catullus, Propertius, Tibullus, and the recently
deceased Gallus (Ch. 6). A proud and outspoken Roman aristocrat, she was
likely inspired by the acclaimed female poets, both Greek and Latin, many
of whose statues stood in Pompey's portico throughout her lifetime and
long afterwards, and whose work we can document in circulation at Rome
in the generation before her birth (Chs. 5–6). In both reading and composing poetry, she enjoyed the support of trained readers and scribes, enslaved
and freed (Chs. 4, 7), and she undoubtedly also had access through her
uncle to literary events at which she could have interacted with his friends
and clients (Chs. 4–7). Her duty to family and fatherland will have required
her to marry, probably in her teens, and to bear children, although we cannot identify with certainty either husband(s) or offspring (Ch. 4). She
ceased to compose poetry if not already at her marriage or upon the birth of
a child, certainly after the passage of Augustus' moral legislation (18–16
BCE). She may have collected her poems into a short cycle, interleaved with
related poems composed by an unknown hand, before her "garland" was
archived with the compositions of other members of Messalla's household
and clientele, including those of Tibullus, the foremost elegist of ancient
Rome, whose poetry survived antiquity in a manuscript tradition of three
books (Ch. 1). In the course of a collecting mission to the south of France
in 1333 CE, the renowned Italian poet Petrarch discovered a codex of
Tibullus' poetry, which was copied for his friend Collucio Salutati forty

years later, just before the latter became Chancellor of Florence. From this codex, it seems, all of our extant manuscripts of Tibullus—and the Tibullan Appendix—derive.

This is a dishearteningly thin account not only of a historical Roman woman's life but also of her literary career, and the narrative has become even shorter in the twenty-first century. For just after Parker revived the view that Sulpicia's corpus should include all the first-person poems in the cycle (Ch. 1), there emerged an equally strong movement to reduce her elegies and epigrams to *pseudepigrapha* ("falsely attributed works"), by categorically denying both female authorship and Augustan date to the cycle.[1] Tränkle, in his 1990 commentary, is a harbinger of this impulse: while he accepted Sulpicia's authorship of elegies 3.13–18, and an early Augustan date of 25–20 BCE for them, he downdated the poems of the "Garland" (elegies 3.8–12) to a period immediately after Ovid's death in exile (16/17 CE).[2] Fernando Navarro Antolín, author of the standard commentary on "Lygdamus" ([Tibullus], elegies 3.1–6), published in the mid-1990s, similarly accepts elegies 3.13–18 as "the only ones from the Augustan period."[3]

At the end of the twentieth century, moreover, T. N. Habinek pursued a line of argument in his 1998 book *The Politics of Latin Literature* that implicitly denied female authorship to the Sulpician corpus by explicitly denying the existence of female authors in ancient Rome.[4] In his provocatively entitled chapter "Roman Women's Useless Knowledge,"[5] he argued that despite the well-documented access of elite Roman women to education and literary study, Roman women were culturally inhibited from literary production. In order to make this argument he had to confine his discussion of the historical record of female authors in ancient Rome—and the modern feminist scholarship that has recovered their names and discussed their works—to the zero-note of the chapter.[6] Instead of treating historical women in his chapter, Habinek focuses on the "learned girls" of the Alexandrian tradition at Rome, the "written women" who appear in idealized if not fictional form in the elegiac poetry of Sulpicia's literary models and contemporaries at Rome:[7]

> The poetry of Catullus, Propertius, Ovid and others invokes the ideal of the *docta puella* precisely in order to regulate and marginalize her, turning the potential evaluator and competitor in the poetic sphere into a mirror that reflects the male's idealized self-image back upon itself. It is the poetry

itself, independent of any external considerations of education, law, or status, that silences the female voice even before it can speak.

In this context, the absence of Sulpicia's poetry from the discussion is a striking, and inexplicable, omission that assimilates her on the one hand to the mostly mute elegiac *puella* and, on the other hand, to M. I. Finley's "silent women of Rome,"[8] the historically recoverable class of elite educated women whom Habinek views as having been denied access to literary production by cultural violence—in the face, in fact, of considerable evidence to the contrary (Ch. 5). By suppressing the evidence of Roman women's literary production and omitting any mention of Sulpicia in his discussion of the "learned girlfriends" of Latin elegiac poetry, Habinek rehearses the very strategies of exclusion and silencing of women that he identified in Roman literary culture.

Niklas Holzberg takes a rather different tack to deny Sulpician authorship to the first-person elegies and epigrams in the cycle.[9] He attributes the Sulpicia cycle (3.8–18) to an anonymous male poet of early imperial, possibly Tiberian, date who designed the Tibullan Appendix to be read—like the pseudo-Vergilian *Culex*—as the early poetry of Tibullus, the background to whose two books of elegies this pseudepigraphic poet supplies. On Holzberg's reading, the twenty poems in the third book of the Tibullan corpus "fill in the blanks" of Tibullus' early work: born into the lap of luxury, a privileged state reflected in the first six elegies in the book where he writes under the pseudonym "Lygdamus," Pseudo-Tibullus suffers the loss of his patrimony during the civil wars and, in need of a patron, writes a panegyric of Messalla (3.7); the story of Sulpicia's love affair with Cerinthus (3.8–18) then unmasks the lovers behind Tibullus' birthday poem for Cornutus,[10] which apparently predicts happiness for the latter in his upcoming marriage, while the final two poems of the book provide a classic explanation for the locked-out lover's elegiac "plaint," and give us a direct link to Tibullus 1.1.

Holzberg's confident assertion that "it is a mistake…to ascribe the poems 8–12, in which the *amicus Sulpiciae* and Sulpicia alternate as speakers, to a different author than the one of poems 13–18, where we hear only Sulpicia's voice"[11] echoes an earlier scholarly tradition which, as Parker (1994, 52) points out, ascribed "the entire group of poems, 3.8–18,…to…a single male author," even though it "require[d] the reader to imagine an unparalleled approach on the part of a Roman poet to love elegy, a friend's love poetry, and her love affair."[12] Holzberg elucidates neither why Pseudo-Tibullus assumes different names in the course of the Tibullan Appendix, nor how the reader is apprised of the game without a preface, or the like. Moreover, the argument for down-dating the third book of the Tibullan corpus to the reign of Tiberius (or even beyond, for Holzberg would accept a Flavian date), relies primarily on Axelsonian methods of word-study,[13] the validity of which has often been called into question and which are in any case problematic in their application to a corpus as small as that of Sulpicia and "Lygdamus." Holzberg's thesis has therefore not gained wide acceptance.

Five years after Holzberg advanced his pseudepigraphic thesis, T. K. Hubbard deftly demolished his arguments in order to clear the ground for his own proposal that the Sulpicia cycle was "written by someone else in the persona of Sulpicia, consciously imitating the style and emotions one might expect from a teenage girl."[14] For Hubbard, it was presumably more inherently plausible that a Roman author (male by definition) should imagine the emotions of a teenage girl than that a Roman woman should herself articulate adolescent emotions—though we have remarkably little evidence of Roman men's interest in the emotions of adolescent girls in general, and in particular in the case of the Roman elegists. Although Hubbard did not adduce Catullus, whose corpus provides two isolated examples in Latin epithalamium of literary interest in adolescent girls' emotions,[15] he argued that the Sulpicia epigrams (3.13–18) were composed as "a kind of epithalamic dedication on the occasion of Sulpicia's wedding…an elegiac equivalent of Fescennine verses, where ribald allusions to sex or to possible infidelity…are common."[16]

In articulating this thesis, Hubbard was primarily exercised by the perceived immorality of the epigrams' content: "What would be embarrassing if the poems were authentic and autobiographical becomes altogether acceptable in a Fescennine context."[17] Yet what he deems unacceptable for a teenage daughter of the Roman aristocracy he finds appropriate in the mouth of a family friend of lesser station: "in light of…more generic examples of assumed female voice in Propertius, Horace, Ovid, and the *Catalepton*, it is not a giant step for a male poet close to Messalla to write a short series of poems in the assumed persona of a young woman known to Messalla and his friends, particularly if she were in on the joke."[18] Indeed Hubbard, like Holzberg, seems committed to a biographical reading of the Sulpician corpus, since he revives the identification of Cornutus, the addressee of Tibullus' elegy 2.2, behind the pseudonym Cerinthus applied to Sulpicia's beloved (Ch. 4). This identification spurs Hubbard on to further biographical speculation that Sulpicia's marriage to Cornutus was the occasion of the performance of the Sulpician epigrams, perhaps even authored by Tibullus, and that a later anniversary provided the occasion for a second epithalamic dedication: "The *Garland* was probably meant as just such an anniversary present, paralleling the earlier wedding gift of the Sulpicia poems."[19] On Hubbard's reading, Sulpicia can be only an elegiac *puella*, not the author herself of elegiac verse.[20]

It is telling, however, that neither Holzberg nor Hubbard has been able to convert critical opinion wholesale and establish a new orthodoxy for either the dating or the authorship of the Sulpicia elegies.[21] Indeed, Laurel Fulkerson, in her 2017 Oxford commentary, even-handedly debates the issues raised by the first- and third-person Sulpicia poems, and cautiously advocates female authorship, at least for the first-person compositions.[22] Nonetheless, the attractions of the genre of *pseudepigrapha* continue to exert a powerful grip on the scholarly imagination, as we can see with the recent publication of another commentary on the *Appendix Tibulliana*, in which the critical tendency to reject the poems' female authorship and Augustan date is confidently reasserted. In his 2021 commentary, Robert Maltby flatly rejects the possibility of an Augustan Sulpicia, proposing rather an unknown Flavian male author's "adoption of a Sulpician mask from the period of the great elegists," on the grounds that it would lend "an air of authenticity to his pseudepigraphic project."[23]

Yet the shifting paradigms that much recent scholarship has adduced for dismissing the hard-won evidentiary gains of earlier eras are themselves vulnerable to the charges of changing critical fashion and excessive skepticism. For example, the critical skepticism of the early twenty-first century is consonant with the prevailing hermeneutic of suspicion brought to bear on biographical criticism in Western literary studies in general, and on ancient biography in classical scholarship in particular.[24] Feminist critics, moreover, have documented a persistent tendency among scholars of European arts, history, and literature to downplay the evidence for, and dismiss the value of, female artistic creation.[25] In 1983, Joanna Russ outlined ten common views that have been adduced to ignore, condemn, and/or belittle the work of female authors of English literature in her ground-breaking study, *How to Suppress Women's Writing*.[26]

She didn't write it.

She wrote it, but she shouldn't have.

She wrote it, but look what she wrote about.

She wrote it, but she wrote only one of it.

She wrote it, but "she" isn't really an artist and "it" isn't really serious, of the right genre—i.e., really art.

She wrote it, but it's only interesting/included in the canon for one, limited reason.

She wrote it, but she had help.

She wrote it, but there are very few of her.

She wrote it, but she's an anomaly.

She wrote it, but she doesn't fit in.

Mutatis mutandis, these views are applicable to female artists working in other cultures, languages, and media—and can be exemplified in the critical literature on the Sulpicia cycle. While the evidence that Emily Hemelrijk, among others, has compiled very clearly shows that there was far from being any kind of prohibition on women writing poetry in ancient Rome, there have been many efforts by classical scholars to "explain [Sulpicia's verse] away, ignore it, downgrade it, in short make it vanish."[27] Certainly, "the first line of defense is to deny that she wrote it."[28] But an even more insidious and effective way to deny the fact of female authorship in Roman antiquity is to deny that a particular speaking or writing woman existed at all.

I shall, therefore, conclude this speculative biography by introducing the seven-piece cycle *Sulpicia's Songs*, a 2015 film-recital project for voice and piano available on YouTube.[29] A feminist tour-de-force, the project showcases the music Jessica Krash composed for English versions of Sulpicia's verse rendered by the scholar/translator Mary Maxwell.[30] Sung by Noelle McMurtry,[31] who is accompanied on the piano by Eric Sedgwick, the songs feature titles that transpose Sulpicia's poems 3.13–18 into an art-song cycle whose lyrics bear thematic resonances with popular music: i. At last, it's come; ii. The hated birthday approaches; iii. Did you hear?; iv. I'm grateful; v. Fever; vi. No longer care for me; vii. Let it be known! (the last, piano only). Illustrated by Roman frescoes, the project is animated by a distinctively feminist sensibility, as McMurtry explains:[32]

Sulpicia's Songs envisions an embodied Sulpicia, manifesting the joys and sorrows of her romantic life. Through her own words, Sulpicia's voice occupies a liminal space between antiquity and our present world. As song cycle, *Sulpicia's Songs* operates as a vital contribution in support of feminist critical attempts to reclaim Sulpicia's personhood, as it textually and musically reframes and performs her first-century poetic voice through the perspectives of twenty-first century creative women as translator, composer, and performer.

While male authors and critics have historically ignored women's artistic production, female artists and scholars have shown a keen compensatory interest in recovering their foremothers' works.[33] Laurie J. Churchill, Phyllis R. Brown, Jane E. Jeffrey, Jacqueline Fabre-Serris, Judith P. Hallett, and Jane Stevenson have been at the forefront of the movement to document and recover women in the Latin literary tradition,[34] and the trio of female artists who have brought Sulpicia's verse to English audiences of western art-song have similarly deepened and enriched the European tradition of women's artistic production. It is my hope that this volume too will contribute to the continuing vitality of feminist scholarship in the exploration of women's artistic traditions.

Sulpicia: Life, Love, and Literature in Ancient Rome. Alison Keith, Oxford University Press.
© Oxford University Press 2026. DOI: 10.1093/9780197607008.003.0009

The Sulpicia Cycle

Unless otherwise indicated, I have reproduced the text of the Sulpicia cycle (3.8–18) from Tränkle 1990; the text of the epitaph of Sulpicia Petale is drawn from *L'année épigraphique* 1928.73; and the text of Tibullus' elegy 2.2 is taken from Maltby 2002. Translations are my own, though I have consulted widely in the commentaries, especially those of Tränkle 1990; Lyne 2007; Fulkerson 2017; Maltby 2002 and 2021.

3.8

Sulpicia est tibi culta tuis, Mars magne, kalendis:
  spectatum e caelo, si sapis, ipse ueni.
hoc Venus ignoscet; at tu, uiolente, caueto,
  ne tibi miranti turpiter arma cadant.
illius ex oculis, cum uult exurere diuos,
  accendit geminas lampadas acer Amor;
illam, quidquid agit, quoquo uestigia mouit,
  componit furtim subsequiturque Decor.
seu soluit crines, fusis decet esse capillis;
  seu compsit, comptis est ueneranda comis.
urit, seu Tyria uoluit procedere palla;
  urit, seu niuea candida ueste uenit.
talis in aeterno felix Vertumnus Olympo
  mille habet ornatus, mille decenter habet.
sola puellarum digna est, cui mollia caris
  uellera det sucis bis madefacta Tyros,
possideatque, metit quidquid bene olentibus aruis
  cultor odoratae diues Arabs segetis,
et quascumque niger Rubro de litore gemmas
  proximus Eois colligit Indus aquis.
hanc uos, Pierides, festis cantate kalendis,
  et testudinea Phoebe superbe lyra.
hoc sollemne sacrum multos †haec sumet† in annos:
  dignior est uestro nulla puella choro.

Sulpicia is dressed for you on the first day of your month, great Mars:
  if you're smart, come from heaven yourself to admire her.
Venus will pardon this; but you, violent god, beware lest your
  weapons fall shamelessly as you gape in admiration.
From her eyes, when he wishes to inflame the gods,   5
  fierce Amor kindles twin torches.
Whatever she does, wherever she moves her steps,
  Elegance attends her, all unawares, and follows in her wake.
If she lets her hair down, her loose hair becomes her;
  or if she styles it, she must be worshipped for her styled locks.   10
She inflames desire, if she wished to step out in a mantle of Tyrian purple;
  she inflames desire, if she comes gleaming in a snow-white dress.
Just so, the blessed god Vertumnus on eternal Olympus
  has a thousand outfits and wears the thousand elegantly.
Alone among girls is she worthy of receiving from Tyre   15
  soft fleeces twice drenched with precious dyes,
and of possessing whatever scented crops
  the wealthy Arabian farmer reaps from his aromatic fields,
and whatever gems from the shore of the Indian Ocean
  the black Indian gathers near Dawn's waters.   20
You Muses, daughters of Pierus, hymn her on the festive Kalends,
  and you, Phoebus Apollo, glorying in your tortoise-shell lyre.
Let her take up this solemn rite for many years:
  no maiden is more worthy of your chorus.

Parce meo iuueni, seu quis bona pascua campi
  seu colis umbrosi deuia montis aper,
nec tibi sit duros acuisse in proelia dentes;
  incolumem custos hunc mihi seruet Amor.
sed procul abducit uenandi Delia cura: 5
  o pereant siluae deficiantque canes!
quis furor est, quae mens densos indagine colles
  claudentem teneras laedere uelle manus?
quidue iuuat furtim latebras intrare ferarum
  candidaque hamatis crura notare rubis?   10
sed tamen, ut tecum liceat, Cerinthe, uagari,
  ipsa ego per montes retia torta feram,
ipsa ego uelocis quaeram uestigia cerui
  et demam celeri ferrea uincla cani.
tunc mihi, tunc placeant siluae, si, lux mea, tecum   15
  arguar ante ipsas concubuisse plagas;
tunc ueniat licet ad casses, inlaesus abibit,
  ne ueneris cupidae gaudia turbet, aper.
nunc sine me sit nulla uenus, sed lege Dianae,
  caste puer, casta retia tange manu;   20
et quaecumque meo furtim subrepit amori,
  incidat in saeuas diripienda feras.
at tu uenandi studium concede parenti,
  et celer in nostros ipse recurre sinus.

Spare my young man, any boar who frequents the good pastures
  of the field or the remote defiles of a shady mountain,
nor have a care to sharpen your hard tusks for battle;
  may his guardian Amor preserve him safe for me.
But the goddess Diana's love of hunting leads him far away:
  O! that the woods might perish and hunting dogs die out!
What madness is it, what sense to wish to harm your tender
  hands by investing the close packed hills with hunting nets?
Or what pleasure is there in entering the haunts of wild beasts by
  stealth and scratching your gleaming shins with prickly brambles?
But yet, should it be permitted to wander with you, Cerinthus,
  I myself would carry the twisted nets over the mountains,
I myself would seek the tracks of a fleet deer
  and strip off their iron chains from the swift dogs.
Then the woods would please me, then my love, if I could
  be proven to have lain with you before the nets themselves;
then, though the boar approach the hunting-nets, he will go away
  unharmed, so as not to disturb the joys of passionate love.
Now without me let there be no love, but by Diana's law,
  chaste youth, touch the nets with a chaste hand;
and whoever stealthily approaches my love,
  let her fall in among savage beasts to be ripped apart.
But you, leave the pursuit of hunting to your father,
  and yourself run swiftly back into my embrace.

3.10

Huc ades et tenerae morbos expelle puellae,
  huc ades, intonsa Phoebe superbe coma.
crede mihi, propera: nec te iam, Phoebe, pigebit
  formosae medicas applicuisse manus.
effice, ne macies pallentes occupet artus
  neu notet informis tabida membra color,
et quodcumque mali est et quidquid triste timemus,
  in pelagus rapidis euehat amnis aquis.
sancte, ueni, tecumque feras, quicumque sapores,
  quicumque et cantus corpora fessa leuant,
neu iuuenem torque, metuit qui fata puellae
  uotaque pro domina uix numeranda facit.
interdum uouet, interdum, quod langueat illa,
  dicit in aeternos aspera uerba deos.
pone metum, Cerinthe: deus non laedit amantes.
  tu modo semper ama: salua puella tibi est.
nil opus est fletu: lacrimis erit aptius uti,
  si quando fuerit tristior illa tibi.
at nunc tota tua est, te solum candida secum
  cogitat, et frustra credula turba sedet.
Phoebe, faue: laus magna tibi tribuetur in uno
  corpore seruato restituisse duos.
iam celeber, iam laetus eris, cum debita reddet
  certatim sanctis laetus uterque focis.
tunc te felicem dicet pia turba deorum,
  optabunt artes et sibi quisque tuas.

Come here and drive out disease from a tender maiden,
  come here, Phoebus Apollo, proud of your unshorn hair.
Believe me, hasten; nor will you ever, Phoebus, regret
  having applied your healing hands to the beautiful girl.
5 See to it that no wasting disease seize her pallid limbs
  nor unsightly complexion stain her weakened body.
Whatever evil there is and whatever sadness we fear,
  let a stream with rapid eddies carry it out to sea.
Holy one, come, and may you bring with you whatever scents
10 and whatever spells relieve exhausted bodies,
nor torture the young man, who feared his girl's death
  and makes vows scarcely to be counted for his mistress.
Sometimes he makes vows; sometimes, because she languishes,
  he utters harsh words against the eternal gods.
15 Lay aside your fear, Cerinthus; god does not harm lovers.
  Only always love! Your girl is safe.
21 There's no need for weeping; it will be more fitting to use tears
22 if ever she will become harsher toward you.
17 But now she is wholly yours; innocently, she thinks
18 of you alone, and a credulous throng besieges her in vain.
Phoebus, be favorable: great praise will be given you
20 for having restored two by saving one person.
23 Now you will be honored, now happy, when each vies
  happily to repay their debts at your sacred hearth.
25 Then the pious throng of gods will call you blessed,
  and each will desire your skills for themselves.

3.11

Qui mihi te, Cerinthe, dies dedit, hic mihi sanctus
atque inter festos semper habendus erit.
te nascente nouum Parcae cecinere puellis
  seruitium et dederunt regna superba tibi.
uror ego ante alias: iuuat hoc, Cerinthe, quod uror,
  si tibi de nobis mutuus ignis adest.
mutuus adsit amor, per te dulcissima furta
perque tuos oculos per Geniumque rogo.
magne Geni, cape tura libens uotisque faueto,
  si modo, cum de me cogitat, ille calet.
quodsi forte alios iam nunc suspiret amores,
tunc precor infidos, sancte, relinque focos.
nec tu sis iniusta, Venus: uel seruiat aeque
  uinctus uterque tibi uel mea uincla leua.
sed potius ualida teneamur uterque catena,
  nulla queat posthac quam soluisse dies.
optat idem iuuenis quod nos, sed tectius optat;
nam pudet haec illum dicere uerba palam.
at tu, Natalis, quoniam deus omnia sentis,
adnue: quid refert, clamne palamne roget?

The day that has given you to me, Cerinthus, I must always
  hold sacred and celebrate amid the festivals.
At your birth the Fates foretold for girls a new
  slavery and gave proud realms to you.

5   I'm on fire before the rest: it pleases me, Cerinthus,
  that I'm on fire, if you have a mutual fire for me.
Let a mutual love be present, I beg you—by our sweetest trysts,
  by your eyes, by your guardian Spirit.

10 Great Spirit, accept incense freely and favor my prayers,
  if only he grows warm when he thinks about me.
But if now he should perhaps sigh over love of another,
  then I pray, holy one, leave his faithless hearth.
Nor should you be unjust, Venus: either let each serve you
  equally bound or release my chains.

15 But rather let us each be held by your strong bond
  which no day afterward may be able to loosen.
My young man desires the same as I, but he desires more secretly;
  for he's ashamed to say these words openly.

20 But you, birthday Spirit, since as a god you perceive everything, grant
  my prayer: what does it matter whether he asks secretly or openly?

3.12

Natalis Iuno, sanctos cape turis aceruos,
  quos tibi dat tenera docta puella manu.
lota tibi est hodie, tibi se laetissima compsit,
  staret ut ante tuos conspicienda focos.
illa quidem ornandi causas tibi, diua, relegat;   5
  est tamen, occulte cui placuisse uelit.
at tu, sancta, faue, neu quis diuellat amantes,
  sed iuueni quaeso mutua uincla para.
sic bene compones: ullae non ille puellae
  seruire aut cuiquam dignior illa uiro.   10
nec possit cupidos uigilans deprendere custos,
  fallendique uias mille ministret Amor.
adnue purpureaque ueni perlucida palla:
  ter tibi fit libo, ter, dea casta, mero.
praecipit et natae mater studiosa, quid optet: 15
  illa aliud tacita, iam sua, mente rogat.
uritur, ut celeres urunt altaria flammae,
  nec, liceat quamuis, sana fuisse uelit.
†sis iuueni grata†, ueniet cum proximus annus,
  hic idem †uotis iam uetus esset† amor.   20

Birthday Spirit, accept the heaps of sacred incense,
  which a learned girl offers you with her tender hand.
She's bathed elegantly for you today, adorned herself most happily for you,
  to stand for all to see before your altars.
Indeed she attributes the reason for her adornment to you, goddess;
  but there's one whom she secretly wishes to have pleased.
And you, holy goddess, show favor, nor let anyone separate lovers,
  but prepare mutual bonds, I beg, for the youth.
So you will well arrange. The youth devotes himself to no maiden
  more worthily, nor the maiden to any man.
Let no watchful guardian be able to catch the lovers,
  and let Amor provide a thousand paths of deception.
Grant my prayer, and come gleaming in a purple cloak: thrice an
  offering of cake is made to you, chaste goddess, thrice of neat wine.
A solicitous mother presupposes what her daughter desires: the girl,
  now her own mistress, asks for something else, with silent mind.
She is inflamed, just as the swift flames burn the altars,
  nor would she wish to be heart-whole, though she could be.
May you be gracious to the youth, and when next year comes,
  may the same love, now of long-standing, remain by these vows.

3.13

Tandem uenit amor, qualem texisse pudore
quam nudasse alicui sit mihi fama magis.
exorata meis illum Cytherea Camenis
attulit in nostrum deposuitque sinum.
exsoluit promissa Venus: mea gaudia narret,   5
dicetur si quis non habuisse sua.
non ego signatis quicquam mandare tabellis,
ne legat id nemo quam meus ante, uelim,
sed peccasse iuuat, uultus componere famae
taedet: cum digno digna fuisse ferar.   10

At last has come love, such as it would disgrace me more to have
   cloaked out of shame than to have exposed to anyone.
Entreated by the Camenae, my muses, the Cytherean goddess
   has brought him and placed him in my lap.
Venus has fulfilled her promises: let them tell of my joys,
   if anyone will be said not to have had their own.
I would not wish to entrust anything to sealed tablets,
   so that none might read it before my lover.
But sin is pleasing; to compose my features for reputation is a bore:
   a worthy woman, I shall be said to have been with a worthy man.

3.14

Inuisus natalis adest, qui rure molesto
et sine Cerintho tristis agendus erit.
dulcius urbe quid est? an uilla sit apta puellae
atque Arretino frigidus amnis agro?
iam, nimium Messalla mei studiose, quiescas;   5
non tempestiuae saepe, propinque, uiae![1]
hic animum sensusque meos abducta relinquo,
arbitrio quoniam non sinis esse meo.

My hateful birthday is here, which will have to be spent unhappily
   in the tiresome countryside and without Cerinthus.
What is sweeter than the city? Or could a country-villa be fit
   for a girl and a cold stream in the fields of Arezzo?
Now please give it a rest, Messalla—too solicitous of me;
   journeys, kinsmen, are often ill-timed.
Carried off, I leave my heart and senses here,
   since you do not permit me to be under my own control.

3.15

Scis iter ex animo sublatum triste puellae?
natali Romae iam licet esse suo.[2]
omnibus ille dies nobis natalis[3] agatur,
qui necopinanti[4] nunc tibi forte uenit.

You know that the dreary journey has been lifted from a girl's heart?
Now it's permitted for her to celebrate her birthday at Rome.
Let that day be celebrated as a birthday by us all,
which now comes to you by chance, against your expectation.

3.16

Gratum est, securus multum quod iam tibi de me
permittis, subito ne male inepta cadam.
sit tibi cura togae potior pressumque quasillo
scortum quam Serui filia Sulpicia:
sollicti sunt pro nobis, quibus illa dolori est,   5
ne cedam ignoto, maxima causa, toro.

I'm glad that you now carelessly permit yourself much leeway
about me, so that I don't suddenly fall into disgrace in my folly.[5]
Be concerned for your toga and a prostitute, weighed down
by a wool-basket, rather than Servius' daughter Sulpicia:
they're solicitous for my interests, whose greatest cause for   5
grief is that I might fall to an ignoble bed.

3.17

Estne tibi, Cerinthe, tuae pia cura puellae,
quod mea nunc uexat corpora fessa calor?
a ego non aliter tristes euincere morbos
optarim, quam te si quoque uelle putem.
at mihi quid prosit morbos euincere, si tu   5
nostra potes lento pectore ferre mala?

Do you have a faithful concern for your girlfriend, Cerinthus,
because a fever now buffets my exhausted body?
Ah! I would not wish to overcome the sad illness,
except if I thought you too wanted it.
But what would it profit me to overcome the illness, if you   5
can bear our ills with an unfeeling heart?

3.18

Ne tibi sim, mea lux, aeque iam feruida cura
  ac uideor paucos ante fuisse dies,
si quicquam tota commisi stulta iuuenta,
  cuius me fatear paenituisse magis,
hesterna quam te solum quod nocte reliqui,
  ardorem cupiens dissimulare meum.

5

May I not now be an equally fevered care for you, my love,
  as I seem to have been a few days earlier,
if I foolishly committed anything in my whole youth
  which I might confess I regretted more
than that I left you alone yesterday night,
  desiring to disguise my passion.

5

L'année épigraphique 1928.73

Sulpiciae cineres lectricis cerne uiator
  quoi seruile datum nomen erat Petale.
ter denos numero quattuor plus uixerat annos
  natumque in terris Aglaon ediderat,
omnia naturae bona uiderat arte uigebat
  splendebat forma, creuerat ingenio.
inuida fors uita longinquom degere tempus
  noluit hanc; fatis defuit ipse colus.

See, passer-by, the ashes of Sulpicia the reader
  to whom the slave name Petale had been given.
She had lived for thrice ten years and four,
  and on earth she had given birth to a son, Aglaos;
she had seen all good things of nature, she flourished in skill,
  she glowed in beauty, she had increased in talent.
Grudging destiny was unwilling for her to spend a long time
  in life; their spindle itself failed the Fates.

5

Tibullus, elegy 2.2

Let us utter auspicious words: the birthday is coming. Anyone
  who is present at the altars, man and woman, guard your tongue.
May holy incense burn on the hearth, let perfumes burn
  which the gentle Arab exports from his wealthy land.
May the birth-spirit himself be present to see his honors   5
  and may soft garlands adorn his sacred hair.
May his temples drip with pure unguent of spikenard, may
  he have his fill of cake and be steeped in neat wine.
May he also nod assent to you, Cornutus, for whatever you ask.
  Go ahead, why do you hesitate? He nods his assent: ask!   10
I augur you will wish for the faithful love of your wife:
  already I think the gods themselves have learned this by heart.
Nor would you prefer for yourself any fields in the whole
  world that a hardy peasant ploughs with his sturdy ox,
nor whatever gems are found in the wealthy Indies,   15
  where the eastern ocean's wave grows red.
The prayers are uttered. Would that the love-god might fly here
  on sounding wings and bear the saffron chains of marriage,
and may those chains ever remain until slow old age
  brings wrinkles and tints the hair.   20
May he, as a birthday bird-omen, come here and supply offspring,
  and may a troop of youngsters frolic before your feet.

Dicamus bona uerba; uenit natalis; ad aras
quisquis ades, lingua, uir mulierque, faue. [6]
urantur pia tura focis, urantur odores
quos tener e terra diuite mittit Arabs.
ipse suos Genius adsit uisurus honores
cui decorent sanctas mollia serta comas.
illius puro destillent tempora nardo,
atque satur libo sit madeatque mero.
adnuat et, Cornute, tibi quodcumque rogabis.
en age, quid cessas? adnuit ille: roga.
auguror, uxoris fidos optabis amores:
iam reor hoc ipsos edidicisse deos.
nec tibi malueris totum quaecumque per orbem
fortis arat ualido rusticus arua boue,
nec tibi gemmarum quidquid felicibus Indis
nascitur, Eoi qua maris unda rubet.
uota cadunt. utinam strepitantibus aduolet alis
flauaque coniugio uincula portet Amor,
uincula quae maneant semper dum tarda senectus
inducat rugas inficiatque comas.
huc ueniat natalis auis prolemque ministret, [7]
ludat et ante tuos turba nouella pedes.

Notes

Introduction

1. Catullus, poem 85. Unless otherwise noted, translations are my own.
2. Skinner 1982; Wiseman 1985, 130–82.
3. We may compare Catullus' complaints in poem 16 that his addressees, Aurelius and Furius, read his verses as evidence of his debauchery (16.2–6): "Obscene Aurelius and pansy Furius, / you thought from my verses that I was / dishonourable, because they're a bit sexy. / It's appropriate for a poet himself to be chaste, / but there's no need for his verses to be pure."
4. Catullus, poem 79.
5. On display in Cicero's speeches *On Behalf of Caelius* 32, 36, 78; *Against Piso* 28; *On Behalf of Sestius* 16; and a letter to his brother Quintus, *To [my] Brother Quintus* 2.3.2. The charge of incest has been variously interpreted as historically true (Rankin 1962), rhetorically strategic (Tatum 1993), and purely metaphorical (Skinner 1982).
6. Skinner 1982; Wiseman 1985, 15–53; Tatum 1993.
7. On arrogance as characteristic of the Claudian family (*gens Claudia*), see Wiseman 1979, 77–103. For Clodia's arrogance and sexual depravity see, e.g., Catullus, poems 11, 37, 58, 76, 83; for her wit and charm see, e.g., Catullus, poems 2–3, 51, 86.
8. Catullus, poem 36.1–10.
9. Catullus, poem 95.
10. Catullus, poem 35.
11. Sappho's writings were organized already in the third century BCE by the male bibliographers of the Museum in Alexandria, and survive, for the most part, in male authors' quotations: see Hadjimichael 2019; Neri 2021. None of Cleopatra's writings survive; for male critics' representations of her, see Wyke 2002, 195–320; Hamer 2008; Roller 2010. On Clodia Metelli, thought to be the historical figure behind Catullus' Lesbia, see Skinner 2011.
12. For the difficulties inherent in constructing the biographies of prominent historical Roman women see, e.g., Fantham 2006; Dixon 2007; Treggiari 2007; Skinner 2011; Osgood 2014.

Chapter 1

1. Quintilian, *Education of the Orator* 10.1.93.
2. Lachmann 1876, 2.150; Smith 1913, 87; Norden 1954, 71; Hanslik 1955; Dettmer 1983; Valvo 1983; Syme 1986, 200–43; Porte 1992; Hallett 2002b.
3. The term is used to characterize Sulpicia in both the third-person poems (3.8.24, 3.10.1, 3.10.16, 3.12.2) and the first-person poems (3.14.3, 3.15.1, 3.17.1).
4. Cerinthus is named at 3.9.11, 3.10.15, 3.11.1, 3.14.2, 3.17.1.
5. The standard Latin edition of the Sulpicia cycle is Tränkle 1990, 43–49. Latin with facing English translation of the cycle is available in Postgate rev. Goold 1988, 322–37; Lee rev. Maltby 1990, 94–103; Maltby 2021, 58–73. Latin text and English translation of 3.13–18 are also available in Lyne 2007, 348–67. English translations of 3.13–18 are available in Snyder 1989 130–4; Lefkowitz and Fant 2016, 11–12.
6. Tibullus celebrates Marathus in his elegies 1.4, 8, 9; his mistress Delia in his elegies 1.2, 3, 5, 6; and Nemesis in his elegies 2.3–6. On Tibullus' elegiac poetry, see Quintilian, *Education of the Orator* 10.1.93; cf. Velleius 2.36.3; Martial 4.68.70, 14.193; Diomedes, *Ars grammatica* 1.484.1–29.
7. On the textual tradition of the Tibullan corpus, see Fisher 1981; Rouse and Reeve 1983; Maltby 2002; Navarro Antolín 1996.
8. Newton 1962, 280–81; Rouse and Reeve 1983, 421.
9. Rouse and Reeve 1983, 412.
10. Ullman 1954, 26; Fisher 1981, 1953.
11. Newton 1962, 258, who confirms (258–89) that the Freising selections "represent faithfully the text and orthography of the complete Tibullus from which they are ultimately derived. This practice extends even to the single words, which have been left in the form in which they appeared in the text."

12. Newton 1962, 277–80.
13. Ullman 1928; Rouse 1979; Rouse and Reeve 1983, 421–22.
14. Ullman 1928; Rouse 1979; Rouse and Reeve 1983, 421–22; Navarro Antolín 1996, 32–33.
15. Rouse and Reeve 1983, 422–23; Navarro Antolín 1996, 33.
16. Ullman 1955, 183–84; Rouse 1967, 1973, and 1979; Navarro Antolín 1996, 34.
17. Rouse and Reeve 1983, 423; Maltby 2002, 21.
18. Rouse and Reeve 1983, 423. On Salutati, see Schwartz 1934; Witt 1983 and 2000.
19. Rouse and Reeve (1983, 423) thank Dr A. C. de la Mare for the observation; they note in addition Salutati's ownership of "the oldest surviving descendant of Petrarch's lost Propertius; and his Catullus too." Ullman 1955, 50, has also argued for the French provenance of the manuscript from which Salutati's codex derived, surmising it to be a copy of Richard de Fourneval's codex, preserved in the Collège de la Sorbonne.
20. Maltby 2002, 21–22.
21. Rouse and Reeve 1983, 423–24; Maltby 2002, 22. On the transmission of Tibullus, see most recently Dixon 2002.
22. Skoie (2002, 29) notes that "In fact, there were three Venetian editions that had to compete for the title *editio princeps*." For the details, see Luck 1998, xx.
23. Lauer 1475: see Skoie 2002, 31–64. My discussion of the early modern commentary tradition on Tibullus is deeply indebted to Skoie 2002.
24. Skoie (2002, 31n29) reports the latest edition as from 1604.
25. Skoie 2002, 53–64. As she puts it, Bernardinus hides Sulpicia "behind a normalizing toga" (2002, 108), the dress of the elite Roman man, thereby "putting a male lover in the place of the female" (2002, 94).
26. On the fragment, see Dixon 2006. Grafton (1983–93, I.166) has identified the fragment as "a medieval remnant from a French library," and Dixon (2006, 59 and 72) supports "an eleventh- or early twelfth-century date for the fragment."
27. Skoie 2002, 94.
28. Skoie 2002, 97–98.
29. Barth 1624, lix.16.coll. 2811–12. Sulpicia the satirist is mentioned in Martial's epigrams 10.35 and 10.38 (Ch. 7).
30. On the iambic fragment (quoted by a scholiast on Juvenal, *Satires* 6.537), see Parker 1992; on the hexameter fragment (*Epigrammata Bobiensia* 37), see Butrica 2006. On Sulpicia the satirist, see also Merriam 1991; Hallett 1992; Richlin 1992.
31. Barth's proposal was accepted by Broukhusius 1708, 384, and revived by Hermann 1951, 17–26.
32. Heyne 1975, 250–51 (translation mine); cited by Skoie (2002, 128n60).
33. Translation by Skoie 2002, 130.
34. My translation of Heyne's Latin (cited at Skoie 2002, 131).
35. Skoie 2002, 179 and 194–96; she notes in particular the endorsement of Karl Lachmann (founder of the science of textual criticism), who had himself published a critical edition of Tibullus in 1829.
36. Rossbach 1855, vi and 55, cited in Lowe 1988, 196n18. Skoie (2002, 231n76) reports that Rossbach was followed by Baehrens (1876, 42) and Postgate (1905). See Cartault 1906, 563–64, for the different scholars and their attributions of 3.13.
37. Haupt 1871, 32–34; accepted by Smith 1913, 79; Tränkle 1990, 299; Hollis 2007, 427–28; Lyne 2007, 344–45. Cf. *PIR*[1] S739 and the stemma at *RE* IVA.1, coll. 879–80, now superseded by Syme 1986, Tables IX ("Messalla Corvinus") and XXIV ("Three Jurists"). Fulkerson (2017, 29n55) seems to accept the identification, *contra* Holzberg 1998/99; Hubbard 2004/5; Maltby 2021 (Ch. 8).
38. Cf. Lyne 2007, 344n8; Treggiari 2019, 105. Cicero refers to Postumia with respect in his eulogy of the dead jurist at *Phil.* 9.5.
39. See Fulkerson 2017, 42, for a summary of the proposals and full bibliography.
40. Smith 1913, 77; Tränkle 1990, 299–302; Tschiedel 1992; Yardley 1992. Cf. Lyne 2007 [2004–5], 344–48.
41. Parker 1994, 46. Parker is anticipated by Doncieux 1891, 78–81; Martinon 1895, xlv–xlvii; Salanitro 1938, 33–34.
42. Hallett 2002a; Dronke 2003; Fabre-Serris 2009, 2017, 2018, 2020a, 2020b, 2022; Hauser 2016.
43. *AE* 1928.73. First proposed by Carcopino 1929; followed by Stevenson 2005, 42–44; Hallett 2009c and elsewhere.

Chapter 2

1. Nepos, *Life of Atticus* 2.1.
2. On the stormy career and violent death of the tribune of 88 BCE, see Broughton 1951, 2.41–42.
3. C. Sulpicius Paterculus, *cos.* 258 BCE; Ser. Sulpicius Galba, *pr.* 187 BCE; L. Supicius, *tr. mil.* 181 BCE; C. Sulpicius Galus, *cos.* 166 BCE; Ser. Sulpicius Galba, *cos.* 144 BCE; Ser. Sulpicius Galba, *cos.* 108 BCE.
4. Cicero, *On Behalf of Murena* 16.
5. On this Sulpicia, see Briscoe 2008, 236; Hallett 2011b, 90–92; Webb 2019, 75; on her father Ser. Sulpicius Paterculus, see *RE* s.v.
6. Valerius Maximus 8.15.12. On the episode, see Langlands 2006, 30, 58–61; Schultz 2006, 144n24; Hallett 2011b, 90–92. On sexual morality in Valerius Maximus, see Langlands 2000 and 2006, 123–91.
7. Fantham 1998, 122 ad Ovid, *Fasti* 4.155–62; see also Hallett 2011b, 92–93.
8. Pliny, *Natural History* 7.120. The story is also related at Solinus, i.126; and by Bocaccio in *On Famous Women*.
9. Briscoe 2008, 236; cf. Webb 2019, 7n45. Schultz (2006, 144) mistakes her for the daughter of the consul, but her father's praenomen Servius distinguishes him from the consul Gaius Sulpicius Paterculus.
10. On Quintus Fulvius Flaccus (*RE* 59), see Briscoe 2008, 154.
11. On Lucius' son, Aulus' grandson, Spurius Postumius Albinus, see *RE* 44; Briscoe 2008, 224, 232–91, 318, 355–56, 372, 519. On Livy's narrative of the Bacchanalia scandal, see Gruen 1990, 34–78; Langlands 2006, 115–22; Panoussi 2019, 120–39; Steinhauer 2020.
12. Livy 39.8–19.
13. Livy 39.11.3.
14. Livy 39.11.4, 12.2.
15. Livy 39.13.3.
16. Livy 39.12.4.
17. Briscoe 2008, 236; cf. Hallett 2011b, 86–88.
18. Livy 39.14.1–3.
19. This discussion reworks Keith 2018.
20. For the debate, see Briscoe 2008, 230–50, with further bibliography.
21. On Roman women inheriting glory from their male kinfolk, cf. Treggiari 2019, 21.
22. Haupt 1871. On Quintus' son Servius Sulpicius Rufus, of the Lemonian tribe, see *RE* 95 (Münzer and Kübler 1931); Meloni 1946; Bretone 1971, 75–87; Frier 1985, esp. 153–55, and index s.v. "Sulpicius Rufus, Ser." On his homonymous son, see Syme 1981.
23. Literary evidence for the family survives in Cicero's orations *On Behalf of Murena* of 62 BCE, defending the incoming consul Murena against charges brought by the defeated candidate, Ser. Sulpicius Rufus, and *Philippics* 9, delivered shortly after Sulpicius' death in 43 BCE; in his history of Roman oratory, *Brutus* (150–56); and in his correspondence *To Friends* (4.3.1, 4.5–6, 4.12; 8.8.3, 9.18.2, 11.71, 11.24.2); and to Atticus (5.4.1, 5.21.14).
24. After Sulla's reforms the earliest age at which the office of *praetor* could be held was 40.
25. Cicero, *To Friends* 4.3.3; *Brutus* 151.
26. Cicero, *Brutus* 154; Pomponius, *Digest* 1.2.2.43.
27. Cicero, *On Behalf of Murena* 18.
28. Cicero, *On Behalf of Murena* 19, 21–22. See Frier 1985, 154.
29. Cicero, *On Behalf of Murena* 15.
30. Cicero, *On Behalf of Murena* 16.
31. In late 60 or early 59 BCE, Cicero floated the possibility of Servius Sulpicius holding the consulship with Gabinius as his colleague: see Cicero, *To Atticus* 2.5.2, with Meloni 1946, 124n13.
32. Meloni 1946, 125.
33. On Clodius, see Tatum 1999. On his sister Clodia, also Cicero's enemy, see Skinner 2011.
34. Asconius 36C; Plutarch, *Life of Pompey* 54.5. The jurist's successful exercise of this magistracy is all the more impressive, since Cicero reports that the first of the year was besieged in his house for five days by Clodius' gangs: Cicero, *On Behalf of Milo* 13; cf. Asconius 33, 36, 43C.
35. Suetonius, *Life of Caesar* 29.1.

36. Saunders 1923, 112.
37. Cicero, *To Friends* 8.10.3.
38. Cicero, *To Friends* 4.1.1.
39. Cicero, *To Friends* 4.2.3.
40. On the jurist's son, see Syme 1981.
41. On Cicero's negotiations for Tullia's third marriage, about which we are extraordinarily well informed because of his surviving correspondence, see Treggiari 1991, 127–34, and 2007, 83–99.
42. Dionysius of Halicarnassus 5.37.1, 6.12.1; Livy 2.16.1. On Postumius, see further *RE* s.v. 24; Broughton 1951, 7–8. He was re-elected in 503 (Livy 2.16.7; Dionysius of Halicarnassus 5.44.1, 6.69.1), and celebrated a triumph for victories over the Sabines (Livy 2.16.1; Dionysius of Halicarnassus 5.37.1–39.4, 6.12.1; Plutarch, *Life of Poplicola* 20.1–3).
43. Cicero jokes to his friend Atticus that one of his legates left his province of Cilicia early in February 50 BCE, "snatched to Rome by Postumius, perhaps also Postumia" (*To Atticus* 5.21.9). Syme (1980, 430) identifies Sulpicius' wife Postumia with the Postumia of Catullus' poem 27.3, in which the poet commends "a Postumia as suitable president for a drinking party." On Catullus' poem, and the identity of the Postumia named there, see Cairns 1975; Treggiari 2019, 105n118, with further bibliography.
44. Suetonius, *Life of Caesar* 50.1.
45. Cicero, *Philippics* 9.3.
46. On Cicero's wife Terentia, see Treggiari 2007. On Servius' wife Postumia, see Münzer 1920, 405n1; Meloni 1946, 141n50; Treggiari 2019, 105–8. Primary evidence comes from Cicero in his correspondence (*To Friends* 4.2.1; *To Atticus* 5.21.14, 10.9.3, 10.10.4, 12.11, 12.22.2) and *Philippics* (9.3.5). Scholars have proposed a tradition of intermarriage between the Postumii and Sulpicii, both families of the "decayed" republican patrician aristocracy (Syme 1986, 17). In this connection, we may recall the relationship between the consul of 186 BCE, Postumius, and his mother-in-law Sulpicia.
47. Treggiari 1991, 127–43; 2007, 87–98. For Postumia's active part in the negotiations, see Cicero, *To Atticus* 5.21.14. Meloni (1946, 141n50) notes that Cicero's references to Postumia in his correspondence almost always show her taking the initiative: *To Friends* 4.2.1; *To Atticus* 5.21.14, 10.9.3, 10.10.4, 12.11, 12.22.2; cf. *Philippics* 9.3.5.
48. On Postumia's promotion of the match, see Cicero, *To Atticus* 5.21.14; on Servilia's promotion of the match, see Cicero, *To Atticus* 5.4.1, 6.1.10; and on Servilia, see further Treggiari 2019.
49. Thus, Cicero reports to Atticus that she is pressing him to meet with her husband at his villa in Cumae early in the civil war (*To Friends* 4.2.1; *To Atticus* 10.9.3, 10.10.4) and some years later, in March of 45 BCE, he suggests that Atticus consult her about details of her sister's family (*To Atticus* 12.22.2). I cannot agree with those scholars who have suggested that it was her husband the jurist who married Messalla's sister Valeria, since Postumia was still alive and actively engaged in the marriage of her son in 50 BCE; actively working for the interests of her husband and son during the ensuing civil war; and praised for her loyalty to her dead husband, the jurist, in Cicero's ninth *Philippic*.
50. For the family connection between the younger Servius Sulpicius and Messalla, cf. Horace, *Satires* 1.10.85–6 (Ch. 5).
51. Cicero, *To Atticus* 9.19.2; cf. 9.9.1, 9.18.2.
52. Cicero, *To Atticus* 10.3a.2; the quotation in the text is from Lockwood 1951, 160.
53. Cicero, *To Atticus* 10.1.4; on the passage, see Meloni 1946, 177.
54. Saunders (1923, 112) notes the oddity of Sulpicius' consultation of Cicero after attending Caesar's senate, "as if, having maintained his neutrality so far, he could still choose his course of action."
55. Cicero, *Philippics* 13.28–29. Meloni (1946, 177) considers Cicero's rhetoric here tendentious and unreliable, and deems it unlikely that Sulpicius was so much a Pompeian adherent that he joined his forces.
56. Meloni 1946, 177, citing Pomponius' *Enchiridion*, preserved in the *Digest* of Roman law (1.2.2.43). Frier (1985, 148) observes that the notice is somewhat garbled, and he therefore prefers (1985, 149n45) the location of Circeii (a promontory on the Bay of Naples) to that of Cercina (a small island in the lesser Syrtes, off the coast of Africa Proconsularis).
57. Cicero, *Brutus* 156.
58. Cicero, *To Friends* 6.6.10.

59. Meloni 1946, 185.
60. Cicero, *To Friends* 4.4.2, 5.
61. Cicero, *Philippics* 9.
62. Cicero, *Philippics* 9.1–2.
63. Cicero, *Philippics* 9.15–17.
64. Reported in the *Digest* (1.2.2.43) and confirmed by Jerome in his *Chronicle* on the year 44 BCE (Helm 1956, 157); cf. Cicero, *Philippics* 8.22, 13.29; *To Friends* 10.28.3, 12.5.3.
65. Cicero, *Orator* 1.48.212; cf. *On Behalf of Murena* 9.19, cited above.
66. Alfenus Varus was suffect consul in 39 BCE, and perhaps an early patron of Vergil (cf. *Bucolics* 6.6–7); cf. Ch. 5.
67. Meloni 1946, 236n16.
68. Meloni 1946, 237n20.
69. *Digest* 1.2.2.42; see Meloni 1946, 238.
70. Gellius, *Attic Nights* 4.1.20; *Digest* 17.2.30; and see further Meloni 1946, 238–40.
71. Gellius, *Attic Nights* 4.3.2[4], 4.4.1[1]; *Digest* 12.4.8[3].
72. Gellius, *Attic Nights* 7[6].12.1.
73. *Digest* 1.2.2.44, 14.3.5.1[7].
74. Meloni 1946, 240–41.
75. If Sulpicius is indeed the "unknown" figure of *On Behalf of Caecina* 80, as Frier (1985, 152–55) proposes.
76. Cicero, *On Laws* 1.5.17.
77. Cicero, *Brutus* 150–56.
78. Cicero, *Philippics* 9.10–12.
79. Cicero, *Philippics* 9.12.
80. If he was, in fact, the young Servius Sulpicius mentioned by Cicero at *On Behalf of Murena* 54; accepted by Syme 1981, 424.
81. Cicero, *To Friends* 4.3.4, 4.4.5, 4.6.1, 13.37.4. Cf. Ch. 5.
82. Cicero, *To Friends* 11.7.1.
83. Syme 1981, 424. Adoption through female family ties was exceedingly common in ancient Rome; we may compare Octavian, the future emperor Augustus, adopted by his maternal great-uncle Julius Caesar; and the younger Pliny, adopted by his maternal uncle, the elder Pliny. For the Roman custom of a maternal uncle (*auunculus*) adopting a sister's son, see Hallett 1984, 163; cf. Ch. 3n127.
84. Jerome, *Against Jovinian* 1.46.
85. Dio 46.55.3.
86. Valerius Maximus 6.7.3.
87. Valerius Maximus 6.7. Hallett (2002b) has argued for a familial relationship between the poet Sulpicia and members of the *gens Valeria*, like Valerius Maximus, which may explain his inclusion of these two Sulpiciae among his exempla.
88. Appian, *Civil Wars* 4.39. On Sulpicia Lentuli, see Milnor 2005, 197–98; Riess 2012, 497; Parker 2005, 164–68; Hallett 2011b, 88–90.
89. Since her mother was a Julia, she cannot have been one of the jurist's daughters.
90. Quintilian, *Education of the Orator* 4.2.106, 6.1.20, 10.1.22, the last naming Messalla as the prosecutor; cf. Festus (p. 140L). Syme (1981, 422) notes that the *Digest* (1.2.44) records the information that Sulpicius senior included among his *auditores* two Aufidii, Tucca and Namusa.
91. Quintilian, *Education of the Orator* 12.10.10.
92. Quintilian, *Education of the Orator* 10.1.116.
93. Quintilian, *Education of the Orator* 12.10.11.
94. Syme 1981, 425.
95. For reasons that will emerge in Ch. 5, I cannot agree with Lewis 2013, who differentiates between Servius Sulpicius Rufus "the orator" and Servius Sulpicius Rufus "the poet."
96. Syme (1981, 425n25) notes his name as "one of the earliest instances of the *gentilicium* ['family name'] of a mother or grandmother used as a cognomen."
97. Frontinus, *On Aqueducts* 99.
98. Cicero, *Philippics* 9.12.
99. Syme 1981, 424–25; *contra* (Münzer and Kübler 1931) *RE* 95, col. 862, dating his demise to the proscriptions, accepted by Shackleton Bailey on *To Atticus* 5.4.1.

100. Münzer and Kübler 1931; Syme 1986, 306n49.
101. Syme (1986, 305) notes that his lineage reveals a "tradition of Roman jurisprudence"; for his patrilineage, see Syme 1986, 305–6.
102. *Digest* I.2.47.
103. *Inscriptiones Latinae Selectae* 3103 = *CIL* I^2 979 = *CIL* VI 361. Syme (1981, 425n23; repeated at Syme 1986, 206) identifies the dedicant as another daughter of the orator—i.e., our poet's sister. In this, he diverges from Münzer (*RE* XIX.40), who identifies her as Sulpicia's aunt: see Table 1 for the stemma.
104. Lyne (2007, 344n7) compares her father's filiation "Servi filius" at Cicero, *To Atticus* 9.18.2.
105. Schultz 2006, 56. On Juno Lucina, see Schultz 2006, 47–57. Pliny (*Natural History* 16.235) reports the dedication of a temple to the goddess on the Esquiline in 375 BCE, though Schultz (2006, 42) interprets this as "the refurbishment or expansion of an already existing site," since there is no firm evidence for women's foundation of public temples in the republican period.
106. Syme 1986, Table XXIVn6, *contra PIR^2* C 502.

Chapter 3

1. Jerome, *Against Jovinian* 1.46.
2. On the legislation, see Raditsa 1980; Galinsky 1981; Gardner 1986; Treggiari 1991, 275–98.
3. On the autonomy and authority of the Roman mother, see Dixon 1988. For the financial autonomy of the Roman *matrona*, see Gardner 1986, 15, and cf., e.g., Cicero, *To Friends* 14.1 about Terentia's financial independence.
4. Cicero, *On the State* 2.53; Livy 2.8.1; Valerius Maximus 4.1.1. On the *gens Valeria*, see Münzer 1891. On Publicola, see Münzer 1891, 9–18 and 34–35, no. 2, with a full register of the ancient sources.
5. Livy 2.7.3; Dionysius of Halicarnassus 5.1.2; Valerius Maximus 1.8.5; Plutarch, *Life of Publicola* 9.5, *Life of Romulus* 16; see further Münzer 1891, 9–12; Broughton 1951, 1.2.
6. Plutarch, *Life of Poplicola* 7.4, 16.2, 17.1, 21.1; Livy 2.2.11, 7.3, 15.1, 16.2.
7. Livy 2.16.2–9; Dionysius of Halicarnassus 5.40.1–43.2; Plutarch, *Life of Publicola* 21.1–23.2: see further Münzer 1891, 9–12; Broughton 1951, 1.7.
8. Dionysius of Halicarnassus 8.39, 40, 43, 55; Plutarch, *Life of Coriolanus* 33; Appian, *Roman History* 5.3. On Valeria's part in the legend, see Münzer 1891, 56; Hallett 1984, 47–48.
9. Livy 2.13.6–11; cf. Dionysius of Halicarnassus 5.32.4–35.2, who includes Publicola's daughter Valeria as one of the hostages rescued by Cloelia.
10. Pliny, *Natural History* 34.28ff.; cf. Plutarch, *Women's Virtues* 14, *Life of Publicola* 18.
11. On Valerius Corvus, see Münzer 1891, 25–34 and 49–50 no. 49, again with a full roster of ancient sources; Broughton 1951, 1.170–71n2.
12. Livy 7.32.15; Pliny, *Natural History* 7.157.
13. Livy 7.26.1–10; Dionysius of Halicarnassus 15.1; Claudius Quadrigarius fr. 12 Peter; Valerius Maximus 3.2.6, 6.15.5; Gellius, *Attic Nights* 9.11; Florus 1.8; Appian, *Gallic Wars* 10; and see further Münzer 1891, 49; Broughton 1951, 1.129.
14. Livy 7.39–41, 10.3.3, 10.5.14; see further Münzer 1891, 18–25; Broughton 1951, 1.133–34, 169–70.
15. Livy (9.41.1) reports four praetorships for Corvus, but the dates of the second and third are not recorded: see Broughton 1951, 1.130, 164.
16. Festus 458L; cf. Livy 27.10.7; Velleius 1.14.4.
17. See the entries in Broughton 1951, vol. 1, for the relevant years; for the triumphs, see Livy 7.27.6–9, 8.16.4–11, 10.3–5.
18. On Corvus' son, M. Valerius M.f. M.n. Maximus, see Münzer 1891, 50 no. 50.
19. Gellius, *Attic Nights* 9.11.1–10; cf. Livy 7.26.1–12.
20. On Valerius Messalla, see Münzer 1891, 50–51 no. 51. For the variation in praenomen, M. (Marcus) vs M'. (Manius), see Broughton 1951, 1.203–4 and esp. 204n1, with further bibliography.
21. Polybius 1.16–17; Livy, *Periochae* 16; Diodorus 23.4; Florus 1.18.6; on the triumph, see Piso fr. 29 Peter; Varro *apud* Pliny, *Natural History* 7.214; Cicero, *To Friends* 14.2.2, *Against Vatinius* 21; Pliny, *Natural History* 35.22; and see further Münzer 1891, 50 [no. 51]; Broughton 1951, 1.203–4.
22. Seneca, *On the Brevity of Life* 13.5; Macrobius, *Saturnalia* 1.6.26.
23. Livy, *Periochae* 18.

24. Valerius Maximus 2.9.7; Frontinus, *Strategemata* 4.1.22; cf. Valerius Maximus 6.3.12; Plutarch, *Roman Questions* 14.
25. On Valerius Antias, see Wiseman 1979.
26. Velleius 2.9.6.
27. Münzer 1891.
28. Valerius Maximus 2.9.9. On Messalla Niger, see *Inscriptiones Italicae* 13.3.77; Münzer 1891, 52–3, no. 59; Broughton 1951, 2.178, 215.
29. M. Valerius M.f. M.n. Messalla, *cos.* 161 BCE: see Broughton 1951, 1.443.
30. Cicero, *Brutus* 246; translation adapted from Hendrickson and Hubbell 1962. In his speech *On Behalf of Roscius Amerinus* (149), Cicero attributes his own defense of Roscius to Niger's persuasion.
31. The relationship is attested by Dio 48.24.3–5.
32. On the age of elite Roman women at marriage, see Hopkins 1965; Treggiari 1991, 398–403.
33. Jerome, *Chronicle* on 12 CE (Helm 1956, 170–71).
34. Ovid, *Letters from the Black Sea* 1.7.29–30, on which see Syme 1986, 217–19.
35. Schulz 1886, 6.
36. Hammer 1925, 10n84; Syme 1986, 201; *contra* Jeffreys 1985.
37. Cicero, *To Atticus* 1.2.1.
38. Suetonius, *Life of Augustus* 5.
39. For the traditional Roman educational curriculum, see Quintilian, *Education of the Orator* 1.1–8, esp. 1.4.4 on the earliest training in grammar and poetry and 1.1.12 on the preference for Greek over Latin. On the declaimers of the period, see Seneca rhetor, *Controversiae* and *Suasoriae*; and on declamation, see Kaster 2002; Gunderson 2003; Langlands 2006, 247–80. On Roman oratorical training see Tacitus, *Dialogus* 34–37; Quintilian, *Education of the Orator*.
40. Cicero, *To Atticus* 12.32.2.
41. Horace, *Odes* 3.21.9–10.
42. Cicero, *To Brutus* 1.15.1–3; on the textual problem ("most severe" or "most true"), see Shackleton Bailey 1980, 246 ad 1.12 *<se>verissimo*.
43. Cicero, *To Atticus* 15.17.2.
44. Kenty (2017) argues that Cicero provided Messalla with a model for both oratory and politics.
45. Cicero, *To Brutus* 1.12.1.
46. Cicero, *To Brutus* 1.15.1–2.
47. Appian, *Civil Wars* 4.38.
48. For Messalla's proscription, cf. Appian, *Civil Wars* 4.38, 5.113; Dio 47.11.4, 49.16.1, 50.10.1.
49. Tacitus, *Annals* 4.34.6; cf. Dio 47.24.5.
50. Hammer 1925, 17–18, citing Dio 47.32.1; Livy, *Periochae* 122.
51. Dio 47.33.3–4; Orosius 6.18.13.
52. Velleius 2.71.1.
53. Plutarch, *Life of Brutus* 40–42, 45, 53. For the extant fragments of Messalla's historical works, see Peter 1914, 65–67.
54. Appian, *Civil Wars* 4.38.162, 5.113.471; Velleius 2.71.1.
55. Appian, *Civil Wars* 4.136, 5.113.
56. Plutarch, *Life of Antony* 25.1, 26.1; cf. Dio 48.24.2.
57. For Messalla's defense, and Antony's decision, see Josephus, *Jewish War* 1.12.5, *Jewish Antiquities* 14.13.1.
58. Appian, *Civil Wars* 4.38; Pliny, *Natural History* 33.50.
59. Horace, *Satires* 1.10.27–30.
60. Syme 1986, 202, citing Appian, *Civil Wars* 5.98.404. On Messalla's role in the Sicilian war, see further Hammer 1925, 28–32; Tansey 2007.
61. Appian, *Civil Wars* 5.102.425.
62. Appian, *Civil Wars* 5.102.
63. Appian, *Civil Wars* 5.110–13.
64. Dio 49.16.1. Hammer (1925, 32) cites an inscription apparently dedicated by two of Messalla's freed slaves in honor of his appointment to the augurate.
65. On Messalla's participation in the Pannonian campaign of 35 BCE, cf. *Panegyric of Messalla* 106–10. On the Salassian campaign, see Appian, *Roman History* 17; Dio 49.38.3.
66. Velleius 2.71.1.
67. Syme 1986, 207.

68. Charisius 104.18, 146.34, 129.7.
69. Cf. Strabo 14, p. 648.
70. Syme 1986, 208, adducing the evidence of the elder Pliny (*Natural History* 33.50) about Antony's court luxury in Alexandria; cf. Hammer 1925, 42n241a.
71. Suetonius, *Life of Augustus* 17.1.
72. Dio 50.10.1; Velleius 2.84.1; *CIL* 1² p. 160; cf. Plutarch, *Life of Brutus* 53.2; Tacitus, *Annales* 13.34.1; *Panegyric of Messalla* 122–23.
73. Appian, *Civil Wars* 4.38.162; cf. Velleius 2.85.2.
74. Plutarch, *Life of Brutus* 53.
75. Velleius 2.85.2.
76. Syme 1986, 209, on the basis of Livy, *Periochae* 122; Dio 47.24.5.
77. Dio 51.7.2–7. For discussion of Messalla's movements after Actium, including his expedition against the gladiators, see Hammer 1925, 46–56.
78. Tibullus 1.3.1–2.
79. Tibullus 1.7.13–18: see Hammer 1925, 58–60.
80. Syme 1986, 209–10, citing Appian, *Civil Wars* 4.61.221, and comparing *CIL* X.704: cf. Hammer 1925, 53–56.
81. Tacitus, *Annals* 11.7.
82. Appian, *Civil Wars* 4.38.161.
83. *CIL* 1², p. 50, for the governorship; *CIL* 1², p. 77, for the triumph, and p. 180 for the date.
84. Cairns 1998, 204–5.
85. Tibullus 1.7.57–60: "Nor let him be silent about the memorial of your road, anyone whom Tusculum and gleaming Alba, of ancient worship, detain; for here the hard gravel has been heaped up and laid at your expense and the stone blocks are skillfully fitted together."
86. Suetonius, *Life of Augustus* 30. See Hammer 1925, 65; Lee rev. Maltby 1990, 136, on Tibullus 1.7.57–58; Maltby 2002, 297–99, on Tibullus 1.7.57–62.
87. Pliny, *Natural History* 34.22.
88. Suetonius, *Life of Augustus* 29.4–5; on Messalla's interest in art, see also Pliny, *Natural History* 35.21.
89. Suetonius, *Life of Augustus* 31. On the close association of the Sibyl with Apollo, see Miller 2009, 239–40.
90. On Tibullus 2.5, see Murgatroyd 1994, 163–235; Maltby 2002, 430–64.
91. Tacitus, *Annales* 6.11.4; Jerome, *Chronicle* on 26 BCE (Helm 1956, 164). On the January dating of his tenure of the post, see Syme 1986, 212.
92. Hammer 1925, 84.
93. Dio 53.27.5. Messalla also seems to have acquired Lucullus' extensive gardens in Rome at some point: see *PIR*¹ V 90; cf. the contrast Tibullus articulates in his elegy 1.1.41–58 between his patron's wealth and his own much more straightened resources.
94. Frontinus, *On Aqueducts* 99.
95. Augustus, *Res Gestae* 35.
96. Suetonius, *Life of Augustus* 58.1.
97. Suetonius, *Life of Augustus* 58.2.
98. Kenty 2017, 468.
99. Velleius 2.36.2.
100. On the poem, see Momigliano 1950; Davies 1973, 28–29; Syme 1986, 200 and 203; and see further Ch. 5.
101. *Panegyric of Messalla* 45–47.
102. Suetonius, *Life of Tiberius* 70.1.
103. Ovid, *Letters from the Black Sea* 2.2.49–51, 2.3.75; cf. Ovid, *Tristia* 4.4.3–4, 27–32.
104. Ovid, *Tristia* 4.4.33; *Letters from the Black Sea* 1.7.27, 2.3.77–78.
105. Seneca rhetor, *Controversiae* 2.4.8, 10; 3 *pr.* 14; *Suasoriae* 1.7; 2.17, 20; 3.6; 6.27.
106. Seneca rhetor, *Controversiae* 2.4.8.
107. Seneca rhetor, *Controversiae* 2.4.8.
108. Tacitus, *Dialogus* 12.6, 17.1, 17.6, 18.2, 20.1, 21.9; Quintilian, *Education of the Orator* 10.1.22, 24.
109. Quintilian, *Education of the Orator* 10.5.4.
110. Quintilian, *Education of the Orator* 1.7.35.
111. Quintilian, *Education of the Orator* 1.7.23; cf. 1.5.15, 61; 1.6.42. For Messalla's grammatical fragments, see Funaioli 1907, 503–7.

112. Quintilian uses the Latin word *dignitas*, "dignity," *Education of the Orator* 12.10.11.
113. Quintilian, *Education of the Orator* 10.1.113; my translation is indebted to that of Kenty 2017, 458. Cf. Tacitus, *Dialogus* 21.9.
114. Quintilian, *Education of the Orator* 4.1.8; Tacitus, *Dialogus* 20.1. On the topos, see Jeffreys 1987; again, I have borrowed my phrasing ("self-effacing") from Kenty 2017, 465.
115. Jeffreys 1987; Kenty 2017. Cf. Messalla's model Cicero, who abandoned his original style of speaking after his health was affected (*Brutus* 91.313–14).
116. Pliny, *Natural History* 7.90. The identification of the Valerius Messalla mocked by Varro is contested: see Jeffreys 1987, 197–98n18, with full discussion and bibliography. He notes that "an aged but vigorous Varro may have found it amusing to twit a rising young orator with lack of stamina" (198n18).
117. [Vergil] *Catalepton* 9.44; cf. Tibullus 1.7.55–56.
118. Syme 1986, 230; cf. Hammer 1925, 92.
119. Dio 55.29.1; Velleius 2.112.2.
120. Dio 55.30.2.
121. Velleius 2.102.2, which omits the defeat.
122. Ovid, *Tristia* 4.1, *Letters from the Black Sea* 1.7, 2.2.
123. Tacitus, *Annals* 1.7.1, 8.6; 3.18.3–5, 33–35.
124. Hammer 1925, 94; cf. Syme 1986, 234.
125. Tacitus, *Annals* 13.34.1.
126. Syme 1986, 230–32; cf. Hammer 1925, 91.
127. Certainty about his identity eludes us: see Syme 1986, 231–32; *contra* Hammer 1925, 96. For the Roman custom of a maternal uncle adopting a sister's son, cf. the younger Servius' cousin D. Junius Brutus, adopted by his maternal uncle Postumius Albinus (Ch. 2n83).
128. For the adoption, see scholia on Persius, *Satire* 2.72; Ovid, *Letters from the Black Sea* 3.2.107–8. For the cognomen, see Velleius 2.112.2.
129. Syme 1986, 236, citing Degrassi in *Epigraphica* 8 (1946), 38.
130. Tacitus, *Annals* 6.5, reports Cotta's use of the diminutive "Tiberiolus."
131. Tacitus, *Annals* 6.6.
132. *IGR* IV.1508 (Sardis); *Forsch. in Ephesos* III.112, no. 22. On the date, see Syme 1986, 237–38.
133. Ovid, *Tristia* 4.5, 9; *Letters from the Black Sea* 1.5, 9; 2.3, 8; 3.2, 5, 8.
134. Ovid, *Letters from the Black Sea* 2.3.83–91; *Tristia* 4.5.
135. Ovid, *Letters from the Black Sea* 1.5.57–58, 3.5.37–39.
136. Ovid, *Letters from the Black Sea* 4.16.41–44.
137. Pliny, *Natural History* 14–15.
138. Juvenal, *Satires* 7.95 and 5.109 respectively.
139. *CIL* 14.2298.
140. Syme 1986, Table IXnn3, 5.
141. Pliny, *Natural History* 35.21. The younger Pedius is named by Horace—along with Messalla and his stepbrother Gellius Publicola—in *Satires* 1.10.28.
142. Suetonius, *Life of Claudius* 13.2.
143. Syme 1986, 240; see *PIR*[1] S 625; Syme 1986, Table IX with n9.

Chapter 4

1. Fundamental are Hallett 1984; Treggiari 1991; Hemelrijk 1999; Caldwell 2015.
2. Rawson 2003, 95–113.
3. Corbier 2001, 54; Rawson 2003, 105 and 121.
4. On the *dies lustricus*, see Festus 107–8 Lindsay; Macrobius, *Saturnalia* 1.16.36; and see further Corbier 2001, 55; Rawson 2003, 110–12.
5. Corbier 2001, 55.
6. Rawson 2003, 122–33.
7. Dixon 1988, 121.
8. On the importance of family traditions in the education of both sons and daughters, see Treggiari 2003 and 2019, 18–22 and 60–61.
9. Treggiari 2019, 61.
10. Treggiari 2019, 61 with nn94–95; cf. Hemelrijk 1999, 39–50.
11. Val. Max. 6.7.3; App. *BC* 4.39.
12. Hemelrijk 1999, 54 with 256n164.

13. Cf. Hemelrijk 1999, 22–23, on the education of Augustus' daughter Julia.
14. Cicero, *To Atticus* 12.33.
15. Hemelrijk 1999, 22 and 231n21.
16. Hemelrijk 1999, 55 and 257n169.
17. Suetonius, *Grammarians* 16. On Attica's marriage, see Nepos, *Life of Atticus* 12.1–2.
18. Hemelrijk 1999, 238n70; cf. Valerius Maximus 6.1.3.
19. Hemelrijk 1999, 64–71.
20. Cited in Stevenson 2005, 44n71. The *OLD*, s.v. *lectrix*, cites only two epigraphic witnesses to the lexeme, to which *l'Année epigraphique* 1928, 73 may be added.
21. Carcopino 1929. His proposal was revived by Stevenson (2005, 43) and is accepted by Hallett (2009c, 188n25; 2010b, 368); Dickison and Hallett 2014, 123; and Hauser 2016, 156–67.
22. On the dress of elite Roman girls, see Olson 2008a, 15–20; Olson 2008b.
23. Harlow 2017, 44.
24. Olson (2008a, 16) observes that "no sculptural representation of *lunulae* exist" and compares "mummy portraits from ancient Egypt [which] often display a crescent-shaped pendant": for an image, see Olson 2008a, 16, Fig. 1.2.
25. Olson 2008b.
26. Dolansky 2017 (quotation at 117) provides extensive bibliography on Roman children's games and toys.
27. Dolansky 2017, 119.
28. Rawson 2003, 128–29, with 129n38.
29. Naples Archaeological Museum inv. 9562; © Erich Lessing/Art Resource, NY.
30. Louvre Museum, Louvre Ma99. © RMN-Grand Palais/Art Resource, NY. According to the fourth-century CE physician and medical writer Oribasius (*Coll. Med. lib. inc.* 18.11–15), the first-century CE physician Rufus of Ephesus recommended ball-playing in his *Regimen for Girls* (a reference I owe to Dolansky 2017, 134n16).
31. J. Paul Getty Museum, Malibu CA, inv. No. 73.AA.II, on which see Bradley 1998, 539; and Dolansky 2012, 258n6.
32. The few literary sources are cited in Dolansky 2012, 257–58n5; the rich material evidence is discussed in Dolansky 2012 and 2017, both with further bibliography.
33. Dolansky 2012, 268, with further bibliography.
34. Cited by Dolansky 2012, 268.
35. Dolansky 2017, 269.
36. Dolansky 2017, 268.
37. Persius 2.70, with the scholiast ad loc.
38. Dolansky 2017, 270.
39. Olson 2008a, 33–36.
40. Pliny, *Natural History* 9.135–41.
41. See Maltby 2021, 453 on 3.8.17–18, for the theme of Arab riches in the poetry of Sulpicia's contemporaries, with further bibliography.
42. On pearls in ancient Rome, see Pliny, *Natural History* 9.54–60.
43. On hairdressers and dressers in the household of Augustus' wife Livia, see Treggiari 1975, 52–53, and Treggiari 1976, 78–80; on imperial household slaves more broadly, see Boulvert 1970.
44. Cf. Treggiari 1975 on Livia's townhouse staff.
45. Gardner 1986, 38; Treggiari 1991, 39–43; Piro 2013.
46. Ancient Roman physicians placed the onset of menarche at thirteen years of age and older: see Amundsen and Diers 1969; Treggiari 1991, 39–41.
47. *Digest* 12.4.8, Ner. citing Sulpicius. On marriage of underage girls, see Frier 2015; Treggiari 2016, 639–40. On dowry, Treggiari 1991, 323–64, is fundamental.
48. Treggiari 1991, 125–60.
49. Treggiari 1991, 85–124.
50. Treggiari 1991, 105–7.
51. Treggiari 1991, 135.
52. Treggiari 1991, 138–60.
53. Fantham 2006, 29–31, 55–67, 79–91.
54. Treggiari 1991, 159.
55. We may note, on the one hand, Ovid's warning that respectable women should not read his *Art of Love* (1.31–4), and on the other, his repeated expressions of blame for his relegation in 8 CE on that poem in his exile poetry (e.g., *Tristia* 1.1.111–16; 2.7–8).

56. My translation is informed by that of Goold 1990, 289.
57. My translation is informed by Treggiari 1991, 160.
58. Treggiari 1991, 160.
59. On erotic tenderness in the frescoes from *cubicula* B and D of the Villa della Farnesina, dated to the decade between 30 and 20 BCE (and so roughly contemporary with the elegiac poetry of Propertius, Tibullus, Ovid, and Sulpicia), see Valladares 2021, 31–65.
60. Treggiari 1991, 275–98; McGinn 1998; Skinner 2005; Langlands 2006.
61. Treggiari 1991, 302–3.
62. On the *Matronalia*, see Gagé 1963; Scullard 1981, 87; Dolansky 2011b; on Roman women's worship of Juno, see Hänninen 2000; on women's religious rites more broadly, see Schultz 2006.
63. For the etymology, see Varro, *Latin Language* 5.69; Isidore, *Etymologies* 8.11.57.
64. On the association of a god's "festival day" with the foundation date of their temple, see Rüpke 2012, 28–29. For the importance of birthdays in the Sulpicia cycle see below; cf. Chs. 6, 7.
65. Pseudo-Acro on Horace, *Odes* 3.8.1.
66. Juvenal, *Satire* 9.53. Scullard 1981, 87; cf. Rüpke 2012, 49. Gagé (1963, 66–80) provides a summary of the festival's proceedings; cf. Dolansky 2011. Ancient authors such as Martial (5.84), Suetonius (*Life of Vespasian* 19.1), and Macrobius (*Saturnalia* 1.12.7) portray the festival as a "women's Saturnalia," because of the role reversals.
67. For the pun on Sulpicia's filiation (*Serui filia Sulpicia*, 3.16.4), see Ch. 6. On the "slavery of love" (*seruitium amoris*), see Copley 1947; McCarthy 1998; Fulkerson 2013.
68. For Greek names among the servile classes in this period, see Solin 1996 and 2003².
69. Apuleius, *Apology* 10. Wiseman (1969, 50–52) traces the notice Apuleius supplies back through the imperial biographer Suetonius' work "On Famous Prostitutes" to a treatise "On the Life and Accomplishments of Famous Men" by Hyginus, the second director of Augustus' Palatine Library, and deems the information inherently plausible. The little that we can verify independently (on the basis of Catullus, poem 79, and Ovid, *Tristia* 2.427–38, quoted in Ch. 5) has been taken to confirm the veracity of his report.
70. Pseudo-Acro on Horace, *Satires* 1.2.64.
71. Hubbard (2004/5, 183n21) notes that "the earliest printed editions actually printed the name *Cerinthe* rather than *Cornute* in [Tibullus, elegy] 2.2.9, based on the reading *cherinthe* in some later manuscripts," and Némethy (1905, 328–29) suggested that this reading derived from an interlinear gloss, itself possibly of ancient origin. Tibullus' nineteenth-century editors accepted the name in their editions, in their notes on Tibullus, elegy 2.2.9; see, e.g., Voss 1811; Heyne 1975; Gruppe 1838.1.27–28.
72. Hubbard (2004/5, 183n21) notes the metrical difference between Greek *kéras*, scanned with short ĕ, and the name of Sulpicia's beloved, *Cêrinthus*, scanned with a long ē, but dismisses it (*contra* Roessel 1990, 244–45) on the grounds that "a poet will be content with even an approximate word-play." See O'Hara 1996, 42–50, on the theoretical underpinnings of Roman etymological practice, including bilingual puns and "the fluidity with which [Varro] suggests that words with different vowel sounds are related etymologically" (50). Ahl 1985 demonstrates the ubiquity of contra-metrical wordplay in the poetry of Sulpicia's contemporary Ovid.
73. Hubbard 2004/5, 183–84.
74. Syme 1986, 46–47; *PIR*² C34. My discussion of M. Caecilius Cornutus is indebted to Scheid 1975, 34–40; Syme 1986, 46–47; Cairns 1998, 227–31.
75. *RE* s.v. Caecilius *no*. 44, with Suppl. I.
76. Scheid 1975, 36.
77. Cairns 1998, 229. The inscriptions are discussed by Scheid (1975, 39, with n1).
78. Syme (1986, 47n98) attributes the identification to C. Cichorius (*Römische Studien* [1922], 261ff.), bolstered by Scheid 1975, 37 with nn3 and 5.
79. Scheid 1975, 37; I owe the reference to Cairns 1998, 229.
80. Cairns 1998, 229; cf. Chs. 3, 5.
81. *CIL* VI 32338. On the inscription, which furnishes the earliest extant evidence for the Arval Brethren (established by Octavian in 29 BCE), see Scheid 1975, 13–40; he offers a tentative biography of Cornutus at 34–40.
82. Cairns (1998, 228) suggests that "the intertwining of the two men in Tibullus Book 2 is… another signal of Messalla's wish to promote Cornutus publicly."
83. Cairns 1998, 229–30; see Hubbard 2004/5 for further bibliography.
84. This proposal is fully worked out in Cairns 1998, which concludes with the suggestion that Messalla recited the poem himself at the wedding. Given the parallel of Messalla's triumph of

27 BCE, held on his birthday (September 25), celebrated in a *genethliakon* with embedded triumph-song in Tibullus, elegy 1.7, I accept this interpretation of Tibullus, elegy 2.2.

85. Following Scheid (1975), 38–39 and 38n4.
86. Murgatroyd 1994, xvi–xvii; Cairns 1998, 229; Maltby 2002, 385–86.
87. Smith 1913, 86–87; Fulkerson 2017, 31–32.
88. Cf. Fulkerson 2017, 31.
89. The Lygdamus cycle spans [Tibullus], 3.1–6, with a wife (*coniunx*) mentioned at elegies 3.1.26–7; 3.2.4, 30; 3.3.32; cf. 3.2.13–14; 3.4.60.
90. Fabre-Serris 2009 provides an intertextual reading of 3.9 in Ovidian reception, interpreting the speaker's role in [Tib.] 3.9 in relation to the mythic models of Venus in *Metamorphoses* 10 and Phaedra in *Heroides* 4: see Ch. 7.
91. Catullus, poem 68.
92. Treggiari 1991, 122. I owe my translation "a suitable match" (for *digna condicio*) to Treggiari 1991, 84. Forms of the adjective *dignus, digna* pervade the Sulpicia cycle: 3.8.15, 24; 3.12.10; 3.13.10: see *infra*, Chs. 6, 7.
93. For the *Genius* as a birth-spirit, see Schultz 2006, 124; cf. Cairns 1998; Fulkerson 2017, 257.
94. For the literary and social resonances of the line, see Ch. 6.
95. For the sentiment in a marital context, cf. Ovid, *Tristia* 1.2.37, "dutiful spouse" (*pia coniunx*) of his wife. Riess 2012, 493, includes the adjective *pia* among the seven adjectives most frequently employed to characterize women in Roman funerary inscriptions.
96. Cf. Propertius, elegy 3.8.9; Vergil, *Aeneid* 8.390; Horace, *Odes* 4.9.11; Ovid, *Art of Love* 1.237.
97. Literary references to the togate prostitute are frequent in this period: cf. Cicero, *Philippics* 2.44; Horace, *Satires* 1.2.63, 82; Martial, *Epigrams* 6.64.4; see Olson 2002, 393–95; McGinn 2004, 157. No visual depiction of a togate prostitute survives; indeed, Strong (2016, 231n26) notes that the sole surviving description of a statue portrait of a togate woman is that of Cloelia (Livy 2.13; cf. Pliny, *Natural History* 34.11).
98. Cf. especially Catullus, poem 68, and Propertius, elegy 2.7; see further James 2003 on the genre's *dramatis personae*.
99. Fatucchi 1976.
100. For luxury villas on the Bay of Naples, see D'Arms 1970; for their scarcity in Tuscany in this period, see Fatucchi 1976.
101. The younger Seneca confirms the gender of the (male) *Genius* and (female) *Juno* (*Epistles* 110.1): see Schultz 2006, 124–25.
102. Pliny, *Natural History* 18.107; see Schultz 2006, 194n45.
103. On the god Vertumnus in Roman religion, see Bettini 2015.
104. For Vertumnus' Etruscan provenance, cf. Pliny, *Natural History* 34.34. On Vertumnus, see further Hutchinson 2006, 86–99 ad Prop. 4.2.
105. Propertius, elegy 4.2.21–22; Ovid, *Metamorphoses* 14.684–85: see Tränkle 1990, 263–64 on 3.8.13–14.
106. Fulkerson 2017, 231–32; Maltby 2021, 449–50.
107. For Apollo as the patron of poetry in the Augustan period, see further Miller 2009, esp. 298–331.
108. Cf. *ueneranda* (3.8.10), with Hinds 1987, 33–34; cf. Fulkerson 2017, 230 ad loc.
109. In these specialized roles the Muses reprise their appearances in the poetry of Lucretius (*On the Nature of the Universe* 4.1) and Vergil (*Bucolics* 3.85), where they are invoked as Pierides, a geographical epithet popularized by the archaic Greek poets Hesiod (*Shield of Herakles* 206) and Pindar (*Olympian* 10[11].96; *Pythian* 1.14). Likewise, the Latin lyric poets apply the title Phoebus to Apollo in his role as patron of the arts (Horace, *Odes* 4.6.29; Statius, *Silvae* 4.6.1).
110. For the popularity of the title in this period, cf. Vergil, *Bucolics* 3.59; Horace, *Secular Hymn* 62; Propertius, elegy 3.10.1; Ovid, *Metamorphoses* 15.482.

Chapter 5

1. Horace, *Satires* 1.10.84–90; on the date of Horace's first collection of *Satires*, see Gowers 2012, 1.
2. Pollio is the brother of the Asinius Marrucinus addressed by Catullus in poem 12, excoriated for stealing a napkin. Vergil addressed *Bucolics* 3, 4, and 8 to Pollio, and Horace his *Ode* 2.1. Pollio governed Cisalpine Gaul for Mark Antony in 43–42 BCE, held the consulship in 40, and celebrated a triumph for his victories in Dalmatia in 39: see André 1949; Bosworth 1972; Nisbet and Hubbard 1978, 7–11 on *C.* 2.1.

3. On the extant fragments, see Courtney 1993, 254–56; Hollis 2007, 215–18; Cairns 2008. Pollio also seems to have been instrumental in establishing recitation at Rome: see Dalzell 1955.

4. Hammer 1925, 87–90; Kenty 2017.

5. The panegyric is included in the Tibullan appendix ([Tibullus] 3.7). The elegist Tibullus himself addresses Messalla in his elegies 1.1, 1.3, and 1.7, and names him in 1.5, 2.1, and 2.5. Ovid recalls Messalla's encouragement of his early literary endeavors in *Letters from the Black Sea* 1.7.27–30, 2.2.5, 97, and 2.3.73–76.

6. Catullus 74, 88, 89, 90, 91, and 116. On the younger Gellius Publicola (*cos.* 36 BCE), see Wiseman 1979, 119–29; Wiseman's *stemma Gelliorum* (1979, 128) also shows the relationships among Messalla Corvinus (*cos.* 31), his sister Valeria (our Sulpicia's mother), and her husband Ser. Sulpicius Rufus (son of the jurist).

7. L. Calpurnius Bibulus was the son of Caesar's colleague in the consulship of 59 BCE, and stepson of the tyrannicide (M. Junius) Brutus, with whom he fought at Philippi in 42. Upon the republicans' defeat he transferred his fealty to Antony, and at his death in 32 was serving as governor of Syria. C. Furnius, like Bibulus a partisan of Mark Antony, served as a tribune of the plebs in 50 and proconsul of Asia in 36/35. After the battle of Actium in 31, he was saved by his son's intercession and eventually adlected to the office of the consulship in 29, twelve years before his son held the office himself. On Furnius' tenure of the proconsulship of Asia in 36/35 BCE, see Appian, *BC* 5.137.567; Dio 49.17.5. For his son's intercession after the battle of Actium in 32, see Seneca, *On Benefits* 2.25.1; Dio 52.42.4.

8. Plutarch, *Life of Brutus* 13.3, 23.6.

9. Plutarch, *Life of Antony* 58. A Horatian commentator preserves the information that the elder Furnius was a historian of great clarity (Comm. Cruq ad Hor. *Serm.* 1.10.86). Jerome (*Chronicle* on 41 BCE) reports that his son also achieved fame as an orator (Helm 1956, 159).

10. Quintilian, *Education of the Orator* 10.5.4.

11. Quintilian, *Education of the Orator* 10.7.30.

12. Ovid, *Tristia* 2.427–42. On the passage, see Hollis 2007, 161, whose enumeration I have followed (2.427–32, 435–6, 433–4, 437–42); Ingleheart 2010 ad loc.; *contra* Lewis 2013.

13. Catullus addresses his friend, the orator and poet C. Licinius Calvus, in poems 14, 50, and 96, and praises his political oratory in poem 53. His speeches against Vatinius were still known, over a century later, to both Quintilian (*Education of the Orator* 10.1.115) and Tacitus (*Dialogus* 21.2); cf. Seneca rhetor, *Controversiae* 7.4.6. On Calvus' life see Castorina 1946; on his poetry, see Courtney 1993, 201–11; Nosarti 1999, 195–201; Hollis 2007, 49–85.

14. Catullus mentions the poet and politician C. Helvius Cinna (*tr. pl.* 44 BCE) in poems 10, 95, 113; cf. Quintilian, *Education of the Orator* 10.4.4; *contra* Gellius, *Attic Nights* 19.9.7. See further Wiseman 1979; Dahlmann 1977; Watson 1982; Courtney 1993, 212–24; Hollis 2007, 11–48.

15. Cornificius (*quaestor pro praetore* 48 BCE, elected augur 47, *pr.* 45) is the addressee of Catullus, poem 38. On Cornificius, see Sumner 1971; Wiseman 1976; Rawson 1978; Courtney 1993, 225–27; Hollis 2007, 149–54; and see below for his relationship to the poet Cornificia.

16. See Catullus, poems 10.9–13, 28.6–13.

17. Lucretius, *On the Nature of the Universe* 1.23–7. On Memmius (*tr. pl.* 66, *pr.* 58) and his poetry, see Courtney 1993, 233; Hollis 2007, 90–92.

18. On the grammarian and poet Valerius Cato (cf. Catullus, poem 56), see Robinson 1923; Neudling 1955; Courtney, 1993, 189–91; Hollis 2007, 429.

19. On Ticida (killed while serving in Caesar's army in 46 BCE as reported in his *African War* 44.1–46.3), see Courtney 1993, 228–29; Hollis 2007, 158–63.

20. On P. Terentius Varro Atacinus, see Courtney 1993, 235–53; Hollis 2007, 165–214.

21. On Hortensius (addressee of Catullus' poem 65) and Servius as the sons of homonymous consular fathers, see Ingleheart 2010, 343–44 on Ovid, *Tristia*. 2.441–42. It is worth noting that the praenomen Servius was used exclusively by the Sulpicii and is therefore often the name under which politicians and writers were recorded in Roman literary and documentary texts. Thus, the jurist Servius Sulpicius Rufus is called Servius in the *Digest*: see Frier 1985, 153.

22. So also Hollis 2007, 427–28; Ingleheart 2010, 343–44 on *Tristia* 2.441.

23. Pliny, *Epistles* 5.3.4–15. Ingleheart 2010, 343–44; Hollis 2007, 427; *contra* Syme 1981.

24. Among them, the speech of 40 BCE on behalf of Herod (Josephus, *Jewish Antiquities* 14.384, *Jewish War* 1.284); the prosecution *Against Aufidia* in the 30s, still extant in Quintilian's day (*Education of the Orator* 10.1.22); the *On Behalf of Pythodoros* mentioned by Seneca rhetor (*Controversiae* 2.4.8); and a speech censuring the inclusion of a Valerius Laevinus among the

ancestor portraits of the Valerii Messallae (Pliny, *Natural History* 35.8). For Messalla's rhetorical fragments, see Malcovati 1955, 529–34.

25. Pliny, *Epistles* 5.3.5.
26. *Catalepton* 9.13–22.
27. Kayachev 2016, 182–86; *contra* Peirano 2012, 120–32.
28. Here I argue against Peirano (2012, 117–72), who views them as *pseudepigrapha*, fictional panegyrics written years later to fill in gaps in the biographies of the long dead poets Vergil and Tibullus. Whether or not the poems are authentic or fictional, however, matters little to my argument. In any case, the poems confirm the verifiable biographical facts of Messalla's cultivation of poets and poetry during his lifetime.
29. Kayachev 2016, 186.
30. Viewed as authentic by Momigliano 1950; Davies 1973, 28–29; Syme 1986, 203; *contra* Peirano 2012, 132–48.
31. Cairns 1998, 204–5; cf. Putnam 1973, 118–19; Murgatroyd 1980, 208–13; Lee rev. Maltby 1990, 133.
32. Syme 1986, 203.
33. Tibullus, elegy 1.3.1–2.
34. Davies 1973, 29–31, comparing M. Fulvius Nobilior's inclusion of Ennius on his military mission to Ambracia in 189 and the poet's subsequent composition of a togate drama, *Ambracia*.
35. Cf., e.g., Caesar's inclusion of Cicero's brother Quintus on his staff in Gaul in the 50s BCE and receipt of laudatory verses about his exploits (Cicero, *To brother Quintus* 2.16.4); Memmius' inclusion of Catullus and Cinna on his staff in Bithynia in 57/56 BCE, though he received nothing but abuse for it (Catullus, poems 10, 28); and the presumed invitation to join his gubernatorial staff in Asia by L. Volcatius Tullus (*cos.* 33 BCE) of the elegist Propertius, who was on friendly terms with his nephew (Propertius, elegies 1.6, 14, 22; 3.22).
36. *Panegyric of Messalla* 179–80. On Valgius (*cos. suff.* 12 BCE), see Nisbet and Hubbard 1978, 134–51; Courtney 1993, 287–90; Hollis 2007, 287–99. For the possibility that the text of Tibullus' elegy 1.10.11–12 conceals an address to Valgius, see Maltby 2002, 344–45.
37. Horace, *Satires* 1.10.82, 85–86.
38. Funaioli 1907, 482–85.
39. Pliny, *Natural History* 25.4.
40. Quintilian, *Education of the Orator* 3.1.18.
41. Seneca, *Epistles* 51.1.
42. Nisbet and Hubbard 1978, 135; *contra* Courtney 1993, 290, who assumes Valgius' work on Aetna was in prose. It is telling that Seneca here associates Messalla and Valgius through their shared use of the adjective *unicum* to describe Aetna (*Epistles* 51.1).
43. On Cornelius Severus' Sicilian war poem, see Quintilian, *Education of the Orator* 10.1.89; on his set piece about Aetna, see Seneca, *Epistles* 79.5; and on Cornelius Severus' poetry more generally, see Courtney 1993, 320–28; Hollis 2007, 338–67. The elder Seneca associates Cornelius Severus with another epic poet, Sextilius Ena, who is recorded as reciting our only extant line of his verse at the house of Messalla (Seneca rhetor, *Suasoriae* 6.27).
44. See frr. 169, 165, 166–68, and 164 Hollis, respectively.
45. For the date, see Nisbet and Hubbard 1978, 138.
46. Vergil, *Bucolics* 7.21–23, 26–28.
47. Valgius fr. 166 Hollis.
48. Hollis 2007, 294.
49. Rostagni 1961, on the basis of *Catalepton* 9.14; accepted by Nisbet 1995, 401–2; Hollis 2007, 294, who compares L. Varius Rufus, writing under the pseudonym Lynceus (so Boucher 1958; accepted by Cairns 2006, 295–319, and Hollis 2007, 281), and Tuscus, writing as Demophoon (Hollis 2007, 428), both in this period; Kayachev 2020, 88–89.
50. Tacitus, *Dialogus* 18.2.
51. The *Appendix Tibulliana* preserves a short *Life*, presumably derived from that of Suetonius in his *On Poets*; and an epigram by Domitius Marsus lamenting Tibullus' death in 19 BCE, the same year as Vergil's (Domitius Marsus, fr. 180 Hollis). On Domitius Marsus, see Courtney 1993, 300–5; Hollis 2007, 300–313. On the date of Tibullus' death, see McGann 1970.
52. Tibullus, elegies 1.1.53; 1.3.1, 56; 1.5.31; 2.1.31, 33; 2.5.119.
53. On Tibullus, see Cairns 1979; Murgatroyd 1980 and 1994; Maltby 2002; Miller 2002, 121–59; further bibliography in Miller 2017.

54. On the *Panegyricus of Messalla*, see Schoonhaven 1983; Tränkle 1990, 172–254; De Luca 2009; Maltby 2021, 337–436.

55. The *Appendix Tibulliana* opens with six poems by a poet who signs himself "Lygdamus," on which see Navarro Antolín 1996.

56. Ovid, *Epistles from the Black Sea* 1.7.28.

57. Ovid, *Epistles from the Black Sea* 2.3.75–78.

58. Ovid, *Tristia* 4.10.15–16; 4.10.57–58.

59. Ovid, *Epistles from the Black Sea* 1.7.23–24; cf. Ovid, *Tristia* 4.4.33.

60. Ovid, *Epistles from the Black Sea* 2.3.69–72.

61. On the Latin love poets from Catullus to Ovid, see Miller 2002; Hollis 2007; McCoskey and Torlone 2013.

62. Vergil, *Bucolics* 6, 10.

63. On elegy and epigram, see Gutzwiller 1998, 4–6; Keith 2011, with further bibliography.

64. On Meleager and his *Garland*, see Gutzwiller 1998, 276–322.

65. Gutzwiller 1998, 4–6.

66. Lausberg 1982, 37–44; Höschele n.d.; cf. Sider 2004. Gow and Page 1965, 2.84 on Antipater of Sidon 64 (*Palatine Anthology* 6.219), bracingly observe that "[t]his long and verbose poem…can hardly be called an epigram."

67. Gow and Page 1968 1.xxxviin2.

68. Ovid, *Art of Love* 3.333–34, 535–38; *Cures for Love* 763–68; *Tr.* 5.1.15–18; cf. *Amores* 1.15.27–30.

69. Quintilian, *Education of the Orator* 10.1.93; cf. Martial, *Epigrams* 8.73.5–7.

70. Cf., e.g., Ovid, *Tristia* 2.427–42, quoted above.

71. Shorter poems (i.e., epigrams): Gallus frr. 144–45 Hollis; Propertius, elegies 1.21–22, 2.11; cf. Catullus, poems 69–116. Longer poems (i.e., elegies): Propertius, elegies 1.1–20, 2.1–10, 12–34; cf. Catullus, poems 65–68.

72. Propertius, elegy 2.34.85–94. Ovid includes Varro of Atax in his roster of earlier Roman love poets at *Tristia* 2.439: see Ingleheart 2010, 342–43.

73. *Palatine Anthology* 4.1.1–12; the translation from Paton rev. Tueller 2014, 175.

74. *Palatine Anthology* 9.66.1–2, 9.506, 9.571.7–8. Sappho is frequently counted among the Muses in Greek epigram: cf. *Palatine Anthology* 7.14 (Antipater of Sidon) and see further Hadjimichael 2019; Kivilo 2021.

75. On Sappho's reception in Rome, see Thorsen and Harrison 2019. The earliest extant evidence for interest in Sappho at Rome is found in an adaptation of her fr. 31 by an otherwise unknown Valerius Aedituus (Gellius, *Attic Nights* 19.9.10; cf. Apuleius, *Apology* 9): see Courtney 1993, 70–72; Nisbet in Thorsen and Harrison 2019, 269–70. For Sappho's reception in classical and Hellenistic Greek literature, see Yatromanolakis 2007; Acosta-Hughes 2010; De Vos 2014; Panagiotopoulou 2022.

76. Catullus, poem 1.1 reworks *Palatine Anthology* 4.1.1. Propertius likewise opens his first book of elegies with an allusion to an epigram of Meleager (Propertius, elegy 1.1–4 ~ *Palatine Anthology* 12.101), on which see Keith 2008b, 45–47. Tibullus, Horace, and Ovid also allude to his epigrams, along with others included in the *Garland*, throughout their erotic poetry. For Tibullus' interest in epigram, see Maltby 2002, 519, Index rerum s.v. "epigram, Greek," and 522, Index locorum notabiliorum s.v. "*Anthologia Palatina*"; for Horace's allusions to epigrams in the *Odes*, see Nisbet and Hubbard 1970, 437, Index rerum s.v. "epigrams."

77. Catullus, poem 51 is a translation/adaptation of Sappho fr. 31.

78. Catullus, poems 11 and 51; cf. Catullus, poem 35.16. On Catullus' reception of Sappho, see Greene 2007; Thorsen and Harrison 2019, 77–136.

79. Homage: Horace, *Odes* 2.13.23–25, 4.9.10–12; *Epistles* 1.19.28. Sapphic stanzas: Horace, *Odes* 1.2, 10, 12, 20, 22, 25, 30, 32, 38; 2.2, 4, 6, 8, 10, 16; 3.8, 11, 14, 18, 20, 22, 27; 4.2, 6, 11. On Sappho's reception in Horace, see also Thorsen and Harrison 2019, 151–84.

80. On Sappho, see Greene 1996a, 1996b, 2005; Finglass and Kelly 2021. On the reception of Sappho in Latin elegy, see Thorsen and Harrison 2019, 185–264.

81. Propertius, elegy 2.3.19; Ovid, *Art of Love* 3.331, *Cures for Love* 761; Tibullus, elegy 1.8.17 adapts Sappho fr. 31.14.

82. Cf. Ovid, *Amores* 2.18.26, 34.

83. On Pompey's Portico, see Gleason 1994; Kuttner 1999; Nisbet in Thorsen and Harrison 2019, 271–74.

84. Kuttner 1999, 348–49. For Silanion's portrait of Sappho, cf. Cicero, *Verrines* 4.57 and see further Rosenmeyer 2007.
85. Catullus, poem 55.6, discussed by Kuttner (1999, 350–51).
86. Augustus, *Res Gestae* 20.
87. Propertius, elegies 2.32, 4.8.75; Ovid, *Art of Love* 1.67, 3.387; Martial, *Epigrams* 2.14, 3.58, 5.10. See further Wiseman 1980; Kuttner 1999, 354–59 and 368–71.
88. Tatian, *Against the Greeks* 33.2–3. Scholars have established that the works of art which Tatian mentions in this passage were originally displayed in the Portico of Pompey: see Kuttner 1999; Dillon 2006, 40–41, 184n28, and 2010, 48; Rosenmeyer 2007, 279; Thorsen 2012.
89. Cicero, *Verrines* 2.4.57.127.
90. On female poets in ancient Greece, see Snyder 1989; Rayor 1991; Balmer 1996; Plant 2004; Greene 2005; Klinck 2008; Natoli, Pitts, and Hallett 2022.
91. On Antipater, see Nisbet in Thorsen and Harrison 2019, 271. On his patron, Piso Pontifex, see Syme 1986, 329–67.
92. GP 19 (= *Palatine Anthology* 9.26); the translation is that of Bowman (2004, 8).
93. Kuttner 1999, 361.
94. On the Hellenistic female authors of epigram, see Gutzwiller 1998, 17–18 and 47–88.
95. On Korinna, see Thorsen 2020, with full bibliography. For her gynocentric perspective, see especially Skinner 1983; Rayor 1993; Larson 2002; on her innovations in mythography, see Collins 2006; Berman 2010; Heath 2017; McPhee 2018.
96. Plutarch, *Greek Questions* 40 (= *Moralia* 300d–f). On Myrtis, see Plant 2004, 36–37.
97. Page 1955, 112–16; Thorsen and Harrison 2019, 14 with n. 44.
98. Pausanias 9.22.3. Aelian (*Various History* 13.25) and the *Suda* (κ 2087) report that she defeated him in five such contests.
99. Propertius, elegy 2.3.21; Ovid, *Amores* 1.5.9, etc.; *Art of Love* 3.538. On Korinna's reception in ancient Rome, see Thorsen 2020.
100. Thorsen 2020, 10–11, with further bibliography.
101. *Poetae Melici Graeci* fr. 717, on which see Bowman 2004, 15.
102. Plutarch, *Moralia* 245d; Pausanias 2.20.8.
103. Eusebius, *Chronicle*, on Olympiad 82.2.
104. *Poetae Melici Graeci* fr. 747.
105. Panagiotopoulou 2022.
106. *Palatine Anthology* 9.190.4.
107. *Palatine Anthology* 9.190.3, 7–8.
108. *Palatine Anthology* 7.11–13, 713.
109. *Palatine Anthology* 7.710, 712; 6.352.
110. *Palatine Anthology* 11.322.
111. *Suda* s.v. "Myro" and "Homerus."
112. Gow and Page 1965, 2.414.
113. *Palatine Anthology* 6.119, 189. Gutzwiller (1998, 17–18) hazards that her epigrams circulated in a mixed collection of her poetry.
114. Athenaeus, *The Learned Banqueters* 9.491b.
115. Gow and Page 1965, 2.90.
116. Gow and Page 1965, 2.89–104; Gutzwiller 1998, 54–73.
117. Pollux 5.48.
118. Gutzwiller 1998, 73–74.
119. Cf. Gutzwiller 1998, 74: "Anyte shifted the focus of the genre from men to women, from adults to children, from humans to animals, and from upper to lower class."
120. *Palatine Anthology* 16.228 (= GP 18); translation from Gutzwiller 1998, 69.
121. On the poetics of Anyte's epigram, see Gutzwiller 1998, 71–73.
122. *Palatine Anthology* 5.169 (= GP 1).
123. Theocritus, *Idyll* 1.1–2, 7.
124. On Nossis, see Skinner 1989, 1991a, 1991b, and 2001; Gutzwiller 1998, 74–88.
125. *Palatine Anthology* 5.170, 6.265, 7.718.
126. *Palatine Anthology* 5.170; translation from Gutzwiller 1998, 76.
127. *Palatine Anthology* 16.228 (Anyte); *Palatine Anthology* 5.169 (Asclepiades).
128. Gutzwiller 1998, 76–77.
129. *Palatine Anthology* 7.718; translation from Gutzwiller 1998, 86.

130. Gutzwiller 1998, 85–86.
131. See Gutzwiller 1998, 282–301. Meleager's *Garland* may well have inspired Roman interest in the genres of elegy and epigram even before Catullus and his friends experimented with them in the mid-50s BCE. Aulus Gellius preserves the strains of three earlier republican amateur poets (Valerius Aedituus, Porcius Licinus, and Lutatius Catulus), at least one of whom enjoyed a distinguished political career (Gellius, *Attic Nights* 19.9.10–14). On these verses, see Courtney 1993, 70–92, with further bibliography.
132. On Cornelia, see Dixon 2007. Cicero mentions her letters in a treatise on Roman oratory (*Brut.* 211) dated ca. 49 BCE, as does Quintilian (*Education of the Orator* 1.1.6) a century and a half later.
133. Two excerpts are preserved in the manuscripts of Nepos' "book on the Latin historians," and included in Dickison and Hallett 2015, 6–7, with commentary at 49–55.
134. Sallust, *War of Catiline* 25.1.
135. Pagán 2009, 43–45, with further bibliography.
136. Appian, *Civil Wars* 4.32.
137. Valerius Maximus 8.3.3; Quintilian, *Education of the Orator* 1.1.6; Appian, *Civil Wars* 4.32–34.
138. Quintilian, *Education of the Orator* 1.1.6.
139. Appian, *Civil Wars* 4.32–4.
140. Jerome, *Chronicle* on 41 BCE (Helm 1956, 159).
141. *CIL* VI 1300a.
142. Wiseman 1976.
143. Catullus, poem 38; Cicero, *To Friends* 12.17–30.
144. Ovid, *Tristia* 2.436, on which see Ingleheart 2010, 333 ad loc.
145. Cicero, *To Friends* 8.7.
146. Sumner 1971, 258.
147. Hollis (2007, 150) adduces the salutation of Cicero, *To Friends* 12.17, addressed to his "colleague Cornificius."
148. Sumner 1971, 358.
149. Rawson 1978, 188.
150. Appian, *Civil Wars* 4.53–57.
151. On Camerius, see Wiseman 1976. He notes the gossip Cicero passes on to Atticus in May 45 BCE (Cicero, *To Atticus* 13.28.4), that Cornificia had turned down an offer of marriage with a Juventius, when she was already "old even for a much-married woman." He assumes that her marriage to Camerius occurred in the 40s, but as we have no other evidence for her marriage(s), we cannot be certain of the date.
152. My translation follows the Latin text of Thomson 1997 and is informed throughout by his commentary on Catullus, poem 55: Thomson 1997, 335–39.

Chapter 6

1. Critics agree on the programmatic valence of 3.13, even if they cannot agree on whether it signals the beginning or end of the cycle: see Voss 1810; Smith 1913; Lowe 1988; Merriam 1990; Tränkle 1990; Flaschenriem 1999; Miller 2002; Milnor 2002; Lyne 2007 [2004–5]; Skoie 2013; Fulkerson 2017, 269. On the editorial organization of the cycle, see Ch. 7.
2. For *amor* as both "love" and "love poem," see *OLD* s.vv. 1 and 5.
3. For the exclusively masculine canon of Latin elegy, though not Latin epigram, see Ch. 5.
4. Propertius, elegy 1.3.35–36: see Skoie 2013, 90n43.
5. Propertius, elegy 1.3.37–46.
6. Propertius has Cynthia's assertion of wretchedness (*me miseram*, elegy 1.3.40) echo his own programmatic assertion (*miserum me*, Propertius, elegy 1.1.1) and that of his predecessor *miser Catulle*, "wretched Catullus" (Catullus, poem 8.1). On the importance of Catullus as a model for Sulpicia, see Santirocco 1979; Hallett 2002a, 47–50.
7. Propertius, elegy 1.3.43–44.
8. The verb "complain" (*queror*) has been recognized as Propertius' idiosyncratic term for his own elegiac poetry, which he consistently represents as "soft" or "slight" (*leuis*) by comparison with the "heavy" strains of martial epic (e.g., Propertius, elegies 1.7 and 1.9). On Propertius' use of "plaint" (*querela*), the substantival cognate of "complain" (*queror*), see Saylor 1967; on Propertius' elegiac poetics, see Keith 2008b, 45–114, with further bibliography. Pichon 1902 collects the conventional lexicon of Latin amatory poetry.

9. Catullus, poem 64.305–87; cf. Tibullus, elegy 1.3.83–88, where Tibullus imagines Delia weaving in his absence.

10. Propertius, elegy 3.2.1–4. On Gallus in Vergil and Propertius, see Ross 1975; on Gallus in Propertius, see Cairns 2006; on Gallus in Sulpicia, see Fabre-Serris 2009, 2017, 2018, 2020a, 2022.

11. Propertius, elegy 1.3.46.

12. Propertius, elegy 1.1.33–38.

13. For *tego* in the sense "cover (with clothing), clothe" (i.e., *uestio*), see *OLD* s.v. 3; for *nudo* in the sense of "divest (of a garment)," see *OLD* s.v. 1c. There is a suggestive parallel with Vergil's representation of Dido in the phrase "with this name she concealed her fault" (*Aeneid* 4.172); on Sulpicia's interest in Vergil's nascent *Aeneid*, and Dido in particular, see Keith 1997; Hallett 2006.

14. *Planudean Anthology* 207.1; Propertius, elegy 1.2.8; Ovid, *Amores* 1.10.15: see Lyne 2007, 351 ad loc. On the rhetoric of disclosure in Sulpicia, see Flaschenriem 1999.

15. *OLD* s.v. *sinus* 1.

16. Cf. Keith 2008a.

17. Fulkerson 2017, 273 ad loc.

18. Sappho, fr. 1; translation mine. Tränkle (1990, 304–5) identified the allusion, which is accepted by Piastri 1998, 139–40; Merriam 2006, 12; Lyne 2007; Fabre-Serris 2009, 150–51, and 2018, 69. Sappho's poem is preserved in manuscript quotation by Dionysius of Halicarnassus, *Arrangement of Words* 173–79; the first twenty-one verses are also fragmentarily preserved in *P.Oxy.* 21.2288. On Sappho's poem, see Page 1955, 3–18; Acosta-Hughes 2010, *Index locorum* s.v. Sappho fr. 1; Neri 2021, 535–46, ad loc.; Mueller 2023, *Index locorum* s.v. Sappho 1V (Hymn to Aphrodite); Nooter 2023, 116–24. Recent bibliography on Sappho is available in DuBois 2015; Ferrari 2010; Budelmann 2018; Tsantsanoglou 2019; Mueller 2023; Nooter 2023.

19. *OLD* s.v. *Camena* 2; cf. Ch. 4.

20. Sappho, fr. 1.26–27.

21. Merriam 2005, 168n8. Sappho uses the epithet at frr. 86, 140a, but it goes back to archaic Greek epic: Homer, *Odyssey* 8.288; Hesiod, *Theogony* 198.

22. Merriam 2006.

23. *OLD* s.v. *gaudium* 2, "physical or sensual delight"; cf. Pichon (1902, 159), who gathers parallels from the erotic poetry of Catullus, Tibullus, and Ovid for the use of *gaudium* in the sense of "physical pleasure."

24. Cf. Treggiari 1991, 84–85.

25. Varro, *On the Latin Language* 6.80: "they used to say they'd been with a woman rather than they'd lain with a woman." The idiom is current already in Plautus (*Amphitruo* 817; *Bacchides* 891, *Truculentus* 688; cf. Terence, *Hecyra* 156), but also occurs in Cicero and the elegists: Cicero, *On Fate* 30; Ovid, *Amores* 2.8.27, *Art of Love* 3.664; cf. *Priapea* 14.3. See further Adams 1982, 177; Fulkerson 2017, 280; Maltby 2021, 519.

26. For the use of the personal pronominal adjective (here *meus*) to denote the poet's beloved, see Pichon 1902, 272, s.v. *suus*; Tränkle 1990, 305–6; Lyne 2007, 353.

27. Pichon (1902, 273), s.v. *tabellae*, adds Tibullus, elegy 2.6.45–46; Ovid, *Art of Love* 3.621, 630.

28. Catullus, poem 42.1–5.

29. The different Latin terms for writing tablets (*codicilli, pugillaria, tabellae*) also confirm the diversity of uses for them. The *OLD* explains that *codicilli* (pl.) denoted "a set of writing-tablets" (*OLD* s.v. *codicillus* 2), including "as the medium of a letter" (*OLD* s.v. 2b); *pugillaria* (pl.) (Catullus, poem 42.5) were "a set of writing-tablets (small enough to hold in the hand)" (*OLD* s.v. *pugillares*); and *tabellae* (pl.) were "wooden, usu. wax-coated, tablets threaded together to form a notebook, etc. (often used as the vehicle for a letter)" (*OLD* s.v. *tabella* 6).

30. Propertius, elegy 3.23.1–2. On the literary anxiety Propertius hints at in the loss of his tablets, see Flaschenriem 1999.

31. Propertius emphasizes his absence in the repetition of the phrase "without me" in a single couplet (3.23.5–6).

32. Propertius, elegy 3.23.21.

33. Milnor 2002, 260 and *passim*; Lyne 2007, 348–50; Fulkerson 2017, 277–78.

34. *OLD* s.v. *pecco* 3b.

35. Horace, *Satires* 1.2.63, 2.7.62; *Odes* 1.27.17, with Nisbet and Hubbard 1970, 315 ad loc.

36. Tibullus, elegy 1.6.16; Propertius, elegy 2.6.40; Ovid, *Amores* 2.5.3; see further Pichon 1902, 227 s.v. *peccare*.

37. *OLD* s.v. *pudor* 2b; cf. *OLD* s.v. *fama* 6a. On the thematic importance of *fama* in the sense of "gossip"—i.e., about her sexual reputation, see Santirocco 1979, 235; Lowe 1988, 203–5.

38. *OLD* s.v. *fama* 7. On the programmatic importance of poetic *fama*, in the sense of "renown," see Santirocco 1979, 234; Lowe 1988, 203–5; cf. Flaschenriem 1999, 39. Cf. Dronke (2003, 85), who interprets 3.13 as reflecting on the range of meanings of *fama*.

39. *Fama* is used here in the sense of *infamia*. Thus, the definition the *OLD* offers for *fama*, s.v. 6b ("ill repute, notoriety"), is the same as appears for *infamia*, s.v. 1 ("bad reputation, ill-fame, notoriety"), and shades all too easily into that for *infamia* s.v. 2 ("discredit, disgrace").

40. Flaschenriem (1999, 39) has a sensitive discussion of Sulpicia's use of *mihi* (3.13.2), dative of the indirect object, as part of her rhetoric of "reticence" in 3.13.

41. The difficulty of the syntax here and throughout 3.13 is the subject of Lowe 1988, and much discussed by the commentators *ad loc.*: see Smith 1913; Tränkle 1990; Lyne 2007; Fulkerson 2017; Maltby 2021. I accept *pudore* (3.13.1) as ablative of cause.

42. Tränkle 1990, 303–4; Lyne 2007, 351; cf. Fulkerson 2017, 272–73.

43. Flaschenriem 1999, 40–41.

44. Tränkle (1990, 305) and Lyne (2007, 353) explain *dicetur*, construed with *habuisse* ("will be said [not] to have had"), as essentially otiose for *habuit* (if anyone didn't "have" their own love).

45. Cf. Fulkerson 2017, 276.

46. Lyne 2007, 353, comparing Catullus, poem 5.2, and Propertius, elegy 2.30.13.

47. Most commentators, following Smith (1913, 508), interpret the verb as present subjunctive; Lyne (2007, 350) views it as future indicative; Fulkerson (2017, 280) discusses the implications of each.

48. As Fulkerson (2017, 280) puts it, "scurrilous gossip has turned into poetic reputation."

49. Flaschenriem 1999; Milnor 2002; Hauser 2016.

50. *OLD* s.v. 2, citing Terence, *Andria* 913; Propertius, elegy 2.3.8; Ovid, *Fasti* 6.573; Seneca rhetor, *Suasoriae* 7.5; Columella 1.11.14; Tacitus, *Annales* 5.3; Gellius, *Attic Nights* 6(7).8.2; Martial, *Epigrams* 6.93.3.

51. The evidence for Gallus' title *Amores* is derived from Vergil, *Bucolics* 10.6, 34, 52–54, with Servius' commentary on *Bucolics* 10.1. Propertius calls his love poems *amores*, in his elegies 1.7.5 and 2.1.1–2. Horace calls Valgius' elegies *amores* at *Odes* 2.9.9–12 (quoted in Ch. 5), while Ovid refers to his love poems by that title in *Art of Love* 3.343–44.

52. First explicitly explored by Lowe 1988; cf. Miralles Maldonado 1990; and the commentaries of Tränkle 1990; Lyne 2007 [2004–5]; Fulkerson 2017; Maltby 2021.

53. Gruppe 1838, 1.49–50; discussion in Lowe 1988, 194–95.

54. Parker 1994, 48–49, following Lowe 1988; cf. Santirocco 1979.

55. Parker 1994, 48, following Lowe 1988, counts only the epigrams (9 out of 20 distichs). I report the tally for the 42 couplets of the first-person poems: 3.9.8, 10, 16, 24; 3.11.16; 3.13.6, 10; 14.6; 15.2; 17.4, 6; 18.2,4, 6.

56. Parker 1994, 48, quoting Lowe 1988, 198. The full count is six, including 3.9.9; 3.13.1, 7, 9; 3.17.3, 5.

57. Parker (1994, 48, quoting Lowe 1988, 198) notes as well the similarly convoluted force of "tmetic *ante...quam*" (3.13.8).

58. Parker 1994, 49, adds the last three stylistic traits enumerated here to Lowe's findings for the epigrams 3.13–18.

59. Parker 1994, 48–49.

60. Santirocco 1979, 236; Tränkle 1990, 301; Parker 1994, 49; Miller 2002, 163 ad loc.

61. Tränkle 1990, 300–302; cf. Lyne 2007, 348. Tränkle (1990, 258–60) dates 3.8–12 two or three decades later, on the grounds that they echo the elegies of Propertius 4 and Ovid's *Heroides*, *Art of Love*, and *Metamorphoses* and probably also the *Letters from the Black Sea*. I agree rather with Fabre-Serris and Hallett that those poets echo Sulpicia: see Ch. 7.

62. Parker 1994; followed by Hallett, Dronke, and Fabre-Serris (Ch. 1n41).

63. The point is wittily made in Parker 2006.

64. Ross 1969.

65. We may note as well the variation in length of the elegies collected in Propertius' first book: the closing epigrams (Propertius, elegies 1.21–22) are both ten lines in length, while the elegies range from twenty lines (Propertius, elegy 1.12) to fifty-two (Propertius, elegy 1.20) and have an average length of 34.3. The elegies of Propertius' first book are considerably shorter than

those of Tibullus' first book, which vary between ninety-eight and sixty-eight lines in length and have an average length of 73.2 lines, or those of his second book, which vary between twenty-two and 122 lines in length and have an average length of 71.3 lines.

66. Carcopino 1929, 85–86; Stevenson 2005, 43–44.

67. Catullus, poem 64.311; Propertius, elegy 4.1.72, 4.9.48. See L-S s.v. *colus*; cf. *OLD* s.v. *colus* 1.

68. Trisyllabic *Petale*, 1928.73.2; quadrisyllabic *ediderat* and *ingenio*, 1928.73.4, 6. The Petale epitaph has only one disyllabic line-ending (*colus*, 1928.73.8).

69. Accepted by Stevenson 2005; Hallett 2009c, 2010a, and 2011b; Hauser 2016, 156–67. I find the attribution of the epitaph to Sulpicia very appealing, and discuss the reference to the Fates' distaff further below, n96, in connection with an allusion to Erinna that has been identified in Sulpicia's choice of the pseudonym Cerinthus for her beloved.

70. Stevenson (2005, 43–44)—followed by Hallett 2009c, 187–89, 2010a, 367–70, and 2011b, 94; Hauser 2016, 160—argues that the first word encodes a pun linking the enslaved "reader" Sulpicia Petale with our author Sulpicia, and translates the phrase *Sulpiciae cineres lectricis* as both "the ashes of the reader Sulpicia" and "the ashes of Sulpicia's reader" (i.e., "of the reader belonging to Sulpicia"). I do not see how the Latin of the epitaph supports this interpretation; cf. the skepticism of L. Morgan, expressed in a blogpost to his site *Lugubelinus*, dated September 8 2018: https://llewelynmorgan.com/2018/09/08/desperately-seeking-sulpicia/.

71. Batstone 2018, 103; cf. Hinds 1987, 30–31, on the similarity between Sulpicia's presentation in [Tib.] 3.8 and Cynthia's in Prop. 1.1.

72. In the first-person poems too, Sulpicia identifies herself as a *puella* (3.14.3, 3.15.1, 3.17.1), the technical term for an elegiac mistress, but always in conjunction with first-person markers (3.14.5, 7, 8; 3.15.3; 3.17.2, 3, 5).

73. Lucretius discusses the metaphorical "bonds of love" in his diatribe against love at the end of the fourth book of *On the Nature of the Universe* (4.1146–48). On *seruitium amoris*, see Copley 1947; Lyne 1979; Murgatroyd 1981; McCarthy 1998; Fulkerson 2013, with further bibliography. On the amatory hunt, see Bréguet 1946, 294–304; Davis 1983; Murgatroyd 1984. On the Roman hunt, see Green 1996.

74. On the *domina* in Latin elegy, see Keith 2012; Fulkerson 2017, 11–12. Hinds (1987, 38–39) notes the "cultural complications" that "inevitably follow" from the gender inversion, but attributes the nuances here to the shadowy figure of the *amicus Sulpiciae*.

75. Ovid, *Art of Love* 1.45–46, 49–50.

76. Propertius, elegy 1.1.9–16: see Ross 1975, 85, 90n1; Cairns 2006, 110–12, 140–43.

77. Vergil, *Bucolics* 10.56: see Fabre-Serris 2020a, 174–75.

78. Fabre-Serris (2009, 158–60) draws on the Milanion exemplum in Propertius 1.1 and Cynthia's departure to the countryside in Propertius 2.19 in her discussion, in addition to passages in Ovid's *Heroides* 4 and *Metamorphoses* 10. A long line of scholars have identified Gallus as the originator of the hunting motif in elegy: see Fabre-Serris 2020a, 172–73, for full discussion and bibliography.

79. Tibullus, elegy 1.4.47–50: see Murgatroyd 1984; Fabre-Serris 2020a, 175.

80. On Marathus in Tibullus, elegies 1.4, 8, and 9, see Maltby 2002, 45–46; Nikoloutsos 2007 and 2011. Racette-Campbell (2023) argues that the suite of activities described in Tibullus' elegy 1.4 better fit freeborn aristocratic youths than enslaved boys. On Catullus' Iuuentius, in his poems 24, 48, 81, 99, see Neudling 1955, 94–96, s.v. Juventius; Wiseman 1976. On Hylas, see Petrain 2000.

81. The gentilician *Iuuentius* was borne by a distinguished Roman family: see Neudling 1955, 94–96.

82. Keith 2016, 74; cf. Boucher 1976, 504–10.

83. Apuleius, *Apology* 10; confirmed by one of Horace's ancient commentators (pseudo-Acro on *Satires* 1.2.64).

84. Randall 1979.

85. Quotation from Lyne 2007, 346. On the ancient sources for beebread, see Roessel 1990, 243.

86. Aristotle, *History of Animals* 623b23; Pliny, *Natural History* 11.17.

87. Waszink 1974; Williams 1978, 92–94; Roessel 1990, 245–46.

88. Roessel 1990, 248–50.

89. Cf. Hubbard (2004/5, 184n22) who suggests "Honeysweet," citing Currie 1983, 1754; Hinds 1987, 38; Roessel 1990, 243–50.

90. Cf. e.g., *Palatine Anthology* 9.187, of Menander, with Waszink 1974; Roessel 1990, 245–46.

91. Respectively *Palatine Anthology* 7.11.1; 7.12.1; and 7.13.1–2.
92. *Palatine Anthology* 9.190.1–2.
93. *Palatine Anthology* 2.110, composed by the late antique epigrammatist Christodorus of Coptus in Egypt, writing under the Byzantine emperor Anastasius 1 (491–518 CE), takes up the same metaphor in relation to a statue of Erinna: "And the maiden Erinna, the clear-humming girl, sat / not plying a braided thread, but in silence / distilling drops of honey from the Pierian bee" (tr. adapted from Paton rev. Tueller 2014, 103).
94. Gutzwiller 1998, 77, with discussion of other evidence for imagery associated with Erinna deriving from her poetry in n80.
95. Roessel 1990, 245.
96. Marilyn Skinner suggests (*apud* Hallett 2009c, 188n25) that the reference to the Fates' distaff in the Sulpicia Petale epitaph (*AE* 1929.73.10) constitutes another reference to Erinna's famous poem. Hallett (2009c, 188n25) paraphrases: "the mention of the distaff in line 8 is an honorific tribute to Erinna, and therefore evidence that the author considers herself to be writing within a female poetic tradition; so, too, in this poem does Sulpicia cast herself as Erinna, and the dead Petale as Erinna's beloved companion, Baucis, an amazing tribute to a freedwoman."
97. Horace, *Satires* 1.2.77–82.
98. Boucher 1976, 504–5.
99. Vergil, *Georgics* 4.63, *cerinthae ignobile gramen*; see further Boucher 1976, 506.
100. Propertius, elegy 2.19.17.
101. Cf. Fabre-Serris 2020a, 175.
102. Propertius, elegy 2.19.1–10. Fabre-Serris (2020a, 184) notes the lexical overlap between Sulpicia (3.9) and Propertius, elegy 2.19, but she attributes their shared vocabulary to their shared reliance on a Gallan model (via the Milanion *exemplum* at Propertius, elegy 1.1.9–16).
103. Good pastureland: 3.9.1 *bona pascua campi* ~ Propertius, elegy 2.19.2–3 *deuia rura...in agris*, 8 *finis pauperis agricolae*, 11–12 *tauros...arantis / et uitem*; hills: 3.9.7 *colles* ~ Propertius, elegy 2.19.7 *montis*, 30 *iugis*; woods: 3.9.6 *siluae*, 15 *siluae* ~ Propertius, elegy 2.19.29 *siluae*.
104. *deuia rura coles*, Propertius, elegy 2.19.2; *colis...deuia montis*, Sulpicia 3.9.2.
105. *castis iuuenis corruptor in agris*, Propertius, elegy 2.19.3.
106. Propertius, elegy 2.19.4.
107. *peccatis*, Propertius, elegy 2.19.10.
108. Propertius, elegy 2.19.17–20.
109. Propertius, elegy 2.19.3–4, 27–32.
110. Vergil, *Bucolics* 7.29.
111. Tibullus, elegies 1.2.71–74, 1.5.21–34.
112. For the view that Sulpicia assumes the role of Phaedra to Cerinthus' Hippolytus, see Fabre-Serris 2009 and 2020a, 183–85.
113. Venus and Diana are named together by Sulpicia at 3.9.19 and by Propertius in his elegy 2.19.17–18. On Propertius' characteristically urban elegy, explicitly indebted to the model of Gallus in his elegies 1.5, 10, 13 (cf. 1.20), see Cairns 1983.
114. Propertius, elegies 1.22, 4.1.63–64: see Boucher 1965, 110–11; Cairns 2006, 142; Keith 2008b, 1–4.
115. Fatucchi 1976.
116. See n18, above.
117. *Palatine Anthology* 7.407.7–8 = 18.1571–2 GP; cf. Paus. 9.29.8.
118. Sappho frr. 140, 168.
119. Sappho fr. 140 (= Heph. *Ench.* 10.4).
120. Cf. Hdt. 1.34.2ff.; Apollod. 3.183; Bion, Ἀδώνιδος ἐπιτάφιος ("Lament for Adonis"). Bréguet (1946, 300–303) discusses Sulpicia 3.9 in relation to Bion's *Lament for Adonis*. Theocritus, in *Idyll* 15, depicts women's engagement with the festival of Adonis in Alexandria.
121. Praxilla, *apud Anthologica Lyrica* II² 5, 1942 fr. 2 Diehl = fr. 747 *Poetae Melici Graeci*.
122. On Praxilla's poem, see Panagiotopoulou 2022 with further bibliography.
123. Stehle 1996, 218; Panagiotopoulou 2022.
124. Ovid, *Metamorphoses* 10.519–739. Before Ovid's *Metamorphoses*, Adonis appears little in extant Latin literature: Plautus, *Menaechmi* 143–44; Catullus, poem 29.8; Cicero, *On the Nature of the Gods* 3.59; Vergil, *Bucolics* 10.18; Propertius, elegy 2.13.53–54; Ovid, *Amores* 3.9.15–16; *Art of Love* 1.75, 1.512, 3.85. On Ovid's echoes of Sulpicia in his treatment of the myth, see Ch. 7.

125. It is likely that Cinna mentioned Adonis in his lost epyllion *Zmyrna* (Catull. 95), which treated the myth of Adonis' mother Myrrha. Fabre-Serris (2009, 2018, 2020a, 2020b) has argued that Gallus addressed the myth somewhere in his lost *Amores*, since Vergil includes Adonis at *B.* 10.18, in an eclogue dedicated to Gallus.

126. Propertius, elegy 2.13.51–58: see Cairns 2006, 144–45.

127. Propertius, elegy 2.13.51–52 employs both the substantive and the verb for "love," *amo, amare*; cf. Sulpicia's use of *Amor* at 3.9.4.

128. Thus Propertius puns on the syllabic echo of the goddess' name in the verb for hunting, *uenantem…Venus* (elegy 2.13.54–56), while Sulpicia redoubles the echo at 3.9.13–23, *ueneris …uenus…uenandi* (3.9.18–23). Neither Maltby 1991 (635 s.v. "Venus") nor O'Hara 1996 offers any ancient comparanda that would support this proposed etymology; but Ahl 1985 amasses copious evidence for contra-metrical wordplay in Ovid.

129. Sarah McCallum suggests to me (*per litteras*) that with elision, the phrase *cum aliquo fuisse* (3.13.10) would sound similar to *concubuisse* as well.

130. Cf. the "chaste maiden" whom Catullus celebrates in epithalamium (Catullus, poem 62.23) and the "chaste maidens" whom Propertius invokes in his early elegies (1.1.5, 1.11.29), by contrast with the latter's "chaste young corruptor in the fields" (Propertius, elegy 2.19.3, discussed above).

131. Adulterous affair with a married woman: Catullus, poem 68; disreputable liaison with an unmarriageable woman: Gallus fr. 145.1 Hollis, Propertius, elegy 2.7.

132. Fulkerson 2017, 245.

133. On the staged hunts in the amphitheater, and the punishment of criminals in the hunt, see Coleman 1990.

134. Fulkerson 2017, 246.

135. Fulkerson (2017, 12) observes that the elegiac *puella* normally serves as the quarry in the metaphor of love's hunt (e.g., Ovid, *Art of Love* 1.46). Cf. the evidence collected in Pichon 1902, s.v. *cassibus* ("hunting-nets"), *nodi* ("knots"), *retia* ("nets"), and *uinculi* ("chains").

136. On 3.11, see especially Fabre-Serris 2022.

137. Song/prophecy: Tibullus, elegy 1.7.1–2; Catullus, poem 64.383. Epithalamium ("wedding song"): Catullus 64.323–81; accompanied by weaving: Catullus, 64.303–22. See further Fulkerson 2017, 256 on Sulpicia 3.11.3–4. On Tibullus, elegy 1.7 as a model for Sulpicia's poem, see Fabre-Serris 2022, 261–65.

138. Fulkerson 2017, 256, citing Batstone 2018. Hinds (1987, 45) suggests that Sulpicia's filiation, *Serui filia*, undermines her assertion of class superiority over her enslaved rival, inasmuch as it could be used to describe a slave's daughter (*serui filia*). The phrase, however, is not attested epigraphically, since slaves could have no filiation (being possessions rather than people).

139. Tibullus, elegy 1.9.80.

140. Pichon 1902, 165–66, s.v. *ignes*.

141. Note the *OLD*'s definition of *caleo* s.v. 6, "to be hot or fired (with love or lust)," citing our line.

142. Catullus, poem 45; Tibullus, elegy 1.6.76. See Pichon 1902, 211, s.v. *mutuus*. Lygdamus offers the closest parallel to Sulpicia's usage, writing of his beloved Neaera ([Tib.] 3.1.19): "she will tell me if her care for me is mutual (*mutua cura*) / or less or if I have fallen from her heart." Elsewhere in elegy, this usage appears in Propertius' elegy 1.5, in a Gallan context, and Tibullus, elegy 1.2.63. Fabre-Serris 2022, 266–67n27, assembles evidence for the Gallan provenance of the cliché. On the elegiac model of erotic domination, by contrast, see Greene 1998. Horace evokes the concept of mutual love always in application to others, first in a parody of elegiac love at *Epodes* 15.10 and then again, apparently alluding to the mutual love of Maecenas and his wife Terentia, at *Odes* 2.12.15–16: see Nisbet and Hubbard 1978, 180–83 and 194–95 ad loc., and Fabre-Serris 2022, 266–67n27; cf. also Hor. *Odes* 3.9.13.

143. See Pichon 1902, 218–19 s.v. *oculi*.

144. of Aeneas and Dido, *furtiuum amorem*, Vergil, *Aeneid* 4.172; *contra*, e.g., Tibullus, elegy 1.5.7, *per te furtiui foedera lecti*: "[I swear to you] by the bonds of a stolen bed." Cf. Catullus, poem 68.136; Vergil, *Georgics* 4.346; Propertius, elegy 2.23.22; Ovid, *Art of Love* 1.33, 2.389. See further Pichon 1902, 158 s.v. *furta*.

145. On jealousy as the elegiac emotion par excellence, see Caston 2012.

146. Fulkerson 2017, 259.

147. Hinds 2006; on the etymology in 3.11, see Fabre-Serris 2022, 268–71.

148. Cf. Propertius, elegy 2.15.25–26, discussed below.

149. Cf. Fabre-Serris 2022, 277.
150. Propertius, elegy 2.14.9–10, 21–32.
151. *gaudia*, Propertius, elegy 2.14.9; cf. Sulpicia's use of the noun at 3.9.18, 3.13.5.
152. Propertius, elegy 2.14.25.
153. Propertius, elegy 2.14.25–28.
154. *Mea lux* occurs twice in Catullus, poem 68.132, 160; and recurs in Propertius' second collection, in elegies 2.14.29, 2.28.59, 2.29.1. Ovid uses the phrase at *Amores* 1.4.25, 2.17.23; *Art of Love* 3.524; *Tristia* 3.3.52. The phrase is not attested in Tibullus.
155. Propertius, elegy 2.15.5–6.
156. Propertius, elegy 2.15.13–16.
157. Propertius, elegy 2.15.5, 13, 15, 16.
158. *quam multa ... narramus uerba*, Propertius, elegy 2.15.3; *mea gaudia narret*, Sulpicia 3.13.5.
159. *narramus*, Propertius, elegy 2.15.3 ~ *narret*, Sulpicia, 3.13.5; *fertur*, Propertius, elegy 2.15.13 ~ *ferar*, Sulpicia 3.13.10; *dicitur*, Propertius, elegy 2.15.16 ~ *dicetur*, Sulpicia 3.13.6.
160. On the Propertian resonances of the opening of the cycle, see Hinds 1987, 30–31.
161. Propertius, elegy 2.3.3–4.
162. Propertius, elegy 2.5.1–2; cf. Propertius, elegy 1.6.26, and Ovid's proud boast at *Amores* 2.1.1–2: "This too was composed by me, that famous Naso / born in the wetlands of the Paelignians, poet of my own profligacy."
163. Propertius, elegy 2.5.27–30.
164. *fama*, Propertius, elegy 2.5.29; Sulpicia 3.13.9. For Sulpicia's interest in the similar elegiac rhetoric of the Vergilian Dido, especially in relation to Dido's *fama*, see Keith 1997.
165. Propertius, elegy 2.24.1–8.
166. *pudor*, Propertius, elegy 2.24.4; *pudore*, Sulpicia 3.13.1.
167. *nequitia*, Propertius, elegy 2.24.6; *peccasse*, Sulpicia, 3.13.9; cf. *peccauerim*, Propertius, elegy 2.16.25.
168. *dicerer*, Propertius, elegy 2.24.6; *dicetur*, Sulpicia, 3.13.6.
169. *fabula*, Propertius, elegy 2.24.1; *infamis*, Propertius, elegy 2.24.7; *fama*, Sulpicia, 3.13.2, 9.
170. *traducerer*, Propertius, elegy 2.24.8; *ferar*, Sulpicia, 3.13.10. Cf. the Vergilian Dido's lament for the loss of her *pudor* and *fama* (*Aeneid* 4.321–23), with Keith 1997.
171. On birthday poems see, Cairns 1972, index s.v. *genethliakon*.
172. *hunc ... diem*, Tibullus, elegy 1.7.1: see Cairns 1998, 204–5.
173. *Genium* [*bis*], Tibullus, elegy 1.7.49; *natalis*, Tibullus, elegy 1.7.63; cf. *Genius*, Sulpicia, 3.11.8, 9, 12; *natalis deus*, Sulpicia, 3.11.19.
174. Tibullus, elegy 1.7.50–53; cf. Sulpicia, 3.11.9.
175. On Tibullus, elegy 2.2, see Cairns 1998.
176. Cairns 1998, 210–14.
177. Hubbard 2004/5, 184–87. For Hubbard's view of the authorship of the Sulpicia cycle, with which I do not concur, see Ch. 8.
178. Lyne 2007, 354, with reference to Propertius, elegy 3.10, and Sulpicia 3.12.
179. On elegy as an urban genre, the opposite of pastoral, see Veyne 1988, 101–15, reprinted in Miller 2002, 366–85; Maltby 2002, 50–54. Catullus sets the standard in his verse by making *urbanitas* ("the qualities typical of a city-dweller"—i.e., "sophistication, polish": *OLD* s.v. 1) a term of high praise and its antonym, *rusticitas* ("the fact or state of being country-born," *OLD* s.v. 1; "uncouthness of manner," *OLD* s.v. 2; "lack of sophistication, provinciality," *OLD* s.v. 3), an insult.
180. *dulcia arua*, Vergil, *Bucolics* 1.3.
181. Anyte, *Palatine Anthology* 16.228.2; Theocritus, *Idyll* 1.1–2, 7.
182. Asclepiades, *Palatine Anthology* 5.169; Nossis, *Palatine Anthology* 5.170.1.
183. I am indebted to the work of Erin M. Hanses on Sulpicia's debt to Epicureanism; on Lucretian motifs in 3.8, see also Fabre-Serris 2018, 68–70.
184. On Epicureanism, see Warren 2009; O'Keefe 2010; Fish and Sanders 2011.
185. On the Epicurean profile of Vergil's *Bucolica*, see Davis 2012; and on the Epicurean ethics of Horace's *Satires*, see Yona 2018.
186. For example, Diogenes, *Lives of the Philosophers* 10.120, reports Epicurus' maxim that "the wise man will love the countryside." Cf. Vergil, *Bucolics, passim*; Horace, *Satires* 2.6.79–117.
187. *OLD* s.v. *quies* 2.
188. Pichon 1902, 86 s.v. *animus*.

189. Pichon 1902, 261 s.v. *sensus*.
190. Helen: Catullus, poem 68.103; Briseis: *abducta Briseide*, Propertius, elegy 2.20.1, cf. *abrepta Briseis*, Propertius, elegy 2.8.29; Ovid, *Amores* 1.9.33, *Heroides* 3.1, *Remedies for Love* 777, *Tristia* 4.1.15; and Andromache: Propertius, elegy 2.20.2. See further Fedeli 2005, 587–92, on Propertius, elegy 2.20.1–4. On *abducere* in the Latin amatory lexicon, see Pichon 1902, 77.
191. Cf. especially Propertius, elegy 2.20.1–4.
192. For the mistress' domineering power (*arbitrium*) over the male poet-lover, see Lygdamus, in [Tibullus], elegy 3.6.14; Propertius, elegy 4.1.143; Ovid, *Art of Love* 1.504. On Sulpicia's recourse to legal terminology here, see Hallett 2009c, 185–86; and cf. Horace's picture of a lovesick girl fearing the lash of her paternal uncle's tongue (*Odes* 3.12.2–3).
193. *natalis*, 3.14 ~ *natali*, 3.15.2; *tristis*, 3.14.2 ~ *triste* 3.15.1; *puellae*, 3.14.3 ~ *puellae*, 3.15.1; *urbe*, 3.14.3 ~ *Romae* 3.15.2; *uiae*, 3.14.6 ~ *iter*, 3.15.1; *animum*, 3.14.7 ~ *animo* 3.15.1; *sinis*, 3.14.8 ~ *licet* 3.15.2; *esse meo*, 3.14.8 ~ *esse suo*, 3.15.2.
194. Caston 2012; cf. Propertius, elegy 1.8.29.
195. The adjective belongs to the Latin lexicon of Epicureanism: Hanses 2024.
196. *OLD* s.v. *toga* 2c; cf. Afranius, fr. 182; Cicero, *Philippics* 2.44; Horace, *Satires* 1.2.63; Martial, *Epigrams* 2.39.2; Juvenal, *Satires* 2.68.
197. Fulkerson 2017, 12.
198. Cf. Catullus, poem 76.25; Tibullus, elegy 2.5.109–10; Propertius, elegies 2.1.58, 2.4.9–16.
199. Tibullus, elegy 1.5.9–20; Propertius, elegies 2.9.25–28, 2.28; Ovid, *Amores* 2.13–14, *Art of Love* 2.315–36. On the *topos* of elegiac lovesickness, see Yardley 1973, 1977, and 1990.
200. *Calor* in the sense of "fever" is drawn from the medical lexicon (*OLD* s.v. 4; cf. *TLL* 3.181.15–39), appropriated by Propertius (3.8.9) and, following him, Vergil (*Aeneid* 8.390) and Ovid (*Art of Love* 1.237; *Metamorphoses* 11.305), to describe amatory "passion" (*OLD* s.v. 6; *TLL* 3.182.25–36).
201. Catullus, poem 76.25–26.
202. Santirocco 1979, 233; Hallett 2002b, 147. Sulpicia's plea that Cerinthus feel "pious devotion" to her may also have a newly acquired Vergilian charge, inasmuch as Vergil worked on the epic of *pius Aeneas* from 29 BCE to his death in 19: see Keith 1997.
203. Cf., e.g., Catullus, poem 64.71, 135. On the so-called "neoteric" *a!*, see Ross 1969, 49–63.
204. Pichon 1902, 244–45, s.v. *puella*.
205. Propertius, elegy 2.28.1–2, 15–16.
206. Propertius, elegies 1.2.15; 3.8.9. See Pichon 1902, 97 s.v. *calor*.
207. Cf. Propertius' use of *morbus*, in elegy 2.1.58.
208. Fulkerson 2017, 291.
209. Propertius, elegies 1.6.12, 15.4; 2.14.14, 2.15.8; 3.8.20, 23.12. See Pichon 1902, 186 s.v. *lentus*.
210. Tränkle 1990, 321 ad loc. Norden (1957, 448) compiles the figures: one instance in the Gallus papyrus (fr. 145.2 Hollis); 32 instances in Propertius; one instance in Tibullus (1.4.63); none in Lygdamus; two in Sulpicia (3.16.1, 3.17.5).
211. Cf. Maltby 2021, 106–7, who notes that the word appears already in the first epigram of Valerius Aedituus (fr. 1.1 Courtney).
212. Catullus, poems 65.1–2, 66.23, 68.18, 51. Vergil, in *Bucolics* 10.22, addresses the phrase "your love/girlfriend Lycoris" (*tua cura Lycoris*) to Gallus; for the bilingual pun, see Ross 1975, 69.
213. Propertius, elegies 1.1.36, 1.3.46, 1.5.10, 1.10.17, 1.13.7, 1.15.31, 1.19.23; 2.12.4, 2.16.2, 2.25.1, 2.34.9; cf. 3.21.3. Tibullus, elegies 1.5.37; 2.3.13, 31; 2.6.51. Ovid, *Amores* 1.3.16; 2.10.12, 2.19.43; 3.9.32. Pichon (1902, 120–21) analyses the different valences of *cura* and its cognate verb *curare* in the Latin elegists.
214. Pichon (1902, 193) notes Sulpicia's gender reversal in these passages, followed by Ovid at *Ars* 3.524; cf. Ovid's conventional use of the phrase at *Amores* 1.4.25, 2.17.23; *Tristia* 3.3.52.
215. Lyne 2007, 365.
216. frequent in Catullus' epigram-series, poems 75, 81, 82, 96, 102, 103.
217. *hesterna, mea lux, cum potus nocte uagarer*: see Lyne 2007, 367.
218. Cf. *sola relicta*, Catullus, poem 64.200; Propertius, elegy 2.24b.46; and see further Lyne 2007, 367; Fulkerson 2017, 293.
219. Lyne 2007, 367; cf. Fulkerson 2017, 293.
220. As Fulkerson (2017, 294) puts it, "S[ulpicia]…uncovers her attempt to cover things over, continuing the elegiac cycle of deferral."

221. Catullus, poem 2.8; Lucretius, *On the Nature of the Universe* 4.1086; Propertius, elegies 1.7.24, 1.10.10, 1.13.28, 1.20.6. See further Tränkle 1990, 322; *OLD* s.v. *ardor* 6; and cf. Pichon 1902, 89, s.v. *ardor.*

222. Commentators from Tränkle 1990 to Maltby 2021 track parallels with Tibullus and Ovid, often to argue for Ovidian priority and, by implication, the inauthenticity of the Sulpicia cycle (Ch. 8).

223. Keith 1997.

224. Hallett 2009c, 186.

225. Davis 1977; cf. McKeown 1989, 309–10 ad Ov. *Am.* 1.11.

226. McKeown (1989, 309) notes Catullus' paired poems (2–3; 5, 7; 37, 39; 70, 72; 107, 109) and examples in the *Palatine Anthology* of Greek epigrams (5.136–37, 151–52, 172–73; 12.82–83).

227. It is worth noting, in this context, that Vergil's Gallus eclogues are conspicuously paired as the opening and concluding poems of the second half of his *Bucolic* collection: see Skutsch 1969.

228. Leach 1978.

229. Propertius, elegies 1.8a–8b; 1.7 and 1.9; 1.11–12; 2.28a–28b; 2.29a–29b.

230. Among them Propertius, elegies 1.8 and 2.16; and 1.14 and 3.22.

231. Davis 1977, 20.

232. A Gallan model has often been proposed for Propertius, elegy 1.8, since Cynthia's proposed departure for Illyria imitates the journey Gallus' mistress Lycoris takes over the Alps with a military general commemorated in Vergil, *Bucolics* 10.45–49 and Servius' report ad loc. that Vergil's lines were shot through with reminiscences of Gallus' verse. Neither the eclogue nor Servius' commentary on it, however, suggests that Gallus paired a poem about Lycoris' journey over the Alps with a second poem about her return to the elegist and/or his triumphant recovery of her love.

233. Maltby 2021, 105.

234. On Propertius, elegy 2.28, see Fedeli 2005, 777–816.

Chapter 7

1. On Hellenistic epigram collections as "poetic garlands," see Gutzwiller 1998.

2. Propertius, elegy 1.1.1. see Hinds 1987, 30–31; Navarro Antolín 2005, 316–17; Kletke 2016; Fulkerson 2017, 224; Maltby 2021, 438. It is important to note, however, the unprecedented use of a Latin gentilician in the context of an elegiac book, where the objects of the poets' erotic interest conventionally bear Greek pseudonyms and the poets themselves bear Roman names. Catullus' Iuuentius is the exception that proves the rule, though he does not give his name to Catullus' elegiac book.

3. These questions are addressed in Hinds 1987, a seminal article in Sulpician studies.

4. Catullus, poem 14.

5. Catullus, poems 35 and 38, respectively.

6. Catullus, poems 65–66.

7. My translation of Catullus, poem 50.1–6, is indebted to the commentary, and glosses, of Fordyce 1961.

8. The title, and subject, of Volk 2021. For the prevalence of a collaborative model of distributed authorship in ancient Rome, see also the abundant evidence collected and discussed in Gurd 2011.

9. Pollio in Vergil, *Bucolics* 3, 4, 8; Gallus in Vergil, *Bucolics* 6, 10.

10. Philodemos in Horace, *Satires* 1.2.90–94, 116–24; distinguished Roman men of letters in Horace, *Satires* 1.10.81–90, partially quoted in Ch. 5.

11. Ovid, *Tristia* 4.10.45–46.

12. Bassus in Propertius, elegy 1.4; Gallus in Propertius, elegies 1.5, 10, 13, 20 (with Cairns 1983); Ponticus in Propertius, elegies 1.7, 9; "Lynceus" (i.e., L. Varius Rufus) in Propertius, elegy 2.34; and Maecenas in Propertius, elegies 2.1, 3.9. On the identity of "Lynceus," see Ch. 5n49.

13. Messalla in Tibullus, elegies 1.1, 1.3; Cornutus in Tibullus, elegies 2.2–3; and Macer in Tibullus, elegy 2.6.

14. Atticus in Ovid, *Amores* 1.9; and Graecinus in Ovid, *Amores* 2.10. On Ovid's wide field of interlocutors in the exile poetry, see Syme 1978.

15. On the identification, see McKeown 1998, 382–83, on Ovid, *Amores* 2.18; cf. Maltby 2002, 466–67, on Tibullus, elegy 2.6.1.

16. Ovid, *Amores* 2.18.27–28; on Sabinus, see McKeown 1998, 383–84.

17. Ovid, *Amores* 2.18.29–34.
18. On Ovid's "single" *Heroides* (1–15), in relation to both Sabinus' "letters from heroes" and his own "double" *Heroides* (16–21), see McKeown 1998, 386–87. McKeown (1998, 386) suggests that Ovid "may have composed individual *Heroides* over a period of years, reciting them to his *sodales*"—i.e., to his literary cronies.
19. Ovid, *Tristia* 2.445–70, 4.10.41–60; *Letters from the Black Sea* 4.16.3–46.
20. Fielding 2020, 190–91.
21. Fielding 2020, 191.
22. Treggiari 1973, 1975, 1976.
23. Gurd 2011; Fielding 2020, 191–92; Volk 2021.
24. Cf. Volk 2021, 39–46, on the roles of Tiro and Atticus in Cicero's preparation, composition and publication of his philosophical dialogues.
25. Hemelrijk 1999, 147–60, 174–80.
26. Catullus, poems 35, 36, 42. Hallett 2009b, §§8–11, reviews evidence from Cicero, Catullus, and Ovid that she takes to imply that both Clodia Metelli, Catullus' "Lesbia," and her daughter Metella might have been poets themselves.
27. Propertius, elegy 2.3.19–22; Ch. 5.
28. Ovid, *Art of Love* 3.1–2; on the addressees of the third book of Ovid's *Art of Love*, see Gibson 2003, 35–36.
29. Ovid, *Tristia* 3.7. See Hemelrijk 1999, 149–51, with 320–22nn15–25; Hallett 2009b.
30. Ovid, *Tristia* 3.7.11–12.
31. Ovid, *Tristia* 3.7.17–18.
32. Ovid, *Letters from the Black Sea* 4.8.90; cf. 4.8.11–12. While Ovid uses pseudonyms throughout the *Tristia* to protect his friends and relations, he names his addressees openly in the subsequent *Letters from the Black Sea* (1.1.17–18), and in 4.8 he attributes his close relationship with Suillius to marriage with his wife's daughter (*Letters from the Black Sea* 4.8.11–12). On Ovid's stepdaughter, see Syme (1978), 79, 89–90, 145. The identification of the pseudonymous "Perilla" of *Tristia* 3.7 with Ovid's stepdaughter is tentatively accepted by Nagle 1980, 150; Raepsaet-Charlier 1987, 860.
33. Ovid, *Tristia* 3.7.23–26.
34. On the passages in Gallus (fr. 145.9 Hollis) and Vergil (*Bucolics* 2.27), and their relationship to one another, see Hollis 2007, 247–52.
35. Horace, *Satires* 1.10.81–90; cf. Horace, *Art of Poetry* 263.
36. On Latin literary culture as gendered masculine, see Farrell 2001, 52–83.
37. Cf. Hemelrijk 1999, 152–53.
38. Fulkerson (2017, 42) lists the following authors as subscribing to the view that Tibullus was the poet of 3.8–12: Scaliger 1577; Gruppe 1838; Némethy 1905, 333–35; Cartault 1906; Smith 1913, 79; Zimmermann 1928; Rostagni 1935, 39–40; Ciaffi 1944, 166–71; Ponchont 1968, 168 and n1. For the view that Tibullus was the poet of 3.8, 10, and 12 alone, Fulkerson (2017, 42) lists Doncieux 1891, 78–79; Salanitro 1938, 31–34. For the view that Ovid was the poet of 3.8–12, see Radford 1920 and 1923; Bréguet 1946, 222, 280, and 333.
39. Butrica 1993.
40. Broukhusius 1708; Hallett 2002a.
41. Cornutus is the addressee of Tibullus' elegies 2.2 and 2.3. Fulkerson 2017, 42, understands Hubbard 2004/5, 186–88, as alluding to Cornutus, though I see Hubbard rather as favoring the identification of Tibullus as the author of the whole of the Sulpicia cycle. It must be noted, however, that in the Appendix to his article, Hubbard (2004/5, 191–92) seems to prefer the thesis of Radford (1920, 1923), taken up by Bréguet (1946), advocating Ovidian authorship of the "Garland" of Sulpicia (3.8–12).
42. Dronke 2003.
43. Tränkle 1990, 258–59; Maltby 2010. Maltby 2021, 82 and 109, allows that the sex of the unitary author (as he believes) of the poems collected in the third book of the Tibullan corpus was "perhaps more likely" (109) to have been female than male.
44. Fabre-Serris 2018, 2020a, 2022.
45. Hinds 1987; Hubbard 2004; Fulkerson 2017, 223; Fabre-Serris 2018, 73–75.
46. Fabre-Serris (2018, 68–70) demonstrates that 3.8 responds to Sulpicia's epigram 3.13 by opening with a potentially erotic scene (3.8.1–6) reminiscent of her successful love (3.13.3–4).
47. Fabre-Serris 2018, 70–71. On 3.10, see especially Fredericks 1976, 761–75.

48. Fabre-Serris 2018, 71–72, 75.
49. Maltby 2021, 104.
50. On the motif of the couple's "worth" across both first- and third-person poems in the cycle, cf. Fabre-Serris 2018, 70–71; on the Catullan resonances of the adjective *digna* in the Sulpicia cycle, see Hallett 2002a, 49–50.
51. On the "broadly hymnic structure" of 3.8, see Fulkerson 2017, 222–23, and cf. Fredericks 1976, 775–76. On 3.10.1–14 as a prayer to Apollo, see Fredericks 1976, 763–70; Fulkerson 2017, 247–51; and for the prayer to Juno Natalis in 3.12.1–14, see Fredericks 1976, 780; Fulkerson 2017, 262–66.
52. On "the elegiac principle of constant change," by contrast with the conventional wish for long-lasting harmony in epithalamium, see Fulkerson 2017, 268 ad 3.12.19–20. Hinds 1987, 32–33, addresses the generic inconcinnity of setting an elegiac poem on the occasion of the *Matronalia*.
53. Cf. Fabre-Serris 2018, 70–73.
54. Here I am especially indebted to the insightful work of Fredericks 1976; Santirocco 1979; Lowe 1988; Fabre-Serris 2018, 70–73, and 2020a, 181–83.
55. On Catullus' elegiac book (poems 65–116), see Skinner 2003.
56. Conte 1992.
57. Parker 1994, 50; cf. Fabre-Serris 2018, 73.
58. Fredericks 1976, 781.
59. Hinds 1987, 34.
60. Hubbard 2004/5, 185–88; Fabre-Serris 2018, 75–78.
61. On Sulpicia's debt to Tibullus' lexicon and phrasing, see the commentators *passim*.
62. Ovid, *Tristia* 4.10.57–58.
63. Ovid, *Tristia* 4.10.59–60.
64. So at least Ovid reports in the epigram that prefaces the *Amores*. On the vexed question of the chronology of Ovid's works, see McKeown 1987, 74–89.
65. Ovid, *Tristia* 4.10.33–36.
66. Jacqueline Fabre-Serris (2009, 2017, 2018, 2020b) and Judith P. Hallett have shed considerable light on intertextual relations between Ovid and Sulpicia, and my discussion is indebted to their research.
67. Fabre-Serris 2009 and 2018.
68. Ovid, *Heroides* 4.19–20.
69. Cf. Wills 1996, 177 on Ovid, *Heroides* 4.19–20 (comparing Calpurnius, *Eclogue* 3.7–8), and 427 on Sulpicia's elegy 3.11.5. Note also *urit/uror*, with alternation of person in epanalepsis, at Tibullus, elegy 2.4.5–6; on the "less striking" repetition there, see Wills 1996, 397.
70. Fabre-Serris 2018, 77. Sarah McCallum reminds me (*per litteras*) that "of the handful of forms of *uror* in the *Aeneid*, one relates to Juno's amatory wound (1.662), one to Dido's suffering (4.68), and one to Circe (7.13)." On Sulpician allusion to the Dido episode of the *Aeneid*, see Keith 1997.
71. Fabre-Serris 2009, 158–59. She sees the evocation of the boar as ultimately indebted to Gallus' use of Milanion, the hero of the Calydonian boar hunt, as an *exemplum* for the elegiac lover (cf. Propertius, elegy 1.1.9–16). In this connection, Sarah McCallum (*per litteras*) compares Ovid, *Art of Love* 2.185ff.
72. Ovid, *Heroides* 4.37–44.
73. Sulpicia's elegy 3.9.15–18, is reworked by Ovid, at *Heroides* 4.85–104.
74. Ovid, *Heroides* 4.93–100.
75. Fabre-Serris 2009, 159–61.
76. Ovid, *Heroides* 4.102–4. Fabre-Serris (2018, 76–77) notes the shared detail of the boar's sharp tusks and the placement of *dentes* in the same metrical sedes in both Sulpicia's elegy 3.9.3 and Ovid, *Heroides* 4.104.
77. Bréguet 1946; Hinds 1987, 36–37; Maltby 2021, 456–73, with further bibliography.
78. Ovid, *Metamorphoses* 10.545.
79. Hinds 1987, 36.
80. Ovid, *Metamorphoses* 1.593.
81. Ovid, *Metamorphoses* 1.508–9; see Hinds 1987, 36.
82. Ovid, *Remedies for Love* 199–200.
83. Bréguet 1946, 269–72.

84. Hinds 1987, 37; Maltby 2021, *passim*.
85. Fabre-Serris 2009, 163–64.
86. Ovid, *Heroides* 15.109–10.
87. Ovid, *Heroides* 15.39–40.
88. Ovid, *Heroides* 15.41–42.
89. Ovid, *Heroides* 15.43–46.
90. Ovid, *Heroides* 15.95.
91. Hallett 2006 and 2009b.
92. Ovid, *Amores* 3.14.1, 5 [*bis*], 11: see Hallett 2009b, §21.
93. Ovid, *Amores* 3.14.15–16; see Hallett 2009b, §23.
94. Hallett 2009b, §20.
95. *Amores* 3.15: see Fear 2000; Keith 2008b, 110–19.
96. Mart. 8.63 cites Propertius, Gallus, Tibullus, Catullus, Ovid, and Vergil (in his guise as a bucolic poet).
97. Cf. *Inscriptiones Latinae Selectae* 3103 (= *CIL* I² 979 = *CIL* VI 361), discussed in Ch. 2. Messalla's friend and fellow Arval Brother, M. Caecilius Cornutus—often proposed as our Sulpicia's husband (Ch. 4)—is known to have fathered a homonymous son (*PIR*² C35), who became in his turn an *arualis* and was *curator locorum publicorum iudicandorum* under Tiberius; accused of treason, he committed suicide in 24 CE.
98. Nisbet 2019, 280.
99. Martial, *Epigrams* 10.35.1–8; on Martial's epigram, see Buongiovanni 2012, 123–82.
100. Martial, *Epigrams* 10.35.9. On Catullus' lexicon, see Ross 1969. On Sulpicia's debt to Catullus, see Hallett 1992, 105–9; Nisbet 2019, 280–81. On Martial's Catullan lexicon in *Epigram* 10.35, see Buongiovanni 2012, 123–82.
101. Nisbet 2019, 281.
102. Martial, *Epigrams* 10.35.21.
103. Nisbet 2019, 282. Moreno Soldevila, Marina Castillo, and Fernández Valverde 2019, 99 s.v. "Calenus¹," tentatively accept his historicity.
104. Martial, *Epigrams* 10.38.1–3.
105. Martial, *Epigrams* 10.38.6 ~ Propertius, elegy 2.15; Martial, *Epigrams* 10.38.4 ~ Propertius, elegy 2.15.1; Martial, *Epigrams* 10.38. 7 ~ Propertius, elegy 2.15.2, and cf. Catullus, poem 6.10; Martial, *Epigrams* 10.38.7–8. Martial, *Epigrams* 10.38 also alludes very precisely a famous epigram by the late Hellenistic Greek poet and Epicurean philosopher Philodemos, celebrating a succession of bodily attributes of the Oscan prostitute Flora (*Palatine Anthology* 5.132 = Philodemos 12 Sider), with sustained anaphora of "ὁ" (thirteen times in three couplets, Philodemos 12.1–6 S; four times in the first nine lines of Martial, *Epigrams* 10.38). On Philodemos' epigram, see Sider 1997, 103–10.
106. See Moreno Soldevila, Marina Castillo, and Fernández Valverde 2019, 99 s.v. "Calenus¹," for the suggestion that the name is a pseudonym for a satirical poet.
107. Cf., e.g., Vergil, *Bucolics* 10.
108. Ausonius, *Cento Nuptialis* 10.9–10 Prete; Sidonius Apollinaris, *Carmina* 9.261–62; Fulgentius, *Mythologies* 1.4, 23. Butrica (2006, 83–87) argues that Ausonius knows Sulpicia because of Symmachus' recent rediscovery of her poem on the Domitianic expulsion of the philosophers (*Epigrammata Bobiensia* 37); that Sidonius knows her through Martial; and that Fulgentius knows her work through Ausonius, since he calls her *Ausoniana* (*Mythologies* 1.4). Butrica (2006, 78–79, 87–88) also discusses the imitation of her two extant poems (*Epigrammata Bobiensia* 36–37) by Prudentius and Claudian.
109. On the Villa dei Papyri at Herculaneum, see Sider 2005. For the continuing importance of family libraries among the pagan aristocrats of late antiquity, cf. Butrica 2006.

Chapter 8

1. Holzberg 1998–99 and 2001; Hubbard 2004–5; Kletke 2016; Maltby 2021. Cf. Habinek (1998, 122–36) who omits Sulpicia from discussion altogether in his chapter on "Roman Women's Useless Knowledge." The seeds of my discussion here lie in Keith 2006.
2. Tränkle 1990, 299–302 and 255–60, respectively.
3. Navarro Antolín 1996, 29.
4. Cf. Russ 1983, 20: "What to do when a woman has written something? The first line of defense is to deny that she wrote it."

5. Habinek 1998, 122–36.
6. Habinek 1998, 209–10.
7. Habinek 1998, 127. The expression "written women" was coined by Maria Wyke in her scholarship on women in Latin elegy now collected in Wyke 2002.
8. Finley 1965 (repr. in Finley 1968).
9. Holzberg 1998–99.
10. Tibullus, elegy 2.2.
11. Holzberg 1998–99, 177.
12. Parker 1994, 46.
13. Axelson 1960a and 1960b.
14. Hubbard 2004–5, 179.
15. Catullus, poems 62 and 64.
16. Hubbard 2001; cf. the fully elaborated argument at Hubbard 2004–5, 184–85.
17. Hubbard 2001, 67; cf. Hubbard 2004–5, 186–87.
18. Hubbard 2004–5, 182.
19. Hubbard 2001; cf. Hubbard 2004–5, 187: "this whole collection can be conceived as Cornutus' Matronalia present to Sulpicia, commissioned by him to renew the hopes and sentiments expressed in poetic form at the beginning of their relationship."
20. We might note, in passing, the curious fact that when male scholars attribute single authorship to the sequence they identify the anonymous poet as male, but when a female scholar proposes single authorship of the sequence, she identifies the poet as Sulpicia: see Hallett 2002b.
21. I do not discuss here Kletke 2016, who attempts to reconcile the differing views of Holzberg 1998–99 and Hubbard 2004–5 to call into question female authorship of the Sulpicia cycle, as I have addressed her points elsewhere in this volume, viz. the textual history of the Tibullan Appendix (Ch. 1), the exemplary conjugal loyalty of Fulvius' wife Sulpicia (Ch. 2), the generic conventions of elegy on display in the cycle (Chs. 4, 5, 6), and its ancient reception (Ch. 7).
22. Fulkerson 2017, 42–43, 47–53.
23. Maltby 2021, 127. In an earlier paper, however, Maltby (2010, 333–34) acknowledges that the bulk of the evidence for dating the Sulpicia cycle to the Neronian or Flavian period is restricted to 3.9 rather than being found consistently across the cycle; and Fulkerson (2017, 237) observes that his "parallels are . . . mostly of rare words, and so may not carry much weight."
24. Peirano 2012 is perhaps the most prominent exponent of this trend. In this regard, it is telling that Fulkerson 2017 was published in a new Oxford University Press series entitled "Pseudepigrapha Latina."
25. Cf. Fulkerson 2017, 52–53, discussing models for Sulpicia's authorship of 3.9, 11, 13–18 from later English literary history.
26. Russ 1983.
27. Russ 1983, 17. For Roman women's literacy, see Hemelrijk 1999; Churchill, Brown, and Jeffrey 2002; Stevenson 2005.
28. Russ 1983, 20.
29. https://www.youtube.com/watch?v=hKWjX2PT7Xg.
30. Maxwell 1995, 83–87.
31. Available on her website: https://www.noellemcmurtry.com/an-ancient-poet-speaks-finding-the-voice-of-sulpicia/.
32. Text from Noelle McMurtry's website as above, my n29.
33. The interlinked phenomena are well discussed in Russ 1983.
34. Hallett 1984, 1989, 1992, 2002a, 2002b, 2006, 2009a, 2009b, 2009c, 2009d, 2010a, 2010b, 2011a, 2011b; Churchill, Brown, and Jeffrey 2002; Stevenson 2005; Fabre-Serris 2009, 2017, 2018, 2020a, 2020b, 2022.

Appendix

1. The text of this line ([Tib.] 3.14.6) is uncertain. Tränkle prints the vulgate between daggers: †neu tempestiue sepe propinque uiet†. I have adopted the text printed by Lee rev. Maltby 1990 and Maltby 2021, 68 (discussed at 522–23), and tentatively accepted by Lyne 2007, 355–56; for a slightly different text, see Fulkerson 2017, 73, with discussion at 283.
2. I print the widely accepted suo in place of the manuscripts' tuo (printed by Tränkle). For discussion, see Lyne 2007, 358; Fulkerson 2017, 285; Maltby 2021, 525.

3. The manuscripts are divided between *natalis* (found in the earlier tradition) and *genialis* (reported in the later tradition). I follow Lee rev. Maltby 1990, Fulkerson 2017, and Maltby 2021 in opting for the reading of the earlier witnesses.
4. I print the text of Lee rev. Maltby 1990, Fulkerson 2017 (discussed at 285), and Maltby 2021 (discussed at 525–26), rather than the conjecture *necopinata*, accepted here by both Tränkle 1990 and Luck 1998.
5. I here adopt the translation of Lyne (2007, 359).
6. In this couplet I adopt the punctuation of Cairns (1998, 217), and adapt the translation he offers.
7. In this couplet, I accept the punctuation and interpretation of Cairns (1998, 221), who has influenced my translation.

Bibliography

Acosta-Hughes, B. 2010. *Arion's Lyre: Archaic Lyric into Hellenistic Poetry*. Princeton: Princeton University Press.

Adams, J. N. 1982. *The Latin Sexual Vocabulary*. Baltimore: Johns Hopkins University Press.

Ahl, F. 1985. *Metaformations*. Ithaca: Cornell University Press.

Amundsen, D. W., and Diers, C. J. 1969. "The Age of Menarche in Classical Greece and Rome," *Human Biology* 41, 125–32.

André, J.-M. 1949. *La vie et l'oeuvre d'Asinius Pollion*. Paris: Libraire C. Klincksieck.

Axelson, B. 1960a. "Lygdamus und Ovid. Zur Methodik der literarischen Priortätsbestimmung," *Eranos* 58, 92–111.

Axelson, B. 1960b. "Das Geburtsjahr des Lygdamus. Ein Rätsel der römischen Elegiendichtung," *Eranos* 58, 281–97.

Baehrens, E. 1876. *Tibullische Blätter*. Jena: H. Dufft.

Balmer, J. 1996. *Classical Women Poets*. Newcastle-upon-Tyne: Bloodaxe Books.

Batstone, W. 2018. "Sulpicia and the Speech of Men," in S. A. Frangoulidis and S. J. Harrison (eds.), *Life, Love and Death in Latin Poetry: Studies in Honor of Theodore D. Papanghelis*, 85–110. *Trends in Classics, Suppl. Vol.* 61. Berlin and Boston: De Gruyter.

Berman, D. W. 2010. "The Language and Landscape of Korinna," *GRBS* 50.1, 41–62.

Bettini, M. 2015. *Il dio elegante: Vertumno e la religione romana*. Turin: Piccola Biblioteca Einaudi.

Bosworth, A. B. 1972. "Asinius Pollio and Augustus," *Historia* 21.3, 441–73.

Boucher, J.-P. 1958. "L'œuvre de L. Varius Rufus d'après Properce II, 34," *REA* 60, 307–22.

Boucher, J.-P. 1965. *Études sur Properce. Problèmes d'inspiration et d'art*. BEFAR 204. Paris: E. de Boccard.

Boucher, J.-P. 1976. "A propos de Cérinthus et de quelques autres pseudonyms dans la poésie augustane," *Latomus* 35.3, 504–1.

Boulvert, G. 1970. *Esclaves et affranchie impériaux sous le haut empire romain: role politique et administrative*. Naples: Jovene.

Bowman, L. 2004. "The 'Women's Tradition' in Greek Poetry," *Phoenix* 58.1/2, 1–27.

Bradley, K. 1998. "The Sentimental Education of the Roman Child: The Role of Pet-Keeping," *Latomus* 57.3, 523–57.

Bréguet, E. 1946. *Le Roman de Sulpicia*. Geneva: Georg.

Bretone, M. 1971. *Tecniche e Ideologie dei Giuristi Romani*. Naples: Edizioni scientifiche italiane.

Briscoe, J. 2008. *A commentary on Livy, Books 38–40*. Oxford: Oxford University Press.

Broughton, T. R. S. 1951. *Magistrates of the Roman Republic*, 3 vols. New York: American Philological Association.

Broukhusius, J. 1708. *Tibullus*. Amsterdam: Westnenius.

Budelmann, F. 2018. *Greek Lyric, A Selection*. Cambridge: Cambridge University Press.

Buongiovanni, C. 2012. *Gli Epigrammata Longa del decimo libro di Marziale: Introduzione, testo, traduzione e commento*. Pisa: Edizioni ETS.

Butrica, J. 1993. "Lygdamus, Nephew of Messalla?," *LCM* 18, 51–53.

Butrica, J. 2006. "The *Fabella* of Sulpicia (*Epigrammata Bobiensia* 37)," *Phoenix* 60, 70–121.

Cairns, F. 1972. *Generic Composition in Greek and Roman Poetry*. Edinburgh: Edinburgh University Press.

Cairns, F. 1975. "Catullus 27," *Mnemosyne* 28.1, 24–29.

Cairns, F. 1979. *Tibullus: A Hellenistic Poet at Rome*. Cambridge: Cambridge University Press.

Cairns, F. 1983. "Propertius 1,4 and 1,5 and the 'Gallus' of the Monobiblos," *PLLS* 4, 61–103.

Cairns, F. 1998. "Tibullus 2.2," *PLILS* 10 (1998), 203–34.

Cairns, F. 2006. *Sextus Propertius: The Augustan Elegist.* Cambridge: Cambridge University Press.

Cairns, F. 2008. "C. Asinius Pollio and the *Eclogues*," *PCPS/CCJ* 54, 49–79.

Caldwell, L. 2015. *Roman Girlhood and the Fashioning of Femininity.* Cambridge: Cambridge University Press.

Carcopino, J. 1929. "Épitaphe en vers de la lectrice Pétalè, découverte à Rome," *Bulletin de la Société Nationale des Antiquaires de France,* 84–86.

Cartault, A. 1906. *A Propos du Corpus Tibullianum: un siècle de philologie latine Classique.* Paris: Félix Alcan.

Caston, R. R. 2012. *The Elegiac Passion: Jealousy in Roman Love Elegy.* Oxford: Oxford University Press.

Castorina, E. 1946. *Licinio Calvo.* Catania: Crisafulli.

Churchill, L. J., Brown, P. R., and Jeffrey, J. E. (eds.) 2002. *Women Writing Latin: From Roman Antiquity to Early Modern Europe,* 3 vols. New York: Routledge.

Ciaffi, V. 1944. *Lettura di Tibullo.* Turin: Chiantore.

Coleman, K. 1990. "Fatal Charades: Roman Executions Staged as Mythological Enactments," *JRS* 80, 44–73.

Collins, D. 2006. "Corinna and Mythological Innovation," *CQ* 56.1, 19–32.

Conte, G. B. 1992. "Proems in the Middle," *YCS* 29, 147–59.

Copley, F. O. 1947. "*Servitium amoris* in the Roman Elegists," *TAPA* 78, 285–300.

Corbier, M. 2001. "Child Exposure and Abandonment," in S. Dixon (ed.), *Childhood, Class, and Kin in the Roman World,* 52–73. London and New York: Routledge.

Courtney, E. 1993. *The Fragmentary Latin Poets.* Oxford: Clarendon Press.

Currie, H. M. 1983. "The Poems of Sulpicia," *ANRW* 2.30.3, 1751–64.

Cyllenius, B. (ed.) 1475. *Tibullus cum commento.* Rome: Georg Lauer.

D'Arms, J. H. 1970. *Romans on the Bay of Naples.* Cambridge, MA: Harvard University Press.

Dahlmann, H. 1977. *Über Helvius Cinna.* Wiesbaden: Franz Steiner.

Dalzell, A. 1955. "C. Asinius Pollio and the Early History of Public Recitation at Rome," *Hermathena* 86, 20–28.

Davies, C. 1973. "Poetry in the 'Circle' of Messalla," *G&R* 20.1, 25–35.

Davis, G. 1983. *The Death of Procris: Amor and the Hunt in Ovid's Metamorphoses.* Rome: Edizioni dell'Ateneo.

Davis, G. 2012. *Parthenope: The Interplay of Ideas in Vergil's Eclogues.* Leiden and Boston: Brill.

Davis, J. T. 1977. *Dramatic Pairings in the Elegies of Propertius and Ovid.* Bern and Stuttgart: Paul Haupt.

De Luca, E. 2009. *Corpus Tibullianum III 7: Panegyricus Messallae.* Soveria Mannelli: Rubbettino.

De Vos, M. 2014. "Sappho and the Female Tradition in Hellenistic Poetry," in J. Ker and C. Pieper (eds.), *Valuing the Past in the Greco-Roman World,* Mnemosyne Supplement 369, 410–34. Leiden: Brill.

Dettmer, H. 1983. "The 'Corpus Tibullianum'," *ANRW* 2.30.3, 1962–75. Berlin.

Dickison, S. K., and Hallett, J. P. 2014. *A Roman Women Reader: Selections from the Second Century BCE through the Second Century CE.* Wauconda, IL: Bolchazy Carducci.

Dillon, S. 2006. *Ancient Greek Portrait Sculpture: Contexts, Subjects, and Styles.* Cambridge: Cambridge University Press.

Dillon, S. 2010. *The Female Portrait Statue in the Greek World.* Cambridge: Cambridge University Press.

Dixon, H. M. 2002. *Studies in the Transmission of Tibullus.* Ph.D. dissertation, University of Cambridge.

Dixon, H. M. 2006. "The Discovery and Disappearance of the *Fragmentum Cuiacianum* of Tibullus," *Revue d'histoire des textes* 1, 37–72.

Dixon, S. 1988. *The Roman Mother*. London: Croom Helm.

Dixon, S. 2007. *Cornelia, Mother of the Gracchi*. London and New York: Routledge.

Dolansky, F. 2011. "Reconsidering the *Matronalia* and Women's Rites," *CW* 104.2, 191–209.

Dolansky, F. 2012. "Playing with Gender; Girls, Dolls, and Adult Ideals in the Roman World," *CA* 31.2, 256–92.

Dolansky, F. 2017. "Roman Girls and Boys at Play: Realities and Representations," in Laes and Vuolanto 2017, 116–36.

Doncieux, G. 1891. "De qui sont les elégies 2–6 du livre IV de Tibulle?," *Revue de Philologie, d'histoire, et de littérature anciennes* 15, 76–81.

Dronke, P. 2003. "Alcune osservazioni sulle poésie di Sulpicia," *Giornate filologiche Francesco Della Corte* 3, 81–99.

DuBois, P. 2015. *Sappho*. London: Bloomsbury.

Fabre-Serris, J. 2009. "Sulpicia: An/other Female Voice in Ovid's *Heroides*: A New Reading of *Heroides* 4 and 15," *Helios* 36, 149–73.

Fabre-Serris, J. 2017. "Sulpicia, Gallus et les élégiaques. Propositions de lecture de l'épigramme 3.13," *EuGeStA* 7, 115–39.

Fabre-Serris, J. 2018. "Intratextuality and Intertextuality in the *Corpus Tibullianum* (3.8–18)," in S. J. Harrison, S. Frangoulidis, and T. Papanghelis (eds.), *Intertextuality and Latin Literature*, 67–79. Berlin: De Gruyter.

Fabre-Serris, J. 2020a. "The Authorship of Tibullus 3.9: Methods and Criteria," in Franklinos and Fulkerson 2020, 170–85.

Fabre-Serris, J. 2020b. "Ovide lecteur de Sulpicia? Déclaration amoureuse et strategies d'énonciation dans le *Corpus Tibullianum* 3.11, 3.13 et l'*Héroide* 4," *Dictynna* 17. http://journals.openedition.org/dictynna/2176.

Fabre-Serris, J. 2022. "Enquête sur l'identité du 'je' féminin de l'élégie 3.11 du *Corpus Tibullianum*: méthodes et conjectures," in L. Cordes and T. Fuhrer (eds.), *The Gendered "I" in Ancient Literature: Modelling Gender in First-Person Discourse*, 257–81. Berlin: De Gruyter.

Fantham, E. (ed.) 1998. *Ovid, Fasti Book IV*. Cambridge: Cambridge University Press.

Fantham, E. 2006. *Julia Augusti, the Emperor's Daughter*. London and New York: Routledge.

Farrell, J. 2001. *Latin Language and Latin Culture from Ancient to Modern Times*. Cambridge: Cambridge University Press.

Fatucchi, A. 1976. "Le ferie aretine di Sulpicia (Nota topografia)," *Orpheus* 23, 145–60.

Fear, T. 2000. "The Poet as Pimp: Elegiac Seduction in the Time of Augustus," *Arethusa* 33, 217–40.

Fedeli, P. (ed.) 2005. *Properzio, Elegie Libro II*. Cambridge: Francis Cairns.

Ferrari, F. 2010. *Sappho's Gift: The Poet and Her Community*. Ann Arbor: Michigan Classical Press.

Fielding, I. 2020. "The Authorship of Sulpicia," in Franklinos and Fulkerson 2020, 186–97.

Finglass, J., and Kelly, A. (eds.) 2021. *The Cambridge Companion to Sappho*. Cambridge: Cambridge University Press.

Finley, M. I. "The Silent Women of Rome," *Horizon* 7 (1965) 57–64; repr. in M. I. Finley, *Aspects of Antiquity* (London: Chatto and Windus, 1968), 129–42.

Fish, J., and Sanders, K. R. (ed.) 2011. *Epicurus and the Epicurean Tradition*. Cambridge: Cambridge University Press.

Fisher, J. M. 1981. "The Transmission of the *Corpus Tibullianum*," *ANRW* II.30.3, 1953–58.

Flaschenriem, B. L. 1999. "Sulpicia and the Rhetoric of Disclosure," *CP* 94, 36–54.

Fordyce, C. J. 1961. *Catullus*. Oxford: Clarendon Press.

Franklinos, T. E. and Fulkerson, L. (eds.) 2020. *Constructing Authors and Readers in the Appendices Vergiliana, Tibulliana, and Ovidiana*. Oxford: Oxford University Press.

Fredericks, S. C. 1976. "A Poetic Experiment in the Garland of Sulpicia (*Corpus Tibullianum* 3.10)," *Latomus* 35.4, 761–82.

Frier, B. W. 1985. *The Rise of the Roman Jurists: Studies in Cicero's* Pro Caecina. Princeton: Princeton University Press.

Frier, B. W. 2015. "Roman Law and the Marriage of Underage Girls," *JRA* 28, 652–64.

Fulkerson, L. 2013. "*Seruitium amoris*," in Thorsen 2013, 180–93.

Fulkerson, L. 2017. *A Literary Commentary on the Elegies of the* Appendix Tibulliana. Oxford: Oxford University Press.

Funaioli, G. 1907. *Grammaticae Romanae Fragmenta*. Leipsig: Teubner.

Gagé, J. 1963. *Matronalia: Essai sur les dévotions et les organisations cultuelles des femmes dans l'ancienne Rome*. Brussels: Latomus.

Galinsky, G. K. 1981. "Augustus' Legislation on Morals and Marriage," *Philologus* 125, 126–44.

Gardner, J. F. 1986. *Women in Roman Law and Society*. London: Croom Helm.

Gibson, R. K. 2003. *Ovid,* Ars Amatoria *Book 3*. Cambridge: Cambridge University Press.

Gleason, K. L. 1994. "*Porticus Pompeiana*: A New Perspective on the First Public Park of Ancient Rome," *Journal of Garden History* 14, 13–27.

Goold, G. P. 1990. *Propertius,* Elegies. Cambridge, MA: Harvard University Press.

Gow, A. S. F., and Page, D. L. (eds.) 1965. *The Greek Anthology: Hellenistic Epigrams*, 2 vols. Cambridge: Cambridge University Press.

Gow, A. S. F., and Page, D. L. 1968. *The Greek Anthology: The Garland of Philip and Some Contemporary Epigrams*, 2 vols. Cambridge: Cambridge University Press.

Gowers, E. 2012. *Horace,* Satires *Book I*. Cambridge: Cambridge University Press.

Grafton, A. 1983–93. *Joseph Scaliger: A Study in the History of Classical Scholarship*. Oxford: Clarendon Press.

Green, C. M. C. 1996. "Did the Romans Hunt?" *CA* 15.2, 222–60.

Greene, E. (ed.) 1996a. *Reading Sappho: Contemporary Approaches*. Berkeley and Los Angeles: University of California Press.

Greene, E. 1996b. *Reading Sappho: Reception and Transmission*. Berkeley and Los Angeles: University of California Press.

Greene, E. 1998. *The Erotics of Domination: Male Desire and the Mistress in Latin Love Poetry*. Baltimore: Johns Hopkins University Press.

Greene, E. 2005. *Women Poets in Ancient Greece and Rome*. Norman: University of Oklahoma Press.

Greene, E. 2007. "Catullus and Sappho," in M. B. Skinner (ed.), *A Companion to Catullus*, 131–50. Malden, MA and Oxford: Wiley-Blackwell.

Greene, E. 2020. *Reading Sappho*, 2 vols. Berkeley: University of California Press.

Gruen, E. S. 1990. *Studies in Greek Culture and Roman Policy*. Leiden: Brill.

Gruppe, O. F. 1838. *Die Römische Elegie*, 2 vols. Leipzig: Wigand.

Gunderson, E. 2003. *Declamation, Paternity and Roman Identity*. Cambridge: Cambridge University Press.

Gurd, S. A. 2011. *Work in Progress: Literary Revision as Social Performance in Ancient Rome*. New York: Oxford University Press.

Gutzwiller, K. J. 1998. *Poetic Garlands: Hellenistic Epigrams in Context*. Berkeley: University of California Press.

Habinek, T. N. 1998. *The Politics of Latin Literature: Writing, Identity, and Empire in Ancient Rome*. Princeton: Princeton University Press.

Hadjimichael, T. A. 2019. *The Emergence of the Lyric Canon*. Oxford: Oxford University Press.

Hallett, J. P. 1984. *Fathers and Daughters in Roman Society: Women and the Elite Family*. Princeton: Princeton University Press.

Hallett, J. P. 1989. "Woman as Same and Other in the Classical Roman Elite," *Helios* 16, 59–78.

Hallett, J. P. 1992. "Martial's Sulpicia and Propertius' Cynthia," *CW* 86.2, 99–123.

Hallett, J. P. 2002a. "The Eleven Elegies of the Augustan Poet Sulpicia," in Churchill, Brown, and Jeffrey, 1.45–84.

Hallett, J. P. 2002b. "Sulpicia and the Valerii: Family Ties and Poetic Unity," in B. Amden et al. (eds.), Noctes Atticae. *34 Articles on Greco-Roman Antiquity and Its Nachleben. Studies Presented to Jurgen Mejer on His Sixtieth Birthday, March 18, 2002*, 141–49. Copenhagen: Museum Tusculanum Press.

Hallett, J. P. 2006. "Sulpicia and Her *Fama*: An Intertextual Approach to Recovering Her Latin Literary Image," *CW* 100, 37–42.

Hallett, J. P. 2009a. "Sulpicia and Her Resistant Intertextuality," in D. van Mal-Maeder, A. Burnier, and L. Núñez (eds.), *Jeux de voix, Énonciation, intertextualité et intentionnalité dans la littérature antique*, 141–53. Bern: Lang.

Hallett, J. P. 2009b. "Ovid's Sappho and Roman Women Love Poets," *Dictynna* 6, 2–10.

Hallett, J. P. 2009c. "Absent Roman Fathers in the Writings of Their Daughters," in S. Hübner and D. Ratzan (eds.), *Growing up Fatherless in Antiquity*, 175–91. Cambridge: Cambridge University Press.

Hallett, J. P. 2009d. "*Corpus Erat*: Sulpicia's Elegiac Text and Body in Ovid's Pygmalion Narrative (*Metamorphoses* 10.238–297), in T. Foegen and M. Lee (eds.), *Bodies and Boundaries in Graeco-Roman Antiquity*, 111–24. Berlin and New York: De Gruyter.

Hallett, J. P. 2010a. "Ovid's Thisbe and a Roman Woman Love Poet," in Barbara W. Boyd and Cora Fox (eds.), *Approaches to Teaching the Works of Ovid and the Ovidian Tradition*. Approaches to Teaching World Literature, Modern Language Association, 170–77. New York: Modern Language Association of America.

Hallett, J. P. 2010b. "Human Connection and Paternal Evocations: Two Elite Roman Women Writers and the Valuing of Others," in R. Rosen and I. Sluiter (eds.), *Valuing Others in Classical Antiquity*, 353–73. Leiden and Boston: Brill.

Hallett, J. P. 2011a. "Recovering Sulpicia: The Value and Limitations of Prosopography and Intertextuality," in J. Nelis (ed.), *Receptions of Antiquity*, 297–311. Ghent: Academia Press.

Hallett, J. P. 2011b. "Scenarios of Sulpiciae: Moral Discourses and Immoral Verses," *EuGeStA* 1, 79–97.

Hamer, M. 2008. *Signs of Cleopatra: Reading an Icon Historically.*[2] Exeter: University of Exeter Press.

Hammer, J. 1925. *Prolegomena to an Edition of the* Panegyricus Messalae*: The Military and Political Career of M. Valerius Messala Corvinus*. New York: Columbia University Press.

Hänninen, M.-L. 2000. *Women as Worshippers of Juno*. Helsinki: University of Helsinki Press.

Hanses, E. 2024. "A Woman's Pleasure: Sulpicia and the Epicurean Discourse on Love," in G. Davis and S. Yona (eds.), *Afterlives of the Garden: Receptions of Epicurean Thought in the Early Empire and Late Antiquity*, 55–79. Berlin: De Gruyter.

Hanslik, R. 1955. "Valerius Messalla Corvinus," *RE* 15.2, 131–57.

Harlow, M. 2017. "Little Tunics for Little People: The Problems of Visualizing the Wardrobe of the Roman Child," in Laes and Vuolanto 2017, 43–59.

Haupt, M. 1871. "Varia," *Hermes* 5, 32–34 = *Opuscula* (Leipzig, 1875–76), 3.502–3.

Hauser, E. 2016. "*Optima tu proprii nominis auctor*: The Semantics of Female Authorship in Ancient Rome, from Sulpicia to Proba," *EuGeStA* 6, 151–86.

Heath, J. 2017. "Corinna's 'Old Wives' Tales,'" *HSCP* 109, 38–130.

Helm, R. (ed.) 1956. *Eusebius Werke, Siebenter Band: die Chronik des Hieronymus*. Berlin: Akademie-Verlag.

Hemelrijk, E. A. 1999. Matrona Docta: *Educated Women in the Roman Elite from Cornelia to Julia Domna*. London and New York: Routledge.

Hendrickson, G. L., and Hubbell, H. M. 1962. *Cicero V: Brutus, Orator*. Loeb Classical Library. Cambridge, MA: Harvard University Press.

Hermann, L. 1951. *L'âge d'argent doré*. Paris: Presses universitaires de France.

Heyne, C. G. 1975 [1815–17]. *Albii Tibulli Carmina libri tres cum libro quarto Sulpiciae et aliorum.*[4] Hildesheim: G. Olms.

Hinds, S. E. 1987. "The Poetess and the Reader: Further Steps towards Sulpicia," *Hermathena* 143, 29–46.

Hinds, S. E. 2006. "Venus, Varro and the *Vates*: Toward the Limits of Etymologizing Interpretation," *Dictynna* 3, 175–210.

Hollis, A. S. 2007. *Fragments of Roman Poetry, c. 60* BC–AD *20*. Oxford: Oxford University Press.

Holzberg, N. 1998–99. "Four Poets and a Poetess or a Portrait of the Poet as a Young Man? Thoughts on Book 3 of the Corpus Tibullianum," *CJ* 94.2, 169–91.

Holzberg, N. 2001. *Die Römische Liebeselegie*.[2] Darmstadt: Wissentschaftliche Buchgesellschaft.

Hopkins, M. K. 1965. "The Age of Roman Girls at Marriage," *Population Studies* 18, 309–27.

Höschele, R. n.d. *Greek Epigram in a Roman Cosmos: The Garland of Philip*.

Hubbard, T. K. 2001. "The Sulpicia Cycle as Epithalamic Dedication," *APA Abstracts* 132, 67.

Hubbard, T. K. 2004–5. "The Invention of Sulpicia," *CJ* 100.2, 177–94.

Hutchinson, G. (ed.) 2006. *Propertius, Elegies Book IV*. Cambridge: Cambridge University Press.

Ingleheart, J. (ed.) 2010. *A Commentary on Ovid*, Tristia, *Book 2*. Oxford: Oxford University Press.

James, S. L. 2003. *Learned Girls and Male Persuasion: Gender and Reading in Roman Love Elegy*. Berkeley and Los Angeles, CA: University of California Press.

James, S. and Dillon, S. 2012. *Blackwell Companion to Women in the Ancient World*. Chichester: Blackwell Publishing.

Jeffreys, R. L. 1985. "The Date of Messalla's Death," *CQ* 35.1, 140–48.

Jeffreys, R. L. 1987. "The 'Infirmitas' of Messalla Corvinus," *Latomus* 46.1, 196–98.

Kaster, R. A. 2002. "Declamation in Rhetorical Education at Rome," in Y. L. Too (ed.), *Education in Greek and Roman Antiquity*, 317–37. Leiden and Boston: Brill.

Kayachev, B. 2016. "'Catalepton' 9 and Hellenistic Poetry," *CQ* 66.1, 180–204.

Kayachev, B. 2020. "Catalepton 9 and Valgius Rufus," in Franklinos and Fulkerson, 83–95.

Keith, A. M. 1997. "*Tandem venit amor*: A Roman Woman Speaks of Love," in J. P. Hallett and M. B. Skinner (eds.), *Roman Sexualities*, 295–310. Princeton: Princeton University Press.

Keith, A. M. 2006. "Critical Trends in Interpreting Sulpicia," *CW* 100, 3–10.

Keith, A. M. 2008a. "Sartorial Elegance and Poetic Finesse in the Sulpician Corpus," in J. Edmondson and A. Keith (eds.), *Roman Dress and the Fabrics of Roman Culture*, 192–201. Toronto: Toronto University Press.

Keith, A. M. 2008b. *Propertius, Poet of Love and Leisure*. London: Duckworth.

Keith, A. M. (ed.) 2011. *Latin Elegy and Hellenistic Epigram: A Tale of Two Genres at Rome*. Newcastle upon Tyne: Cambridge Scholars Publishers.

Keith, A. M. 2012. "The *Domina* in Roman Elegy," in B. Gold (ed.), *Blackwell Companion to Roman Love Elegy*, 285–302. Malden, MA: Wiley-Blackwell.

Keith, A. M. 2016. "Naming the Elegiac Mistress: Elegiac Onomastics in Roman Inscriptions," in A. Keith and J. Edmondson (eds.), *Roman Literary Cultures: Domestic Politics, Revolutionary Poetics, Civic Spectacle*, 73–111. Toronto: Toronto University Press.

Keith, A. M. 2018. "Historical Roman Courtesans," in R. Berg and R. Neudecker (eds.), *The Roman Courtesan: Archaeological Reflections of a Literary Topos*, 73–86. Acta Instituti Romani Finlandiae 46. Rome: Institutum Romanum Finlandiae.

Kenty, J. 2017. "Messalla Corvinus: Augustan Orator, Ciceronian Statesman," *Rhetorica* 35.4, 445–74.

Kivilo, M. 2021. "Sappho's Lives," in Finglass and Kelly 2021, 11–21.

Kletke, S. 2016. "Why Is Sulpicia a Woman?," *Mouseion* 13, 625–53.

Klinck, A. L. 2008. *Women's Songs in Ancient Greece*. Montreal and Kingston: McGill-Queen's University Press.

Kuttner, A. L. 1999. "Culture and History at Pompey's Museum," *TAPA* 129, 123–45.

Lachmann, K. 1876. *Kleinere Schriften*, 2 vols. Berlin: G. Reimer.

Laes C., and Vuolanto, V. (eds.) 2017. *Children and Everyday Life in the Roman and Late Antique World*. Routledge: London and New York.

Langlands, R. 2000. *Gender and Exemplarity in Valerius Maximus*. Ph.D. dissertation, University of Cambridge.

Langlands, R. 2006. *Sexual Morality in Ancient Rome*. Cambridge: Cambridge University Press.

Larson, J. 2002. "Corinna and the Daughters of Asopus," *Syllecta Classica* 13, 47–62.

Lauer, G. (publ.) 1475. *Albii Tibulli Elegiarum libri IV cum commentario Bernardini Cillenii Veronensis*. Rome.

Lausberg, M. 1982. *Das Einzeldistichon: Studien zum antiken Epigramm*. Munich: W. Fink.

Leach, E. W. 1978. "Vergil, Horace, Tibullus: Three Collections of Ten," *Ramus* 7, 79–105.

Lee, G., rev. Maltby, R. 1990. *Tibullus: Elegies*.[3] Leeds: Francis Cairns.

Lefkowitz, M. R., and Fant, M. B. 2016. *Women's Life in Greece and Rome: A Source Book in Translation*.[4] London: Bloomsbury.

Lewis, A.-M. 2012. "Reconsidering Ovid's Relationship to Perilla (*Tristia* III, 7)," in C. Deroux (ed.), *Studies in Latin Literature and Roman History* 16, 367–97. Brussels: Latomus.

Lewis, A.-M. 2013. "The Family Relationships of Ovid's Third Wife: A Reconsideration," *Ancient Society* 43, 151–89.

Lockwood, J. F. 1951. Review of *Servio Sulpicio Rufo e I Suoi Tempi* by Piero Meloni, *JRS* 41, 159–60.

Lowe, N. J. 1988. "Sulpicia's Syntax," *CQ* 38, 193–205.

Luck, G. (ed.) 1998. *Tibullus*.[2] Stuttgart and Leipzig: Teubner.

Lyne, R. O. A. M. 1979. "*Seruitium amoris*," *CQ* 29, 117–30.

Lyne, R. O. A. M. 2007 [2004–5]. "[Tibullus] Book 3 and Sulpicia," *Collected Papers on Latin Poetry*, 341–67. Oxford: Oxford University Press.

Malcovati, H. 1955. *Oratorum Romanorum Fragmenta*.[2] Milan: I. B. Paraviae.

Maltby, R. 1991. *A Lexicon of Ancient Latin Etymologies*. Leeds: Francis Cairns.

Maltby, R. (ed.) 2002. *Tibullus: Elegies*, with text, introduction and commentary. Leeds: Francis Cairns.

Maltby, R. 2010. "The Unity of *Corpus Tibullianum* Book 3: Some Stylistic and Metrical Considerations," *PLLS* 14, 319–40.

Maltby, R. 2021. *Book Three of the* Corpus Tibullianum. Newcastle upon Tyne: Cambridge Scholars Publishing.

Martinon, P. 1895. *Les élégies de Tibulle, Lygdamus et Sulpicia*. Paris: Thorin.

Maxwell, M. 1995. *Latin Lyric and Elegiac Poetry: An Anthology of New Translations*. New York: Garland Publishing.

McCarthy, K. 1998. "*Servitium Amoris: Amor Servitii*," in S. Murnaghan and S. Joshel (eds.), *Women and Slaves in Greco-Roman Culture*, 174–92. London: Routledge.

McCoskey, D., and Torlone, Z. 2013. *Latin Love Poetry*. London: I. B. Tauris.

McGann, M. J. 1970. "The Date of Tibullus' Death," *Latomus* 29, 774–80.

McGinn, T. A. 1998. *Prostitution, Sexuality, and the Law in Ancient Rome*. Oxford: Oxford University Press.

McGinn, T. A. 2004. *The Economy of Prostitution in the Roman World: A Study of Social History and the Brothel*. Ann Arbor: University of Michigan Press.

McKeown, J. C. 1987–98. *Ovid*: Amores, *Text, Prolegomena and Commentary*, in 3 vols. Leeds: Francis Cairns.

McMurtry, N. 2015. "Reflections on Jessica Krash's *Sulpicia's Songs* (2015)," https://www.noel-lemcmurtry.com/an-ancient-poet-speaks-finding-the-voice-of-sulpicia/.

McPhee, B. D. 2018. "Mythological Innovations in Corinna's Asopides Poem (fr. 654.ii–iv *PMG*," *GRBS* 58.2, 198–222.

Meloni, P. 1946. *Servio Sulpicio Rufo e i suoi Tempi. Annali della Facoltà di Lettere e Filosofia della Università di Cagliari* XIII. Cagliari: University of Cagliari.

Merriam, C. U. 1990. "Some Notes on the Sulpicia Elegies," *Latomus* 49, 95–98.

Merriam, C. U. 1991. "The Other Sulpicia," *CW* 84, 303–5.

Merriam, C. U. 2005. "Sulpicia and the Art of Literary Allusion: [Tibullus] 3.13," in E. Greene (ed.), *Women Poets in Ancient Greece and Rome*, 158–68. Norman: University of Oklahoma Press.

Merriam, C. U. 2006. "Sulpicia: Just Another Roman Poet," *CW* 100.1, 11–16.

Miller, J. F. 2009. *Apollo, Augustus, and the Poets*. Cambridge: Cambridge University Press.

Miller, P. A. (ed.) 2002. *Latin Erotic Elegy: An Anthology and Reader*. New York: Routledge.

Miller, P. A. 2017. *Oxford Bibliographies. Classics. Tibullus*. New York: Oxford University Press.

Milnor, K. 2002. "Sulpicia's (Corpo)reality: Elegy, Authorship, and the Body in [Tibullus] 3.13," *CA* 21.2, 259–82.

Milnor, K. 2005. *Gender, Domesticity, and the Age of Augustus: Inventing Private Life*. Oxford: Oxford University Press.

Miralles Maldonado, J. C. 1990. "La Lengua de Sulpicia: *Corpus Tibullianum* 4.7–12," *Habis* 21, 101–20.

Momigliano, A. 1950. "*Panegyricvs Messallae* and 'Panegyricvs Vespasiani': Two References to Britain," *JRS* 40, 39–42.

Moreno Soldevila, R., Marina Castillo, A., and Fernández Valverde, J. 2019. *A Prosopography to Martial's Epigrams*. Berlin: De Gruyter.

Mueller, M. 2023. *Sappho and Homer: A Reparative Reading*. Cambridge: Cambridge University Press.

Münzer, F. 1891. *De Gente Valeria*. Ph.D. dissertation, University of Berlin.

Münzer, F. 1920. *Römische Adelsparteien und Adelsfamilien*. Stuttgart: J. B. Mettzlersche Verlagsbuchhandlung.

Münzer, F., and Kübler, B. 1931. "Sulpicius," *RE* s.v. 95, 851–60.

Murgatroyd, P. (ed.) 1980. *Tibullus I*. Natal: University of Natal Press; repr. 1991, Bristol Classical Press.

Murgatroyd, P. 1981. "*Servitium Amoris* and the Roman Elegists," *Latomus* 49, 589–606.

Murgatroyd, P. 1984. "Amatory Hunting, Fishing and Fowling," *Latomus* 43, 362–68.

Murgatroyd, P. (ed.) 1994. *Tibullus, Elegies II*. Oxford: Clarendon Press.

Nagle, B. R. 1980. *The Poetics of Exile: Program and Polemic in the* Tristia *and* Epistulae ex Ponto *of Ovid*. Coll. Latomus 170. Brussels: Latomus.

Natoli, B., Pitts, A., and Hallett, J. P. 2022. *Ancient Women Writers of Greece and Rome*. London and New York: Routledge.

Navarro Antolín, F. 1996. *Lygdamus:* Corpus Tibullianum *III.1–6*, translated by J. J. Zoltowski. Leiden: Brill.

Navarro Antolín, F. 2005. "Propercio en el libro tercero del *Corpus Tibullianum*," in C. Santini and F. Santucci (eds.), *Properzio nel genere elegiaco: modelli, motivi, riflessi storici*, 301–24. Assisi: Accademia Properziana del Subasio.

Némethy, G. 1905. *Albii Tibulli Carmina*. Budapest: Academia Litterarum Hungaricae.

Néraudau, J.-P. 1983. "Asinius Pollion et la poésie," *ANRW* 2.30.3, 1732–50.

Neri, C. 2021. *Saffo—testimonianze e frammenti*. Berlin: De Gruyter.

Neudling, C. L. 1955. *A Prosopography to Catullus*. Oxford: Oxford University Press.

Newton, F. L. 1962. "Tibullus in Two Grammatical Florilegia of the Middle Ages," *TAPA* 93, 253–86.

Nikoloutsos, K. P. 2007. "Beyond Sex: The Poetics and Politics of Pederasty in Tibullus 1.4," *Phoenix* 61.1–2, 55–82.

Nikoloutsos, K. P. 2011. "The Boy as Metaphor: The Hermeneutics of Homoerotic Desire in Tibullus 1.9," *Helios* 38.1, 27–57.

Nisbet, G. 2019. "Sappho in Roman Epigram," in Thorsen and Harrison 2019, 265–88.

Nisbet, R. G. M., and Hubbard, M. 1970. *A Commentary on Horace, Odes, Book I*. Oxford: Clarendon Press.

Nisbet, R. G. M., and Hubbard, M. 1978. *A Commentary on Horace, Odes, Book II*. Oxford: Clarendon Press.

Nisbet, R. G. M., and Hubbard, M. (ed. S. J. Harrison) 1995. *Collected Papers on Latin Literature*. Oxford: Oxford University Press.

Nooter, S. 2023. *Greek Poetry in the Age of Ephemerality*. Cambridge: Cambridge University Press.

Norden, E. 1954. *Die römische Literatur*.[3] Leipzig: Teubner.

Norden, E. 1957. *Vergil. Aeneis Buch VI*. Leipzig: Teubner.

Nosarti, L. 1999. *Filologia in Frammenti*. Bologna: Pàtron.

O'Hara, J. J. 1996. *True Names: Vergil and the Alexandrian Tradition of Etymological Wordplay*. Ann Arbor: University of Michigan Press.

O'Keefe, T. 2010. *Epicureanism*. Berkeley: University of California Press.

Olson, K. 2002. "Matrona and Whore: The Clothing of Women in Roman Antiquity," *Fashion Theory* 6.4, 391–95.

Olson, K. 2008a. *Dress and the Roman Woman: Self-Presentation and Society*. London and New York: Routledge.

Olson, K. 2008b. "The Appearance of the Young Roman Girl," in J. Edmondson and A. Keith (eds.), *Roman Dress and the Fabrics of Roman Culture*, 139–57. Toronto: University of Toronto Press.

Osgood, J. 2014. *Turia: A Roman Woman's Civil War*. New York and Oxford: Oxford University Press.

Pagán, V. 2009. *A Sallust Reader: Selections from* Bellum Catilinae *and* Bellum Iugurthinum, *and* Historiae. Wauconda, IL: Bolchazy-Carducci Publishers.

Page, D. L. 1955. *Sappho and Alcaeus*. Oxford: Clarendon Press.

Panagiotopoulou, M. 2022. "Praxilla's *Adonis* and the Female Voice: An Erotic 'Reverse Priamel' in Sappho's Shadow and Nossis's Light," *ILS* 47.1, 24–44.

Panoussi, L. 2019. *Brides, Mourners, Bacchae: Women's Rituals in Roman Literature*. Baltimore: John Hopkins University Press.

Parker, H. N. 1992. "Other Remarks on the Other Sulpicia," *CW* 86.2, 89–95.

Parker, H. N. 1994. "Sulpicia, the *Auctor de Sulpicia* and the Authorship of 3.9 and 3.11 of the *Corpus Tibullianum*," *Helios* 21, 39–62.

Parker, H. N. 2005. "Loyal Slaves and Loyal Wives: The Crisis of the Outsider-Within and Roman Exemplum Literature," in S. R. Joshel and S. Murnaghan (eds.), *Women and Slaves in Greco-Roman Culture: Differential Equations*, 152–73. New York: Routledge.

Parker, H. N. 2006. "Catullus and the 'Amicus Catulli': The Text of a Learned Talk," *CW* 100.1, 17–29.

Paton, W. R. (tr.), rev. Tueller, M. A. 2014. *The Greek Anthology, Books 1–5*. Cambridge, MA: Harvard University Press.

Peirano, I. 2012. *The Rhetoric of the Roman Fake: Latin Pseudepigrapha in Context*. Cambridge: Cambridge University Press.

Peter, H. 1914. *Historicorum Romanorum Reliquiae*. Leipzig: Teubner.

Petrain, D. 2000. "Hylas and *Silua*: Etymological Wordplay in Propertius 1.20," *HSCP* 100, 409–21.

Piastri, R. 1998. "I carmi di Sulpicia e il repertorio topico dell'elegia," *Quaderni del Dipartimento di Filologia Linguistica e Tradizione Classica* 11, 137–70.

Pichon, R. 1902. *Index Verborum Amatoriorum*. Paris: Hachette.

Piro, I. 2013. *Spose bambine. Risalenza, diffusione e rilevanza giuridica del fenomeno in età romana dale origini all'epoca classica*. Milan: Giuffrè.

Plant, I. M. (ed.) 2004. *Women Writers of Ancient Greece and Rome, an Anthology*. Norman: University of Oklahoma Press.

Ponchont, M. 1968. *Tibulle et les auteurs du* Corpus Tibullianum.[7] Paris: Les Belles lettres.

Porte, D. 1992. "Messalla," *Orphea Voce* 4. Bordeaux.

Postgate, J. P. 1905/15.[2] *Tibulli aliorumque carminum libri tres*. Oxford: Clarendon Press.

Postgate, J. P., rev. G. P. Goold. 1988. "Tibullus," in *Catullus, Tibullus, Peruigilium Veneris*.[2] Loeb Classical Library. Cambridge, MA: Harvard University Press.

Putnam, M. C. J. (ed.) 1973. *Tibullus, A Commentary*. Norman: University of Oklahoma Press.

Racette-Campbell, M. 2023. *The Crisis of Masculinity in the Age of Augustus*. Madison: University of Wisconsin Press.

Radford, R. S. 1920. "The Juvenile Works of Ovid and the Spondaic Period of His Metrical Art," *TAPA* 51, 146–71.

Radford, R. S. 1923. "Tibullus and Ovid: The Authorship of the Sulpicia and Cornutus Elegies in the Tibullan Corpus," *AJP* 44, 1–26, 230–59, 293–318.

Raditsa, L. F 1980. "Augustus' Legislation Concerning Marriage, Procreation, Love Affairs and Adultery," *ANRW* II.13, 278–329.

Raepsaet-Charlier, M.-Th. 1987. *Prosopographie des femmes de l'ordre sénatorial (Ier–IIe siècles)*, 2 vols. Louvain: Peeters.

Randall, J. G. 1979. "Mistresses' Pseudonyms in Latin Elegy," *LCM* 4, 27–35.

Rankin, A.V. 1962. "*Odi et Amo*: Gaius Valerius Catullus and Freud's Essay on 'A Special Type of Choice of Object Made by Men'," *American Imago* 19, 437–47.

Rawson, E. 1978. "The Identity Problems of Q. Cornificius," *CQ* 28.1, 188–201.

Rawson, E. 2003. *Children and Childhood in Roman Italy*. Oxford: Oxford University Press.

Rayor, D. 1991. *Sappho's Lyre: Archaic Lyric and Women Poets of Ancient Greece*. Berkeley: University of California Press.

Rayor, D. 1993. "Korinna: Gender and the Narrative Tradition," *Arethusa* 26.3, 219–31.

Richlin, A. 1992. "Sulpicia the Satirist," *CW* 86.2, 125–40.

Riess, W. 2012. "*Rari exempli femina*: Female Virtues on Roman Funerary Inscriptions," in S. L. James and S. Dillon (eds.), *A Companion to Women in the Ancient World*, 491–501. Malden, MA and Oxford: Wiley-Blackwell.

Robinson, R. P. 1923. "Valerius Cato," *TAPA* 54, 98–116.

Roessel, D. 1990. "The Significance of the Name Cerinthus in the Poems of Sulpicia," *TAPA* 120, 243–50.

Roller, D. W. 2010. *Cleopatra: A Biography*. Oxford and New York: Oxford University Press.

Rosenmeyer, P. 2007. "From Syracuse to Rome: The Travails of Silanion's Sappho," *TAPA* 137.2, 277–303.

Ross, D. O., Jr. 1969. *Style and Tradition in Catullus*. Cambridge, MA: Harvard University Press.

Ross, D. O., Jr. 1975. *Backgrounds to Augustan Poetry: Gallus, Elegy and Rome*. Cambridge: Cambridge University Press.

Rossbach, A. (ed.) 1855. *Albii Tibulli libri quattuor*. Leipzig: Teubner.

Rostagni, A. 1935. "La *Vita* Suetoniana di Tibullo e la costituzione del *Corpus Tibullianum*," *RFIC* 13, 20–51; repr. in *Scritti Minori* 2.2 (Turin 1956), 304–41.

Rostagni, A. 1961. *Virgilio minore*,[2] 405–27. Rome: Edizioni di storia e letteratura.

Rouse, R. H. 1967. "The Early Library of the Sorbonne," *Scriptorium* 21, 42–71, 227–45.

Rouse, R. H. 1973. "Manuscripts Belonging to Richard de Fournival," *RHT* 3, 253–69.

Rouse, R. H. 1979. "*Florilegia* and Latin Classical Authors in Twelfth- and Thirteenth-Century Orléans," *Viator, Medieval and Renaissance Studies* 10, 131–60.

Rouse, R. H., and Reeve, M. D. 1983. "Tibullus," in L. D. Reynolds (ed.), *Texts and Transmission: A Survey of the Latin Classics*, 420–25. Oxford: Clarendon Press.

Rüpke, J. 2012. *Religion in Republican Rome*. Philadelphia: University of Pennsylvania Press.

Russ, J. 1983. *How to Suppress Women's Writing*. Austin, TX: University of Texas Press.

Salanitro, N. 1938. *Tibullo*. Naples: Luigi Loffredo.

Santirocco, M. S. 1979. "Sulpicia Reconsidered," *CJ* 74, 229–39.

Saylor, C. F. 1967. "*Querelae*: Propertius' Distinctive, Technical Name for his Elegy," *Agon* 1, 142–49.

Saunders, C. 1923. "The Political Sympathies of Servius Sulpicius Rufus," *CR* 37.5/6, 110–13.

Scaliger, J. J. (ed. and comm.) 1577. *Catulli, Tibulli, Properti nova editio*, in id. *Castigationum liber*. Paris: Rob. Stephanus.

Scheid, J. 1975. *Les frères arvales. Recrutement et origine sociale sous les empereurs julio-claudiens*. Bibliothèque de l'école des hautes études. Section des sciences religieuses 77. Paris: Presses universitaires de France.

Schoonhaven, H. 1983. "The *Panegyricus Messallae*: Date and Relations with *Catalepton 9*," *ANRW* II.30.3, 1681–1707.

Schultz, C. 2006. *Women's Religious Activity in the Roman Republic*. Chapel Hill: University of North Carolina Press.

Schulz, H. 1886. *De M. Valerii Messalae Aetate*. Stettin.

Schwartz, T. G. 1934. *A Biography of Coluccio Salutati (Feb 16, 1331–May 4, 1406)*.

Scullard, H. H. 1981. *Festivals and Ceremonies of the Roman Republic*. Ithaca: Cornell University Press.

Shackleton Bailey, D. R. (ed.) 1965–70. *Cicero's Letters to Atticus*, 7 vols. Cambridge: Cambridge University Press.

Shackleton Bailey, D. R. (ed.) 1980. *Cicero*: Epistulae ad Quintum Fratrem et M. Brutum. Cambridge: Cambridge University Press.

Shumka, L. 1993. *Children and Toys in the Roman World: A Contribution to the History of the Roman Family*. M.A. Thesis, University of Victoria.

Sider, D. (ed.) 1997. *The Epigrams of Philodemos: Introduction, Text, and Commentary*. Oxford: Oxford University Press.

Sider, D. 2004. "Posidippus Old and New," in B. Acosta-Hughes, E. Kosmetatou, and M. Baumbach (eds.), *Labored in Papyrus Leaves: Perspectives on an Epigram Collection Attributed to Posidippus (P.Mil. Vog. VIII 309)*, 29–41. Washington, DC: Center for Hellenic Studies.

Sider, D. 2005. *The Library of the Villa dei Papiri at Herculaneum*. Los Angeles: J. Paul Getty Museum.

Skinner, M. B. 1982. "Pretty Lesbius," *TAPA* 112, 197–208.

Skinner, M. B. 1983. "Corinna of Tanagra and Her Audience," *Tulsa Studies in Women's Literature* 2, 9–20.

Skinner, M. B. 1989. "Sapphic Nossis," *Arethusa* 22, 5–18.

Skinner, M. B. 1991a. "Nossis *Thelyglossos*: The Private Text and the Public Book," in S. B. Pomeroy (ed.), *Women's History and Ancient History*, 20–47. Chapel Hill: University of North Carolina Press.

Skinner, M. B. 1991b. "Aphrodite Garlanded: Eros and Poetic Creativity in Sappho and Nossis," in F. de Martino (ed.), *Rose di Pieria*, 79–96. Bari: Levante.

Skinner, M. B. 2001. "Ladies' Day at the Art Institute: Theocritus, Herodas, and the Gendered Gaze," in A. Lardinois and L. McClure (eds.), *Making Silence Speak*, 201–22. Princeton: Princeton University Press.

Skinner, M. B. 2003. *Catullus in Verona: A Reading of the Elegiac libellus, Poems 65–116*. Columbus: Ohio State University Press.

Skinner, M. B. 2005. *Sexuality in Greek and Roman Culture*. Oxford and Malden, MA: Wiley-Blackwell.

Skinner, M. B. 2011. *Clodia Metelli, the Tribune's Sister*. New York and Oxford: Oxford University Press.

Skoie, M. 2002. *Reading Sulpicia: Commentaries 1475–1990*. Oxford: University of Oxford Press.

Skoie, M. 2013. "'The Woman,'" in Thorsen 2013, 83–96.

Skutsch, O. 1969. "Symmetry and Sense in the *Eclogues*," *HSCP* 73, 153–68.

Smith, K. F. 1913. *The Elegies of Albius Tibullus, the Corpus Tibullianum Edited with Introduction and Notes on Books I, II, and IV.2–14*. New York: American Book Company.

Snyder, J. M. (ed. and tr.) 1989. *The Woman and the Lyre: Women Writers in Classical Greece and Rome*. Carbondale: Southern Illinois University Press.

Solin, H. 1996. *Die Stadtrömischen Sklavennamen: Ein Namenbuch*. Stuttgart: Franz Steiner Verlag.

Solin, H. 2003. *Die Griechischen Personennamen in* Rome,² 3 vols. Berlin and New York: De Gruyter.

Stehle, E. 1996. "Sappho's Gaze: Fantasies of a Goddess and Young Man," in Greene 1996a, 2.193–225; originally published in *differences* 2 (1990), 88–125.

Steinhauer, J. 2020. "Dionysian Associations and the Bacchanalian Affair," in F. Mac Góráin (ed.), *Dionysus and Rome*, 133–56. Berlin: De Gruyter.

Stevenson, J. 2005. *Women Latin Poets: Language, Gender, and Authority, from Antiquity to the Eighteenth Century.* Oxford: Oxford University Press.

Strong, A. K. 2016. *Prostitutes and Matrons in the Roman World.* Cambridge: Cambridge University Press.

Sumner, G. 1971. "The *Lex Annalis* under Caesar," *Phoenix* 25.3–4, 246–71, 357–71.

Syme, R. 1978. *History in Ovid.* Oxford: Clarendon Press.

Syme, R. 1980. "No Son for Caesar?," *Historia* 29.4, 422–37.

Syme, R. 1981. "A Great Orator Mislaid," *CQ* 31, 421–27.

Syme, R. 1986. *The Augustan Aristocracy.* Oxford: Clarendon Press.

Tansey, P. 2007. "Messalla Corvinus and the 'Bellum Siculum,'" *Latomus* 66.4, 882–90.

Tatum, W. J. 1993. "*C.* 79: Personal Invective or Political Discourse?," *PLILS* 7, 31–45.

Tatum, W. J. 1999. *The Patrician Tribune: Publius Clodius Pulcher.* Chapel Hill: University of North Carolina Press.

Thomson, D. F. S. (ed.) 1997. *Catullus.* Toronto: University of Toronto Press.

Thorsen, T. S. 2012. "Sappho, Corinna and Colleagues in Ancient Rome: Tatian's Catalogue of Statues (*Oratio ad Graecos* 33–4) Reconsidered," *Mnemosyne* 65, 695–715.

Thorsen, T. S. (ed.) 2013. *The Cambridge Companion to Latin Love Elegy.* Cambridge: Cambridge University Press.

Thorsen, T. S. 2020. "'Divine Corinna': Pre-Twentieth Century Receptions of an Artistic Authority," *EuGeStA* 10.

Thorsen, T. S. and Harrison, S. (eds.) 2019. *Roman Receptions of Sappho.* Oxford: Oxford University Press.

Tränkle, H. (ed.) 1990. *Appendix Tibulliana.* Berlin and New York: De Gruyter.

Treggiari, S. 1973. "Domestic Staff at Rome in the Julio-Claudian Period," *Social History/ Histoire sociale* 6, 241–55.

Treggiari, S. 1975. "Jobs in the Household of Livia," *PBSR* 43, 48–77.

Treggiari, S. 1976. "Jobs for Women," *AJAH* 1, 76–104.

Treggiari, S. 1991. *Roman Marriage: Iusti Coniuges from the Time of Cicero to the Time of Ulpian.* Oxford: Clarendon Press.

Treggiari, S. 2003. "Ancestral Virtues and Vices: Cicero on Nature, Nurture and Presentation," in D. Braund and C. Gill (eds.), *Myth, History and Culture in Republican Rome. Studies in Honour of T. P. Wiseman*, 139–64. Exeter: University of Exeter Press.

Treggiari, S. 2007. *Terentia, Tullia and Publilia, the Women of Cicero's Family.* London and New York: Routledge.

Treggiari, S. 2016. "Training for Marriage," review of Caldwell 2015 in *JRA* 29, 635–41.

Treggiari, S. 2019. *Servilia and Her Family.* Oxford: Oxford University Press.

Tsantsanoglou, I. 2019. *Studies in Sappho and Alcaeus.* Berlin and New York: De Gruyter.

Tschiedel, H. J. 1992. "Die Gedichte der Sulpicia (Tib. 3.13–18)—Frauenlyrik?," *GB* 18, 87–102.

Ullman, B. L. 1928. "Tibullus in the Mediaeval *Florilegia*," *CP* 23, 128–74.

Ullman, B. L. 1954. "A List of Classical MSS (in an Eighth Century Codex) Perhaps from Corbie," *Scriptorium* 8, 24–37.

Ullman, B. L. 1955. *Studies in the Italian Renaissance.* Rome: Edizioni di storia e letteratura.

Valladares, H. 2021. *Painting, Poetry, and the Invention of Tenderness in the Early Roman Empire.* Cambridge: Cambridge University Press.

Valvo, A. 1983. "M. Valerio Messalla Corvino negli studi più recenti," *ANRW* II.30.3, 1663–80.

Veyne, P. 1988. *Roman Erotic Elegy: Love, Poetry, and the West*, tr. D. Pellauer. Chicago: University of Chicago Press. [Originally published in French as *L'élégie rotique romaine: l'amour, la poésie et l'Occident*, Paris 1983: Editions du Seuil.]

Volk, K. 2021. *The Roman Republic of Letters*. Princeton: Princeton University Press.

von Barth, K. 1624. *Aduersariorum commentariolum*. Frankfurt.

Voss, J. H. 1810. *Albius Tibullus und Lygdamus*. Tübingen: J.G. Cottaische Buchhandlung.

Voss, J. H. (ed.) 1811. *Albius Tibullus und Lygdamus nach Handschriften berichteget bei J. H. Voss*. Heidelberg: Mohr und Zimmer.

Warren, J. (ed.) 2009. *The Cambridge Companion to Epicureanism*. Cambridge: Cambridge University Press.

Waszink, J. H. 1974. *Biene und Honig als Symbol des Dichters und der Dichtung in der griechisch-römischen Antike*. Opladen: Rhein.-Westfäl. Akad. Der Wiss. Geisteswiss. Vortr.

Watson, L. C. 1982. "Cinna and Euphorion," *SIFC* 54, 93–110.

Webb, L. 2019. *Gloria Muliebris: Elite Female Status Competition in Mid-Republican Rome*. Ph.D. dissertation, University of Gothenburg.

Werner, E. 2022. *Erzählen der Macht—Macht des Erzählens: Eine Analyse der sog. Sulpicia-Elegien* (Corpus Tibullianum *III.8–18*). IPHIS 13. Trier: Wissenschaftlicher Verlag Trier.

Williams, F. 1978. *Callimachus, Hymn to Apollo*. Oxford: Oxford University Press.

Wills, J. 1996. *Repetition in Latin Poetry: Figures of Allusion*. Oxford: Oxford University Press.

Wiseman, T. P. 1969. *Catullan Questions*. Leicester: Leicester University Press.

Wiseman, T. P. 1974. *Cinna the Poet, and Other Roman Essays*. Leicester: Leicester University Press.

Wiseman, T. P. 1976. "Camerius," *BICS* 23, 15–17.

Wiseman, T. P. 1979. *Clio's Cosmetics: Three Studies in Greco-Roman Literature*. Leicester: Leicester University Press.

Wiseman, T. P. 1980. "Looking for Camerius: The Topography of *c.* LV," *PBSR* 48, 6–16 [= *Roman Studies* (1978), 176–86].

Wiseman, T. P. 1985. *Catullus and His World*. Cambridge: Cambridge University Press.

Witt, R. G. 1983. *Hercules at the Crossroads: The Life, Works, and Thought of Coluccio Salutati*. Duke Monographs in Medieval and Renaissance Studies, No. 6. Durham, NC: Duke University Press.

Witt, R. G. 2000. "Coluccio Salutati," in R. G. Witt, *In the Footsteps of the Ancients: The Origins of Humanism from Lovato to Bruni*, 292–337. Leiden: Brill.

Wyke, M. 2002. *The Roman Mistress: Ancient and Modern Representations*. Oxford: Oxford University Press.

Yardley, J. C. 1973. "Sick-Visiting in Roman Elegy," *Phoenix* 27, 283–88.

Yardley, J. C. 1977. "The Roman Elegists, Sick Girls, and the *Soteria*," *CQ* 27, 394–401.

Yardley, J. C. 1990. "Cerinthus' *Pia Cura* ([Tib.] 3.17.1–2)," *CQ* 40, 568–70.

Yardley, J. C. 1992. *Minor Authors of the Corpus Tibullianum*. Bryn Mawr Commentaries. Hackett Publishing.

Yatromanolakis, D. 2007. *Sappho in the Making: The Early Reception*. Washington, DC: Center for Hellenic Studies.

Yona, S. 2018. *Epicurean Ethics in Horace: The Psychology of Satire*. Oxford: Oxford University Press.

Zimmermann, R. 1928. "Die Autorschaft Tibulls an den Elegien 2-6 des IV Buches," *Philologus* 83, 400–18.

Index Locorum

For the benefit of digital users, indexed terms that span two pages (e.g., 52–53) may, on occasion, appear on only one of those pages.

Index Rerum

For the benefit of digital users, indexed terms that span two pages (e.g., 52–53) may, on occasion, appear on only one of those pages.